THE BEATLES ARE COMING!

The Birth of Beatlemania in America

By
Bruce Spizer

Foreword
by
Walter Cronkite

Copyright ©2003 by 498 Productions, L.L.C.

498 Productions, L.L.C.
P.O. Box 70194
New Orleans, Louisiana 70172
Fax: 504-524-2887
email: 498@beatle.net

All rights reserved. No part of this book may be used or reproduced in any form or by any means, or stored in a database or retrieval system without written permission of the copyright owner, except in the case of brief quotations embodied in critical articles and reviews. Making copies of any part of this book for any purpose other than your own personal use is a violation of United States copyright laws.

This book is sold as is, without warranty of any kind, either express or implied. While every effort has been made in the preparation of this book to ensure the accuracy of the information contained herein, the author and 498 Productions, L.L.C. assume no responsibility for errors or omissions. Neither is any liability assumed for damages resulting from the use of the information contained herein.

The *Billboard* chart data used in this book is ©1930-1965 by BPI Communications.

The Watcher and the distinctive likeness thereof appearing on pages 210-211 is a trademark of Marvel Characters, Inc. and is used with permission. TM and © 2003. All rights reserved. www.marvel.com.

This book is published by 498 Productions, L.L.C. It is not an official product of Apple Corps Ltd., Capitol Records, Inc. or EMI Records Ltd.

Library of Congress Control Number: 2003106746
Paperback ISBN 0-9662649-8-3   Hardcover ISBN 0-9662649-9-1
1 2 3 4 5 6 7 8 9 0   1 2 3 4 5 6 7 8 9 0

Printed in Singapore

TABLE OF CONTENTS

Foreword

Friday, February 7, 1964. The day the Beatles arrived in America. We at CBS News decided to send a film crew over to Kennedy Airport to cover the event. I wasn't thinking of any historical aspect. They were a bunch of guys who were packing in the hits in the entertainment industry. It didn't occur to me that it would be of any historical importance whatsoever. After viewing the footage, I chose to close our Evening News with film of the large crowd greeting the Beatles and a bit of their press conference. And then I gave my traditional sign-off, "And that's the way it is, Friday, February 7, 1964."

I first heard about the Beatles in October or November of 1963, when Alexander Kendrick, one of our leading correspondents in London, sent us a story about a group of young musicians called the Beatles. This surprised me because Kendrick was a very serious minded fellow who was interested in foreign affairs. It was not like him to do feature stories. He had read in the London papers about the Beatles, who were just beginning to make a splash, and in pursuit of another story in Manchester, he spent an evening at an appearance by these long-haired musicians. The audience was largely of girls screaming and hollering with some new form of worship. He suggested that his camera crew film a report. He wasn't a fan of that kind of music, so he got another reporter, Josh Darsa, to interview the band.

Kendrick sent the story to us, and we looked at it in New York. I was semi-interested, but I did not immediately run the story because it was a busy news week. I put it on the shelf until we had time for that sort of feature. As it turned out, a few days after we got the story on the Beatles, President Kennedy was assassinated in Dallas. For the next few weeks, the President's death dominated the news.

By the second week in December, I thought it was once again appropriate to run feature stories. We decided to broadcast Kendrick's Beatles piece on our Evening News program. Shortly after we were off the air, I got a call from Ed Sullivan, who was a friend of mine. He was excited about the story we had run on the long-haired British group. He said, "Tell me more about those, what do they call them? Those bugs or whatever they call themselves." I didn't remember the group's name and had to look down on my copy sheet for the Evening News broadcast to tell him, "They are called the Beatles." Ed wanted to know what I knew about the group, which was next to nothing. I told Ed I would query our guy in London. I sent my query to Alexander Kendrick and requested that he contact Ed. I don't know what happened after that, but soon Ed was announcing he would have the Beatles on his show.

A few days before the Beatles were on *The Ed Sullivan Show*, I was talking to Ed and he asked if I wanted to bring my daughters by. He would invite them backstage to meet the Beatles. Although it wasn't my type of music, I knew it would mean a lot to my daughters.

The Sunday after we covered the Beatles arrival in America, I took my wife and daughters to CBS Studio 50 for the show. We went backstage and were introduced to the Beatles. I was not particularly impressed, but my two young daughters were very impressed. I think that meeting the Beatles made my daughters the heroines of their school for the next few weeks. Even now, they still mention that they met the Beatles in person. I was glorified in their eyes by my ability to introduce them to the Beatles.

Although my daughters loved the Beatles, I did not share their enthusiasm. I was offended by the long hair. That was a pretty minor point, of course, but I did not care for the appearance of the Beatles very much. Their music did not appeal to me either. My music was Dixieland jazz, one of the great forms of music with its improvisation. As far as music goes, my daughters viewed me as an old fuddy duddy. I was not a Beatlemaniac by any means. But I got used to it.

Bruce Spizer is from New Orleans, which is famous for its Dixieland jazz. But he, like my daughters, grew up listening to the Beatles. His passion for the group is obvious. *The Beatles Are Coming!* is a thoroughly researched and entertaining account of the group's first U.S. visit, full of interesting and little known stories about how the Beatles caught on in America. The text is effectively matched with hundreds of pictures and documents. The devotion and effort Bruce Spizer put into this book is rare these days.

Seeing the pictures of the girls chasing after the Beatles in New York and the group's appearance on *The Ed Sullivan Show* brought back memories of my initial reaction. I remember thinking, "Look at those silly girls." I was amazed that these figures on the stage could generate such hysteria.

The text and images of the Beatles arrival at Kennedy Airport bring back the excitement of that day. The rows of girls up on the roof of the Kennedy Airport terminal waiting for the plane. The CBS News station wagon with its heavy camera and sound equipment strapped on its roof poised to capture the event. The Beatles exiting the plane and waving to the crowd. The Beatles apparently charming most of the tough New York reporters at their airport press conference. And that's the way it was, Friday, February 7, 1964.

Walter Cronkite
CBS News
July, 2003

Acknowledgments

Putting together a book of this magnitude would not have been possible without the help of several individuals. I was fortunate to have many people enthusiastically contribute their time, memories and memorabilia to this project. I have attempted to list them all. I have also listed many of the individuals whose contributions to my prior books carried forward to this book. I apologize in advance to anyone I have inadvertently left out.

Gay Linvill spent a considerable part of her summer vacation working on this project. She served as a research assistant, sounding board and proof reader. She also provided editorial suggestions. Her television-oriented ideas and perspectives were particularly helpful for the chapters on *The Ed Sullivan Show*. She not only set up several interviews with former Sullivan staff members, but also personally conducted many of them.

The following people were kind enough to share their memories and insights by taking part in interviews in person or by telephone, email or fax: Walter Cronkite and Mike Wallace of CBS News; Edwin Newman of NBC News; Alan Livingston, former president of Capitol Records; former *Ed Sullivan Show* staff members Robert Arthur, Bill Bonhert, Vince Calandra, Emily Cole, Ann Cremmons, Kathie Kuehl and John Moffitt; George Martin; Dick Clark; Albert Maysles; Lou Harrison; attorneys Paul Marshall, Thomas Levy and Nat Weiss; Sid Bernstein; Peter Prichard; Billy J. Kramer; Tony Barrow; Tony Bramwell; Alistair Taylor; Randy Paar; Harry Benson; Gilda Weissberger of Carnegie Hall; Dick Biondi; Bruce Morrow; Robert Freeman; Debbie Gendler; Joan Schulman; David Picker, former vice president of United Artists; George Osaki, former head of the art department for Capitol Records; and former Queens Litho employees Eric Kaltman and Richard Roth.

Once again, several Beatles dealers came to my aid by either sending me digital files or lending me items. Gary Hein of Beatles4me.com provided several images, including *Sullivan Show* and United Artists documents. Other key contributors include Jeff Augsburger, Perry Cox, Marty Eck, Paul and Staci Garfunkle of Blackbird Records, Paul Grenyo, Tom Grosh of Very English and Rolling Stone, Jim Hansen of Blue Jay Way Galleries, Gary and Wayne Johnson of Rockaway Records, Craig Moore of Younger Than Yesterday, Alan Ould of Good Humour, Rick Rann, Bob Richerson, John Tefteller, Thomas Vanghele of Fab 4 Collectibles; Paul Wayne of Tracks; and Cliff Yamasaki of Let It Be Records.

Many individuals helped me obtain images from either their personal collections or from photo and research archives. Others assisted me with my research. These helpful people include Frank Absher, Marlene Adler, Jason Anjoorian, Dave Ash of Mirror Syndication International, Andy Babiuk, Jerry Bishop, William Brown, Margaret Burke of BBC Library Sales at CBS News, Frank Caiazzo, Mike Calahan, Joe Caldwell, Betty Chiapetta, Bud Connell, Andrew Croft of *Beatlology*, Dennis Dailey, Frank Daniels, George Edmonds, Walter Everett, Gino Francesconi of Carnegie Hall, Rob Friedman, Neil Gallacher, Mark Galloway, Andy Geller, Barbara Gottlieb of Stock Photo, Rod Griffith, John Guarnieri, Chuck Gunderson, Terri Hammert, Bill Hathaway of Record Research Publications, Piers Hemmingsen, Joe Hilton, Rob Hudson of Carnegie Hall Archives, Matt Hurwitz, Charles Iscove, Richard Jeffery of the BBC, Joe Johnson of Beatle Brunch, Jim Kirkpatrick, David Klein, Kent Kotal, Allan Kozinn, Barbara Kramer of NBC News Archives, Eric Kulwright, Mark Lapidos, Jude Law, Russ Lease, Gay Linvill, Bud Loveall, Michael Macchio of the American Federation of Musicians, Cliff Malloy, Mike Mashon of the Library of Congress, Anne Mathews, Pat Mathews, Gabe McCarty, Mitch McGeary, Maury Mollo, Steve Moore, Mark Naboshek, Tim Neely of *Goldmine*, Bob Nichols, Dave Nichols, Lisa Oberhofer of BBC Library Sales at CBS News, Tony Perkins of ABC's *Good Morning America*, Susan Petersen, Casey Piotrowski, Wally Podrazik, Cary Pollack, Linda Pollack, Simon Postbrief, Heather Preston, Randy Price, Johnny Rabbit, Marilyn Rader of AP/Wide World Photos, Michael Randolf, Ann Rausher of the Newseum, Vickie Rehberg, Ron Riley, Elias Savada, Roland Scherman, Ed Schwartz, Ron Simon of the Museum of Television & Radio, Barry Spizer, Al Sussman, Angela Troisi of Daily News Pix, Tom Vitucci, Mark Wallgren, Michael White, John C. Winn, Robert Wolk, Michelle Wood and Robert York.

Much of the information regarding the Beatles studio activities comes from Mark Lewisohn's *The Beatles Recording Sessions* and *The Complete Beatles Chronicle*. Mark's well-researched books set the standard for Beatles books and belong in every Beatles library. Mark frequently gave me quick answers when I needed to resolve conflicting data. Additional details about the recordings came from Walter Everett's *The Beatles As Musicians* and George Martin's *All You Need Is Ears*. John C. Winn's *Way Beyond Compare* provided information on recording sessions as well as extensive details of interviews with members of the group. Andy Babiuk's *Beatles Gear* provided fascinating details about the instruments and amplifiers used by the band.

Martin Lewis assisted me with matters pertaining to the Beatles and Great Britain. Alex Games researched British newspapers of 1963.

As usual, my friends and colleagues provided much appreciated moral support. Trish Morgan, the Coach and the Papa helped me get through my morning runs and stairwell training that prepared me for climbing the Inca Trail up to Machu Picchu, giving me a much needed one-week break from the Beatles and tax law. Roblynn Sliwinski kept things going at 498 Productions and my law practice while I was writing this book. Eloise Keene and Lisa Wagner keep assisting me in selling my books at the Fest for Beatles Fans and other Beatles conventions. Good listeners include a gang of characters known as DC, the Burgs, Junior, Scrunge, Big Puppy, the bears, Doc, Kili, NASA, Commander Columbo and others too numerous and crazy to mention.

My gang of "assistant editors" included Frank Daniels, Eloise Keene, Jim Kendall, Martin Lewis, Mark Lewisohn, Gay Linvill, Maury Mollo, Diana Thornton of Crescent Music Services and Trish Morgan of the East Jefferson Hospital Emergency Room. Once again I received guidance from Susan McDaniel on marketing matters.

As always, I relied heavily my prepress person, Diana Thornton. She converted the images in my brain to the images in the book, reviewed text and spent many hours working closely with me on layouts. Other key people who assisted me on the production end include: Michael Ledet and Kaye Alexander, who lined up and coordinated communications with the printer; Rick Randall of Harvey Press, who provided support and expertise; and Jim Filo of Garrison Digital Color, who photographed some of the larger items seen in the book.

I would also like to thank all those good people who purchased my previous books, and for those of you who haven't, get with the program! And, of course, I must thank my sisters, Dale Aronson and Jan Seltzer, and my parents, David and Jean Spizer, for their love, understanding and guidance.

PHOTOGRAPHY AND IMAGE CREDITS

AP/Wide World Photos (pages 5, 180, 203 top) • BBC Photograph Library (page 89) • Bill Bohnert (page 150) • Carnegie Hall Archives (page 188 bottom) • CBS News Archive (pages 61 and 220) • CBS Photo Archive (198, 201 and 219 middle) • Corbis (pages 51 right, 65, 151, 154 top, 157 top, 177 bottom, 191 top, 197 bottom, 203 bottom) • Daily News Pix (pages 2, 144, 148, 178, 186 bottom, 187, 188 top, 191 bottom, 193, 204, 207) • Bill Epperidge (pages 136-137, 138, 140 and 141 top) • Hulton/Getty (page 176 top, 219 top and bottom) • Gabe McCarty (page 49 bottom) • Miami Herald (196) • Ira Kaltman/Alan Kaltman (page 185) • Mirror Syndication International (pages 4, 113, 115, 142, 145 right, 147) • Michael Ochs Archive (page 31) • www.popsiephotos.com (pages 79 top, 160, 164, contact prints on 166-167, 192) • rowland.scherman@verizon.net (page 181) • Stock Photo Black Star (pages 182, 183, 186 top) • *The Washington Times* (page ix) • John Williams, greenlight_graphics@cox.net (page 210-211) • Zuma Press (197 top).

Information from various *Billboard* record charts appears through the courtesy of Billboard Productions, Inc. (BPI) and Joel Whitburn's Record Research Publications. *Billboard* and *Record World* charts were based on a combination of sales and airplay. During the sixties, *Cash Box* based its chart positions solely on sales. Unless stated otherwise, chart positions in this book refer to the peak position the record achieved.

The chart information for the New York and Miami radio stations summarized on page 217 was provided by the following websites: WMCA www.musicradio.computer.net/wmca; WABC www.musicradio77.com; and WQAM www.560.com/html/wqam_surveys.html.

ERRORS AND OMISSIONS POLICY

Although every effort was made to ensure that the information contained in this book is accurate and complete, errors, omissions and typos do occur. At an early age, my extensive comic book reading taught me that writers often make mistakes. Marvel Comics addressed this problem by awarding a "no prize" to the first reader to write a letter informing the editor of the mistake. For those readers of this book unfamiliar with this marvelous tradition, a "no prize" is just what it sounds like—you get no prize. However, the person receiving a no prize is given credit for spotting the error.

In continuation of the errors and omissions policy adopted by me for my previous books, I will award a no prize to each person who is the first to inform me of a particular mistake. I will also award no prizes for new information pertaining to the subject matter and time frame covered by this book.

I must caution readers that you will not get a no prize merely by informing me that my book has information in it contradictory to what you have read in every other book on the Beatles. This book will have some facts different from what has previously been written. To get a no prize, you must prove me wrong. Also, you must be the first person to inform me of the error.

Please write or email me (bruce@beatle.net) if you think you have what it takes to win a no prize.

It's been a long, long, long time...

TIME–JANUARY, 1964

I remember an afternoon in early January, 1964, when I first heard *I Want To Hold Your Hand* on the school bus radio. There was something fresh and exciting about the record that grabbed my attention. After weeks of hearing the song and others by the Beatles, I persuaded my mother to take me to Studio A record store where I then purchased my first album, *Meet The Beatles!* From start to finish, it was one great song after another. I was further impressed when I learned that all but one of the album's selections were written by members of the band.

Towards the end of January I began hearing exciting news: "The Beatles Are Coming!" They would be arriving in early February and would be on *The Ed Sullivan Show*. I remember sitting in front of the television on the evening of February 9, 1964, watching the program while eating a macaroni & cheese TV dinner. For me and millions of other Americans, it was an event never to be forgotten. The Beatles on *Ed Sullivan* was one of those "Where were you when...?" memories, right up there with the Kennedy assassination and Neil Armstrong setting foot on the moon.

Thirty-nine years after first hearing *I Want To Hold Your Hand* I began this book. A lot had happened during that time, but one thing hadn't changed. I still find the Beatles early music as fresh and exciting now as I did in 1964.

"TIMING IS SO IMPORTANT" — Brian Epstein

In describing his writing of the song *While My Guitar Gently Weeps*, George Harrison stated that he was influenced by the *I Ching*, the Chinese *Book of Changes*. Harrison believed that the book was based on the Eastern concept that everything is relative to *everything* else, as opposed to the Western view that things are merely coincidental.

In researching and writing this book, I was fascinated by how certain key events affecting the birth of Beatlemania in America took place on either the same date of the year or the same day as other key events. My cultural upbringing led me to describe these occurrences as an incredible string of coincidences. But I also realized that each event had an effect on other events that followed. Everything *was* relative to *everything* else.

I also began wondering what if some of these key events had occurred at different times. I imagined that things certainly would have turned out differently. It reminded me of the "imaginary" stories that occasionally appeared in Superman comics of the sixties and the *What If?* comic book series published by Marvel. To me, these stories were based on the concept that things happen for a reason. If something, no matter how seemingly insignificant, had happened differently or at a different time, it would have affected everything else.

The birth of Beatlemania in America is best understood by recognizing all of the above concepts. It is a story full of events happening at coincidental times that shows that everything is relative to everything else and that things happen for a reason.

TIME–JANUARY, 2003

When I began putting this book together in January, 2003, I recognized the importance of each event and how it affected what was to follow. Thus, I made every effort to get to the truth and debunk the myths and misinformation about Beatlemania in America that have circulated for years.

As was the case with my previous books, I approached this project the same way I prepare a lawsuit. I went through a discovery process in which I familiarized myself with the subject matter by: reading books, articles, magazines and newspaper stories; watching videos as well as archival news stories and raw footage of the events; interviewing people who were there at the time; working with people who had access to archival materials; reviewing documents; and discussing my findings and interpretations of events with experts and other individuals. I sorted through the material and began making judgments as to which stories could be corroborated and/or supported by documents.

After completing the preliminary discovery phase, I began putting together the story and time line best supported by the documents and recollections of individuals deemed to be reliable. I spent several months fine-tuning the text, sometimes changing my conclusions after conducting additional research.

You may recognize that some information in this book conflicts with accounts that have been accepted as gospel for years. You may also notice that the book downplays or ignores some stories from people who were there at the time. I intentionally left out first-hand recollections when they conflicted with documentary evidence. While memories change over time, original documents do not.

THE TIME COMPRESSION FACTOR

In researching my previous books on the Beatles, I noticed that people had difficulty not only remembering when things occurred, but also remembering the time span between events and even the order of when things took place. I began calling this the "time compression factor." The further back one goes, the stronger the effect. For example, if someone asks you what you did last week, you can probably remember the order in which things occurred. But when you try to recall what you did during a summer several years ago, you may remember what you did, but you will probably have great difficulty in getting the order right.

The time compression factor applies to our memories of the Beatles. Many people insist that they first became aware of the Beatles when they appeared on *The Ed Sullivan Show*. But by that time, the Beatles had the number one single in America. Their songs had dominated the airwaves for over a month. But time compressed the events of January, 1964, into February. The late Beatles historian Gareth Palowski recalled purchasing *Introducing The Beatles* the week President Kennedy was assassinated. We now know that was not possible; however, these events were so imbedded in Palowski's mind that he remembered them occurring the same week. Time had compressed them.

Because people have difficulty remembering exactly when certain things occurred, it is difficult to place every piece of the puzzle in its proper order when researching events that took place four decades earlier. Fortunately there are surviving documents. They tell the true order of events and are more reliable than people's memories. But documents can not tell the full story. The trick in writing about the past is to choose the stories that make sense and are supported by the documents, and not to rely on stories presented as fact when documents or logic tell otherwise.

TIME CAPSULES

We are fortunate that the Beatles first U.S. visit was a well documented event. There are surviving memos, press releases and invitations from Capitol Records, CBS, *The Ed Sullivan Show* and United Artists. There are stories in newspapers and magazines published at the time that give first-hand contemporary accounts. There are teen fanzines that may be hokey, but contain informational gems and pictures packed with details that would otherwise have been long forgotten. There are interviews of the Beatles and their fans recorded by newsmen and disc jockeys. And there are video images and sound of many of the key events filmed by news organizations, CBS and documentary crews.

Albert and David Maysles, a pair of film-makers known as the Maysles Brothers, were hired by Britain's Granada Television to film an inside view of the group's first U.S. visit. The project had the blessing of Beatles manager Brian Epstein. The Maysles Brothers filmed the group's arrival at the airport, the boys in their hotel suite during their first few evenings in New York, a photo session held in Central Park, a limousine ride, a train ride, a night out at the Peppermint Lounge, the group preparing to leave Miami and their arrival back in London. They also filmed disc jockey Murray the K during his *Swingin' Soiree* program, Brian Epstein on the telephone and a New York family watching *The Ed Sullivan Show* on their television set.

Footage from the first few days shot by the Maysles was flown to London by David Maysles and quickly edited for broadcast on the evening of February 12, 1964. The program, which ran 36 minutes and 25 seconds, was titled *Yeah! Yeah! Yeah! The Beatles In New York* (though it is also known as *Yeah! Yeah! Yeah! New York Meets The Beatles*). On November 13, 1964, Americans got to see an expanded version of show, which added footage shot during the later parts of the visit. The documentary (edited down to 45 minutes for television) was shown on the weekly CBS series *The Entertainers*, which was hosted by Carol Burnett. The show was called *The Beatles In America*, though it is also known as *What's Happening! The Beatles In The USA* and *The Beatles In New York*.

The Beatles appearances on *The Ed Sullivan Show* were taped as was the practice at the time. In addition, CBS filmed the Beatles first concert appearance in Washington, D.C., for closed circuit theater broadcasts on March 14 and 15, 1964.

Significant portions of these filmed events were released on video. *The First U.S. Visit*, which was prepared by the Beatles's company Apple Corps Ltd., mixes bits of film shot by the Maysles Brothers with performances from the *Sullivan Show* and the Washington Coliseum concert. The video is entertaining and gives an excellent overview of the group's two weeks in America, although some segments are edited out of sequence. The first visit is covered in parts three and four of the Beatles *Anthology* video. The three *Sullivan Show* appearances from February, 1964, are part of a DVD titled *The Four Complete Historic Ed Sullivan Shows Featuring The Beatles*. All of these videos serve as fascinating time capsules and are highly recommended.

TIME–FEBRUARY 7, 1964

In a few pages you will be taken back to February 7, 1964, when the Beatles first arrived in America. It's been a long, long, long time, but the memories live on. And so does the music.

Bruce Spizer
August, 2003

About The Author

Bruce Spizer is a first generation Beatles fan and a life-long native of New Orleans, Louisiana. A "tax man" by day, Bruce is a board certified tax attorney and non-practicing certified public accountant. A "paperback writer" by night, he is the author of the critically acclaimed books *The Beatles Records on Vee-Jay,* the two-book set *The Beatles' Story on Capitol Records* and *The Beatles on Apple Records.* He is also a regular feature writer for *Beatlology Magazine, Beatlefan* and *Goldmine*.

Bruce was eight years old when the Beatles invaded America. He began listening to the radio at age two and was a diehard fan of WTIX, a top forty station that played a blend of New Orleans R&B music and top pop and rock hits. His first two albums were *The Coasters' Greatest Hits*, which he permanently "borrowed" from his older sisters, and *Meet The Beatles!*, which he still plays on his vintage 1964 Beatles record player.

During his high school and college days, Bruce played guitar in various bands that primarily covered hits of the sixties, including several Beatles songs. Due to the limited range of his baritone voice, his singing was primarily restricted to Ringo songs such as *With A Little Help From My Friends*. He was allowed to sing *Like A Rolling Stone* because his band mates didn't think Bob Dylan had a good voice. He was given the task of singing the Rolling Stones' *Get Off My Cloud* because he was the only one who could remember the words.

Although Bruce was the phototography editor for the Newman High School yearbook, he decided against a career in photography because he didn't want to do weddings and bar mitzvahs. He wrote numerous album and concert reviews for his high school and college newspapers, including a review of *Abbey Road* that didn't claim Paul was dead. While at Tulane University, he served on the Board of Directors of the Mushroom, which was a highly-successful student-run record store.

Bruce received his B.A. (in economics), M.B.A. (concentrating in marketing and finance) and law degree from Tulane University. Upon graduation, he clerked for a judge at the Louisiana Supreme Court. During his tenure at the Court and for the first part of his legal career, he managed the Cold, which was a pop rock band that dominated the New Orleans music scene in the early eighties. Two of the group's singles, *You* and *Mesmerized*, received extensive airplay on New Orleans' top rated radio stations, including B-97, WQUE-FM and his childhood favorite WTIX.

Bruce has had his own law practice for nearly 20 years, specializing in tax and estate planning and administration. He has given numerous lectures on tax, retirement plans and estate planning matters. In his other life, Bruce is a frequent guest speaker at The Fest for Beatles Fans (the event formerly known as "Beatlefest") and other Beatles conventions. He has appeard on numerous national and local television and radio programs as a Beatles historian.

Bruce has an extensive Beatles collection, concentrating primarily on United States and Canadian first issue records, record promotional items, press kits and posters. His varied interests, background and training have made him uniquely qualified to detail the history of the Beatles in America.

In November, 2000, Bruce traveled to the site of the Beatles first U.S. concert, the Washington Coliseum, only to find that the place was literally a garbage dump. This picture, which originally appeared in *The Washington Times,* shows Bruce wearing a Beatle wig. Notice the garbage truck backing into the waste management facility.

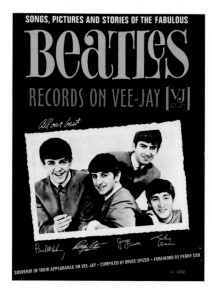

ALL FOUR BOOKS NAMED "BEATLES BOOKS OF THE YEAR" BY *GOLDMINE* MAGAZINE

Visit the Beatles American Records website
www.beatle.net
for information about all the books in this series.
The site also contains enhanced and updated versions of Bruce Spizer's articles appearing in *Beatlology*, *Beatlefan* and other magazines.

ONLINE ORDERING AVAILABLE

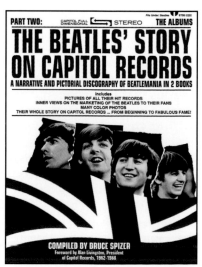

The stories behind the entire Beatles catalog on Apple Records — From Hey Jude and The White Album through Anthology and Beatles 1

COMPILED BY BRUCE SPIZER
Foreword by Ken Mansfield, First U.S. Manager of Apple Records

"*The Beatles Records on Vee-Jay* is a landmark book that will easily rate as a "must have" addition to the library of any serious Beatles collector or music historian. Even casual fans of the group will no doubt find this book to be extremely entertaining, enjoyable and enlightening." (*Goldmine*)

"This photo-rich, exhaustively researched book offers the reader a comprehensive look at the Beatles' first releases in the U.S. It's a must-have for any serious Beatles fan or collector." (*Billboard*)

"A visual feast with every label variation, sleeve design, advert, document and mailer presented in full, glorious colour, and in an easily accessible form. No Beatles collector can afford to be without this masterpiece of a book." (*Record Collector*)

"A stunning and masterful work—one of the most useful and informative books about The Beatles ever published. Lavishly appointed and extremely detailed, the book is an enormously satisfying volume of tremendous historical importance documenting this extremely complicated and often misunderstood chapter in the history of The Beatles in America. This is one book that is certainly of significant interest to every Beatlefan concerned—a souvenir of their appearances on Vee-Jay that is well worth the price of admission." (*Beatlefan*)

"A gorgeously presented, thoroughly researched and lovingly detailed book that anyone interested in The Beatles' career from 1968 on must have. After working your way through this handsome, hefty volume, you'll be impressed with Spizer's work, and thankful he cared enough to do it right." (*Beatlefan*)

"Congratulations to respected Beatles historan Bruce Spizer for producing the most collosal, comprehensive and collectibles-crammed coffee-table tomb documenting the history of the Beatles on Apple Records ever published. *The Beatles On Apple Records* is an absolute must for fans, historians and collectors alike." (*Goldmine*)

"Comprehensive, lavishly illustrated.... *The Beatles On Apple Records* deserves a place on any Beatles fan's bookshelf." (*Billboard*)

"You may be thinking, 'Why would I possibly need another Beatles book?', but trust me, you need this one." (*Discoveries*)

"Visually stunning and awe inspiring. Author Bruce Spizer redefines 'perfection' with each new book that he writes." (*The World Beatles Forum*)

"The rare photos, promo artwork and foreign picture sleeves are addictive enough." (*Rolling Stone*)

Follow the story of **THE BEATLES AMERICAN RECORDS** IN THESE BOOKS FROM **498** PRODUCTIONS

"If you don't own these detailed chronicles of the Beatles recording history, buy them!" (*Daytrippin'*)

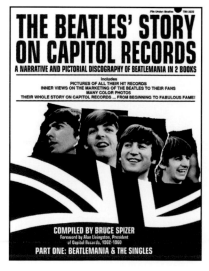

"A mind-blowing compendium of the most carefully researched, full documented, historically accurate, acutely insightful and extremely entertaining account of The Beatles' Capitol Records catalog ... a visual delight to behold ... offers readers a number of extremely important historical revelations concerning The Beatles' Capitol releases (and non-releases!). Casual and serious fans alike will warmly embrace this eye-popping assortment of the rarest Beatles record-related memorabilia and collectibles ever assembled between two book covers. Both books deserve to share the formal title as **Goldmine's 'Beatles Books of the Year - 2000.'** (*Goldmine*)

"Comprehensive . . . beautiful . . . lavish . . . offers the reader a time capsule of [The Beatles] U.S. releases and how first-generation American fans were exposed to the music." (*Billboard*)

"... a bonanza of highly descriptive and visually stunning information... your ticket to recounting a most incredible time in the history of popular music. From Beatle collectors to casual fans, this book is a standout read in the new millennium." (*Daytrippin'*)

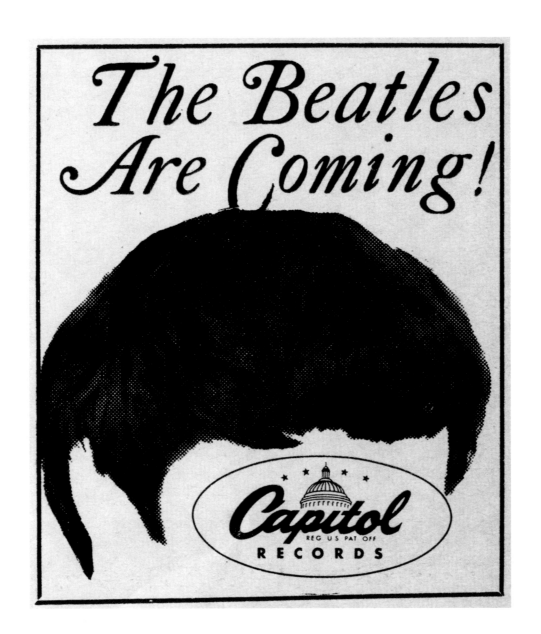

FEBRUARY 7, 1964

On Friday, February 7, 1964, Pan American Airways Flight 101 lifted off the runway at London Airport at 11:00 a.m. and headed across the Atlantic for New York. On board the Boeing 707 jetliner were the Beatles and their entourage. When the Beatles exited the plane at Kennedy International Airport shortly after 1:20 p.m. (shown left), they were greeted by over 3,000 teenagers who had assembled on the airport's upper arcade to welcome their heroes.

The Beatles Are Coming! When Capitol Records began spreading the word in December, 1963, most Americans did not know who or what the Beatles were. But that was before radio, the youth of America and the press took over.

The Beatles Are Coming! It started innocently enough, with a 2⅛" x 1⅝" ad (shown on page 1) that appeared twice in the December 28, 1963, issue of *Billboard*, which hit the newsstands shortly before Christmas Eve.

The Beatles Are Coming! As the new year began, the Beatles first Capitol single, *I Want To Hold Your Hand*, began blasting out of radios all across America. It was soon followed by *Please Please Me*, *She Loves You* and other songs by the band.

The Beatles Are Coming! Preteens, teenagers and young adults were flocking to record stores in record numbers to buy Beatles singles and albums.

The Beatles Are Coming! This was a story the American press couldn't resist. And while the youth of America was anxiously awaiting the group's arrival, others were dreading the day. An editorial in the December 30, 1963, edition of Baltimore's *Evening Sun* lamented:

"'The Beatles are coming.' Those four words are said to be enough to jelly the spine of the most courageous police captains in Britain.... Since, in this case, the Beatles are coming to America, America had better take thought as to how it will deal with the invasion.... Indeed, a restrained 'Beatles, go home,' might just be the thing."

The Beatles Are Coming! Friday, February 7, 1964. The youth of America knew this was the day the Beatles would finally arrive in America. They had been counting the days for weeks and they were not alone. Many parents were dreading it. The police forces in New York, Washington, D.C., and Miami were planning crowd control strategies. Members of the press were preparing to cover the event, expecting to dismiss the band as a curiosity.

Anticipation was greatest in New York where the group would first touch down on American soil. Radio stations were given details of their itinerary to ensure the band's arrival would not go unnoticed. Disc jockey Murray the K informed WINS listeners that the Beatles would arrive at Kennedy Airport on Pan American Airways Flight 101 from London on Friday at 1:20 p.m. and that the group would be staying at the Plaza Hotel near Central Park. Radio stations WMCA and WABC also began spreading the word.

On the day of the invasion, stations gave reports of the plane's progress. WMCA reported, "It is now 6:30 a.m. Beatles time. They left London 30 minutes ago. They're out over the Atlantic Ocean, headed for New York. The temperature is 32 Beatle degrees." Listeners were told, "It's B-Day!" Radio was giving the Beatles the kind of publicity that their manager and Capitol Records could only dream of.

Those on board the Pan Am 707 jetliner had no idea of the reception awaiting them in New York. Prior to boarding the plane at London Airport (which subsequently reverted to its original name Heathrow Airport), the Beatles paused to wave good-bye to the thousand or so screaming fans who had come to see them off. They never dreamed an even larger and more vocal crowd would soon gather at New York's Kennedy Airport to welcome them to the States.

The Beatles sat in first class with their manager, Brian Epstein. Others in the front of the plane included producer Phil Spector, who was returning home from a British promotional visit (pictured above with John and wife Cynthia), reporters Maureen Cleave of the *Evening Standard* and George Harrison (no relation), who wrote for the *Liverpool Echo*. Road managers Neil Aspinall and Mal Evans sat in coach with members of the press, including photographers Dezo Hoffmann, Robert Freeman and Harry Benson.

The Beatles were fully aware that no British act had ever made it big in America. In England, Cliff Richard was a true star, but he never made it big in America despite having a few of his records released in the U.S. on Capitol. George Harrison, who had previously been to America to visit his sister, summed up the group's concern. "They've got everything over there. What do they want us for?"

Still, the Beatles had hopes that things would be different for them. Their latest single, *I Want To Hold Your Hand*, was number one in America. Other songs were racing up the charts as anything Beatles was getting played. They were selling tons of records. Maybe they could defy the odds.

Meanwhile, in New York, teenagers began making their own preparations. Encouraged by New York radio stations, many young fans flocked to Kennedy Airport to meet the Beatles. Never mind that it was a school day. *The New York Times* later reported that more than 3,000 teenagers stood four deep on the airport's upper arcade in anticipation of the group's arrival. An airport official was quoted as saying, "We've never seen anything like this here before. Never. Not even for kings and queens." A security officer added, "I think the world has gone mad."

As their plane got closer to New York, the Beatles apprehension gave way to excitement. When Pan Am Flight 101 landed, the group was clueless as to what was waiting at the terminal. It was only when the jet neared the gate that the huge crowd became visible. At first the Beatles thought the mass of people was for someone else. Perhaps the President was arriving. But as they left the plane and headed down the steps towards the tarmac, the thundering roar of the crowd, the uniformed police and legions of photographers snapping pictures from behind barricades made it clear that this was their reception – louder and larger than anything they had experienced in England. This gave them an adrenaline rush and a boost of confidence that they could defy the skeptics. Although no one noticed, the plane they exited was appropriately named *Jet Clipper Defiance*.

After waving to their fans and quickly being cleared through customs, the group was led into a packed room for their first American press conference. Brian Sommerville, the group's press agent, tried desperately to maintain order. *The New York Times* reported that the Beatles were met by 200 reporters and photographers from newspapers, magazines, foreign publications, radio and television stations and teenage fan magazines. The press conference was described as bedlam. A March 21st story in *The Saturday Evening Post* detailed the event in similar terms. Disc jockeys equipped with tape recorders were pointing microphones at the mob. Flash bulbs exploded. From the back of the lobby came word that two girls had fainted. Sommerville, realizing that the press conference had gotten totally out of control, momentarily lost his cool and shouted, "Gentlemen, would you please shut up!" Once order was restored, questions began and the Beatles were able to show their wit and charm.

Reporter: Are you embarrassed by the lunacy you cause?
John: No. It's great!
Reporter: Would you please sing something?
Group: No!
Ringo: Sorry!
Reporter: There's some doubt that you can sing.
John: No, we need money first.

Reporter: How many are bald that you have to wear wigs?
Paul: I am. I'm bald.
John: Oh, we're all bald, yeah.
Paul: Don't tell anyone, please.
John: And deaf and dumb, too.
Reporter: Are you gonna get a haircut while you're here?
Ringo, Paul and John (separately): No.
George: I had one yesterday.
Ringo: And that's no lie, it's the truth.... You should have seen him the day before!

Reporter: What do you think your music does for these people?
Ringo: It pleases them, I think. It must be cause they're buying it.
Reporter: Why does it excite them so much?
Paul: We don't know, really.
John: If we knew we'd form another group and be managers.

Reporter: What do you think of Beethoven?
Ringo: Great. Especially his poems.

The New York Times of February 8, 1964, reported that when confronted with the statement that the group was keeping kids out of school, John laughed and replied, "That's a dirty lie." The newspaper's coverage of the press conference ended with the following description: "Mr. McCartney beamed. 'We have a message,' he said. Suddenly there was a moment of silence. 'Our message is,' he began, 'buy more Beatles records!' The Beatle wit was contagious. Everyone guffawed. Photographers forgot about pictures they wanted to take. The show was on and the Beatle boys loved it."

After the press conference, the Beatles were driven in four black Cadillac limousines hired by Capitol Records to the Plaza Hotel, where the chaos continued. As the group's motorcade arrived, thousands of fans were waiting. Stacked up against police barricades, the mob chanted, "We want the Beatles! We want the Beatles!" Twenty members of New York's police force were on horseback to control the crowd.

The Maysles Brothers filmed the group in their Plaza Hotel suite watching themselves on the *CBS Evening News with Walter Cronkite*. As they exit the plane, Cronkite states that, "The British invasion this time goes by the code name Beatlemania. D-Day has been common knowledge for months, and this was the day." The group is then shown at the press conference as Cronkite continues, "The invasion took place at New York's Kennedy International Airport." After a few sound bites from the Beatles press conference, Cronkite gives his traditional sign-off, "And that's the way it is, Friday, February 7, 1964."

And that's the way it was. But the events leading up to the Beatles triumphant arrival in America began exactly one year earlier with the unheralded release of the group's first American single, *Please Please Me*.

Let me take you back ...

FEBRUARY 7, 1963

Exactly one year before the Beatles arrived in New York, Vee-Jay Records released the group's first American disc. The 45 RPM record, designated VJ 498, contained *Please Please Me* and *Ask Me Why*. The band's name was misspelled "THE BEATTLES" on first pressings of the disc (shown left).

Although Capitol Records coined the slogan "The Beatles Are Coming!" and issued the group's breakthrough U.S. single, *I Want To Hold Your Hand*, the first Beatles records released in America were not on Capitol. The Beatles first appeared on Vee-Jay, a Chicago-based independent label that specialized in R&B and gospel recordings. For years, the official release date of the first Beatles single in America remained unknown, but a recently discovered document solved the mystery. In a telegram dated February 1, 1963 (shown on page 6), Vee-Jay president Ewart Abner informed publisher Concertone Songs that "PLEASE, PLEASE ME BY THE BEATLES WILL BE RELEASED FEBRUARY SEVEN." While the release of the Beatles first single took place exactly one year before the group's February 7, 1964, arrival in America, the events leading up to Vee-Jay obtaining the Beatles began in 1961.

The story of how the Beatles ended up on Vee-Jay is literally a story of international proportions. To obtain revenue from foreign sales of its recordings, Vee-Jay, through its subsidiary, Vee-Jay International, Inc., leased its master recordings to record companies in other countries. Assisting Vee-Jay in this endeavor was New York attorney Paul Marshall, whose client list also included EMI (Electrical and Musical Industries, Ltd.), a worldwide recording organization based in England.

On April 1, 1962, Vee-Jay entered into a licensing agreement with EMI under which Vee-Jay granted to EMI the sole and exclusive right and license to use every master recording owned by Vee-Jay during the term of the agreement for the purpose of manufacturing and selling records in specified foreign territories. The covered countries were nations in which EMI owned record companies, including Afghanistan, Gibraltar, India, Iran, Iraq, Jordan, Kuwait, Malaysia, Nepal, Nigeria, Pakistan, Saudi Arabia and, most important, the United Kingdom. In consideration for these rights, EMI agreed to pay Vee-Jay a royalty of nine percent (9%) of the retail selling price of ninety percent (90%) of the records sold under the agreement. The agreement was for a term of three years retroactive from November 1, 1961. It was quickly amended to add Angola, East Africa, Kenya, Tanganyika and the Republic of South Africa, but at a royalty rate of ten percent (10%). Pursuant to this agreement, recordings by Vee-Jay artists such as Jerry Butler, Dee Clark and Jimmy Reed appeared throughout the world on EMI-controlled labels such as Stateside.

Transglobal Music Co., Inc, served as EMI's agent in America. The company was incorporated in the state of New York by Mortimer Edelstein, an attorney for EMI, at the request of Roland Rennie, assistant to EMI president L.G. Wood. Although formed in 1961, Transglobal did not become active until the following April. In an ad appearing in the *1963-1964 International Music-Record Directory* published by *Billboard*, Transglobal described itself as an organization established to assist record manufacturers and music publishers in the placement and acquisition of masters and copyrights in the U.S.A., Europe and throughout the world. Its initial president was Joseph Zerga, a former employee of both Capitol Records and EMI. Although EMI did not own the stock of Transglobal, the company was subsidized by EMI, which was the company's only foreign client. Its primary function was to obtain master recordings from American labels for licensing foreign rights to EMI for worldwide distribution. In addition, it attempted to place foreign records made by EMI artists with American companies when recordings were turned down by Capitol which, as an EMI subsidiary, had first refusal for the United States' rights to all EMI product. Paul Marshall summed up the relationship between the companies by stating that "Transglobal was nothing more than EMI doing business in America."

In January of 1955, EMI had purchased a 95% interest in Capitol Records for eight and a half million dollars. EMI made the deal to obtain access to Capitol's recordings of popular American artists for its worldwide family of labels. For Capitol, the deal provided much needed capital enabling the company to better compete in the industry. It also gave Capitol the right of first refusal for the United States release of all recordings by EMI artists. For the most part, this arrangement was a one-way street. While EMI enjoyed great success selling records by American artists in the U.K. and foreign markets, Capitol was not very successful in breaking British and other foreign acts in America. A rare exception was Laurie London's *He's Got The Whole World In His Hands*, originally issued on EMI's Parlophone label. When released on Capitol 3891 in 1958, the song charted for 19 weeks, including four weeks atop the *Billboard Most Played by Jockeys* chart. The label's experience with Cliff Richard was more typical. Although Richard was a true star in England, neither of his late 50s Capitol releases, *Move It* or *Livin' Lovin' Doll*, charted in America.

A Brief History of Capitol Records

Capitol Records was founded in 1942 by Johnny Mercer, Glenn Wallich and Buddy DeSylva at a time when the record industry was dominated by three companies: Decca, RCA-Victor and Columbia. The story behind its creation is pure Hollywood. Ginger Mercer, wife of Johnny Mercer, was looking for a birthday gift for her husband when a friend suggested she have a radio installed in his car. Johnny Mercer was so impressed with the car radio that he visited Glenn Wallich, the man who installed the radio. The two quickly became friends. Mercer was an accomplished songwriter who believed that neither performers nor songwriters were presented at their best on records. Wallich, who owned a successful music store in Hollywood, was looking to expand the custom recording service provided by his store. The two decided that they could form their own record company if they could obtain financing. In a classic case of "let's do lunch," Mercer arranged a meeting at Lucey's restaurant in Hollywood with Buddy DeSylva, a Paramount Studios executive. DeSylva became interested and put up $25,000 in capital to get the label started. It was from this lunch meeting in the winter of 1941 that Capitol Records was born.

The three founders went through many potential names before Ginger Mercer came up with Capitol Records. Wallich designed the original logo of four stars around the Capitol dome in Washington, D.C.

Starting a new record company in 1942 turned out to be more of an adventure than the principals envisioned. Less than two months after Capitol released its first record, the American Federation of Musicians instituted a ban on recording over concerns that records were destroying job opportunities for musicians. Capitol was also handicapped by a wartime shortage of shellac, the principal ingredient used in manufacturing 78 RPM records. Wallich proved to be a creative, hardworking leader, helping the company overcome these and other hardships.

Early on, Capitol was an innovator. While other record companies frowned on radio stations playing their records on the mistaken belief that air play would cut into sales, Capitol issued free DJ copies. The strategy paid off as stations eagerly played Capitol discs, giving the records exposure and helping sales. In 1948, Capitol became the first company to record with magnetic tape, leading to improved fidelity and the ability to edit. The following year, Capitol became the first label to issue records in three different formats — 78 RPM 10" shellac discs, 33⅓ RPM Long Playing records and 45 RPM 7" vinyl singles.

The company experienced remarkable growth, quickly becoming a leader in the music industry. Its artists included Nat King Cole, Benny Goodman, Peggy Lee, Johnny Mercer, Kay Starr, Jackie Gleason, the Four Freshmen, the Kingston Trio, Les Paul & Mary Ford, Dean Martin and Frank Sinatra.

Capitol's artist roster made the company a suitable acquisition target for EMI which, in January of 1955, purchased a 95% interest in the company. The deal provided much needed capital enabling Capitol to better compete and gave Capitol the right of first refusal for the U.S. release of all recordings by EMI artists.

During the early sixties, Capitol was slow to move away from its roster of adult-oriented artists, although the label did have success with the Beach Boys before signing the Beatles. During the second half of the decade, the Hollywood-based label worked to become more "hip" by signing more rock artists. The company continues to be a force in the music industry.

Capitol can look back proudly on its history. The company revolutionized the industry with innovations in recording techniques, promotion, marketing and distribution and released landmark records by two of the most important recording artists of all time: Frank Sinatra and the Beatles.

In 1962, Alan Livingston became president of Capitol Records. He explained the arrangement between Capitol and EMI as follows:

"Out of courtesy, 'cause we had no obligation, I would occasionally take an EMI record, English in particular, and release it in the United States with no success whatsoever. There was just no interest in English artists here. And they would pressure me somewhat, but not too bad, and I'd keep trying something every now and then. We had no success at all, but because of the relationship, I felt we had to screen everything they sent us. I couldn't just brush it off, so I gave one of my producers at Capitol the assignment of listening to every EMI record that was sent to us. His name was Dave Dexter. And Dave was a good musicologist, he was a writer, he was a producer, and I trusted Dave's ears and was not concerned about it."

Dexter, who was then in his mid-to-late-forties, grew up with big band music and jazz and was not particularly fond of rock 'n' roll music. He routinely rejected EMI recordings as not being suitable for the American market. Neither Dexter nor anyone at Capitol recognized any interest in foreign product at that time.

Capitol's skepticism towards British acts led the label to pass on Frank Ifield who, in the summer of 1962, was enjoying a number one hit in England on EMI's Columbia label with *I Remember You*. Capitol reasoned that if British pop star Cliff Richard couldn't sell in America, then why should it be any different with Ifield, a popular Australian singer who moved to London in 1959. EMI wanted *I Remember You* released in America, so it transferred the licensing rights of Frank Ifield's master recordings to Transglobal, requesting that the company find an American label to issue the single. Paul Marshall, who, at the time, was serving as counsel for EMI, Transglobal and Vee-Jay, recalls unsuccessfully offering the Ifield master to MGM and other labels before approaching Vee-Jay.

A Brief History of Vee-Jay Records — The First Decade

The Vee-Jay Records story is about talented people with promotional savvy and human frailties who briefly turned a small business into a corporate giant, only to see it self-destruct. Vee-Jay was founded by Vivian Carter and her husband, Jimmy Bracken, owners of a record shop in Gary, Indiana. Vivian also had her own radio show, which featured music by black artists. Acting upon the suggestion of Chicago disc jockey and friend Sid McCoy, the Brackens developed a plan to record black artists and issue the recordings on their own label, which was named Vee-Jay from the initials of their first names.

Another key player in the Vee-Jay story was Vivian's brother, Calvin Carter. He served as the company's A&R (artists and repertoire) man, signing acts and producing sessions. His signings for the label included the Staple Singers, Jimmy Reed, John Lee Hooker, the Spaniels, the Dells, the El Dorados, Jerry Butler and Betty Everett.

After borrowing $500 from a pawn shop to finance their first studio session, the Brackens recorded four songs by the Spaniels, a group of five singers who had attended the same high school in Gary as Vivian and Calvin. Shortly after the May 5, 1953, session with the Spaniels, Vee-Jay held its first session with Jimmy Reed, a blues singer from Mississippi who had migrated north to Gary, where he worked in the steel mills, and then to Chicago seeking work as a full-time musician. These sessions gave birth to the company and its first two releases, *High & Lonesome* by Jimmy Reed on VJ 100 and *Baby, It's You* by the Spaniels on VJ 101.

Both of these records sold well locally and were leased to Chance records of Chicago for broader distribution. *Baby, It's You* (not the Shirelles song later recorded by the Beatles) reached the number ten spot on *Billboard's Rhythm & Blues Records* chart in September of 1953.

The success of these records enabled Vee-Jay to push forward and issue more records. The Spaniels' third single, *Goodnight Sweetheart, Goodnight* entered *Billboard's Rhythm & Blues Records* chart on May 1, 1954, and climbed to number five.

In 1955, Vee-Jay gained another key man in Ewart Abner, who had worked for Chance Records until the company went out of business. He initially served as Vee-Jay's business manager and was named president in 1961. His impact was immediate as his promotional talents helped Vee-Jay rack up two number one hits on *Billboard's Rhythm & Blues Records* chart during his first year with the company: Jay McShann's *Hand's Off* featuring Priscilla Brown on vocals and the El Dorados' *At My Front Door*. The El Dorados song became Vee-Jay's first song to crossover to the pop charts, reaching the number 17 spot on *Billboard's Best Sellers in Stores* chart on November 12, 1955.

Vee-Jay continued to release R&B hits that would become staples in the repertoire of British bands such as the Rolling Stones and the Animals. These songs included: Jimmy Reed's *Ain't That Lovin' You Baby*, *Honest I Do*, *Baby What You Want Me To Do*, *Big Boss Man* and *Bright Lights, Big City*; Gene Allison's *You Can Make It If You Try*; and John Lee Hooker's *Boom Boom*. Although Jimmy Reed's recording of *Take Out Some Insurance On Me Baby* did not chart, it captured the attention of bands and singers in England. Tony Sheridan, backed by the Beatles, recorded the song in Germany in June of 1961.

In 1956, Vee-Jay released the Dells' doo wop classic *Oh What A Night*, which was a number four R&B hit. Towards the end of the fifties and continuing into the early sixties, the label became more successful at having its records crossover to the pop charts.

The three key players in Vee-Jay's early success (from left to right): Vivian Carter Bracken, the "V" in Vee-Jay; Jimmy Bracken, the "J" in Vee-Jay; and Calvin Tollie Carter, the soul of Vee-Jay.

Although Vee-Jay was known for its R&B and gospel records, Marshall thought the Chicago-based label might be a good fit for Frank Ifield. By the early sixties, some of Vee-Jay's black artists were achieving considerable success on the pop charts. Examples include Jerry Butler's *He Will Break Your Heart* (VJ 354; R&B #1, Pop #17), Dee Clark's *Raindrops* (VJ 383; R&B #3, Pop #2), Gladys Knight & the Pips' *Every Beat Of My Heart* (VJ 386; R&B #1; Pop #6) and Gene Chandler's *Duke Of Earl* (VJ 416; R&B #1; Pop #1). Having broken into the lucrative pop market with crossover hits, Vee-Jay was interested in taking the next logical step by issuing records by pop artists.

At the time Marshall offered *I Remember You* to Vee-Jay, the label had just signed the Four Seasons, a white vocal group from New Jersey led by Frankie Valli. Vee-Jay realized that by entering into a leasing agreement with Transglobal for the Ifield single, the company could add another pop artist to its roster in a low-risk, low-cost way. In the summer of 1962, Vee-Jay signed a licensing agreement with Transglobal for *I Remember You*. The contract also gave Vee-Jay a right of first refusal for future EMI recordings of Frank Ifield. Some of the first pressings of *I Remember You* misspelled the artist's first name as "Farnk" (shown below).

Both of Vee-Jay's moves into the pop market proved successful when singles by the Four Seasons and Frank Ifield were assigned consecutive record numbers and released in August of 1962. The Four Seasons' *Sherry* (VJ 456) became the group's first of three consecutive number one pop hits, topping the charts for five weeks and selling over one million copies. Ifield's *I Remember You* (VJ 457) charted at number five in the *Billboard Hot 100*, demonstrating that Vee-Jay was capable of successfully promoting a British artist in America–something Capitol had been unable to do for years.

At the same time Frank Ifield entered the top ten in America, the Beatles first record, *Love Me Do*, was released on EMI's Parlophone subsidiary on October 5, 1962. Capitol's Dave Dexter was sent a copy of the single later that fall. Dexter was not impressed and recommended that Capitol pass on the song and the Beatles. He would later say that John's harmonica playing influenced his decision to reject *Love Me Do*. Having produced several R&B discs for Capitol, Dexter believed that the harmonica was a blues instrument that had no place in pop music. Because the Beatles first single was only a moderate hit in England (peaking at number 17), EMI was neither surprised nor concerned when Capitol declined to issue the 45 in America.

The Recording Of The First Two Beatles Singles

The song selected for the Beatles first single was *Love Me Do*. It was recorded at Abbey Road studios on three different occasions, each time with a different drummer!

After being turned down by several companies, the Beatles finally landed a record deal with EMI's Parlophone label, which was run by producer George Martin. The band's audition and first recording session took place on June 6, 1962, while Pete Best was still the drummer. Four songs were recorded that day: *Besame Mucho, Love Me Do, P.S. I Love You* and *Ask Me Why*. The first tune, written by Consuelo Velazquez and Sunny Skylar, was a Latin standard that came to the attention of the Beatles by way of the Coasters, who issued the song in two parts on a 45 in 1960. The other three songs were Lennon-McCartney originals. The tape containing the songs was erased shortly after the session; however, acetates of *Besame Mucho* and *Love Me Do* survived. The songs were released in 1995 on *Anthology 1*.

Although George Martin set up the session, Ron Richards initially served as producer because he was more familiar with rock 'n' roll than Martin, whose background encompassed classical and comedy recordings. Upon hearing *Love Me Do*, engineer Norman Smith was impressed and had Martin brought to the studio. He immediately took control, reassigning the singing of the "Love me do" refrain that ended each verse from John to Paul. This was done because John's harmonica playing prevented him from actually singing the word "do." It would be the first of many suggestions Martin would make over the years.

After completing four songs, the group met with Martin in the control room to listen to the tapes. Afterwards he lectured about recording studio equipment and techniques as the group sat silently and impassively. When he finished talking, he asked the group if there was anything they didn't like. George Harrison took a long look at Martin and said, "Yeah, I don't like your tie!" His wisecrack broke the ice, and the Abbey Road personnel were then treated to the Beatles at their entertaining best. Although none of the songs recorded that day was deemed suitable for release, the exploratory session marked the beginning of the group's successful union with producer George Martin.

Prior to the band's return to the studio, Pete Best was fired and replaced by Ringo Starr on drums. Best got the news on August 16, a date that would later gain even more notoriety in rock history as the day that Elvis Presley died.

The reasons behind the group's dismissal of Best have been debated for years. Some early fans believed the other members of the group were jealous of his good looks and popularity with their female fans. It is also quite possible that, for whatever reason, the others just did not think Pete fit in well with them. And, of course, the Beatles may have realized his drumming was inadequate.

The June 6, 1962, recording of *Love Me Do* supports the belief that Pete Best could not provide the Beatles with the strong drumming needed for their sound. His performance on the song is weak, particularly in the middle eight where it sounds like he falls off the bridge. George Martin took notice and told manager Brian Epstein that although Best could remain the drummer for live appearances, a session drummer would replace him for studio recordings. It is likely that Pete Best's sacking resulted from a combination of the reasons mentioned above.

Based upon the three Lennon-McCartney songs performed at the group's initial session, George Martin was not convinced the pair could write a hit single. He sent the band a demo of *How Do You Do It*, a song written by tunesmith Mitch Murray, and insisted that the group learn the song for their upcoming recording session. The demo, prepared with Adam Faith (a popular British singer) in mind, featured Barry Mason on vocals backed by the Dave Clark Five, who at the time were virtually unknown. The Beatles rearranged the song to give it more of a rock sound.

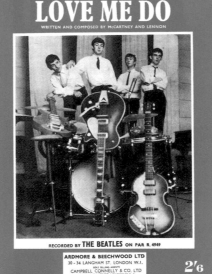

On September 4, 1962, the Beatles, with Ringo Starr on drums, returned to Abbey Road studios to record their first single. Because Pete Best had been replaced, Martin did not book a session drummer, instead opting to see what Ringo could do. That afternoon, the group rehearsed six songs, including *How Do You Do It, Love Me Do, P.S. I Love You, Ask Me Why* and P*lease Please Me*. The latter song sounded drastically different at that time. According to Martin, P*lease Please Me* was "a dreary song," which "was like a Roy Orbison number, very slow, bluesy vocals." He suggested that the group rearrange the song by speeding up the tempo and working out tight vocal harmonies.

After a break for dinner, the Beatles reluctantly recorded *How Do You Do It*. George Martin produced the session. As was the practice at that time, the group performed the song live with vocals and instruments being played and recorded at the same time. The song, which features John and Paul on lead vocals, John on acoustic guitar, George on his Gretsch Duo-Jet electric guitar, Paul on his Hofner 500/1 violin-shaped bass and Ringo on drums, was apparently captured in one take. The group then superimposed hand claps over the instrumental break to form Take 2. Although some people, including Ron Richards, believe the Beatles deliberately played poorly on the song in an attempt to prevent its release, this does not appear to be the case. While the Beatles lack of enthusiasm is somewhat apparent, their playing and singing is quite competent.

Having completed Martin's initial choice for the A side, the Beatles were allowed to record one of their original compositions, *Love Me Do*. Although studio logs no longer exist, it is believed that the group took over 15 takes on the backing track. The finished master may consist of an edit of two or more takes. Hand claps were overdubbed during the harmonica solo.

Both songs were mixed for mono by George Martin and engineer Norman Smith at the end of the session. Over the next few days, Martin listened to the acetates of the songs, trying to decide if they were worthy of being the group's debut single. Although the Beatles had competently performed *How Do You Do It*, he knew that the group wanted to release their own songs on the single. As for *Love Me Do*, Martin thought it could be improved. He booked studio time on September 11, 1962, for the Beatles to record a remake of *Love Me Do*, along with one of their own compositions for the flip side. Due to a scheduling conflict, Martin had to miss the start of the session. He arranged for Ron Richards to produce the session until his arrival.

Although Ringo's drumming was a big improvement over that of Pete Best, neither Martin nor Ron Richards were satisfied with the drum sound on *Love Me Do*. Without consulting or warning the Beatles, Richards hired Andy White, a reliable studio drummer, to sit in with the band for the session.

The first song recorded on September 11 was *P.S. I Love You*, which featured Paul on lead vocals, supported by John and George. To the surprise and disappointment of the group, Richards insisted that Andy White play the drums. Ringo, making the best of a humiliating situation, dutifully shook maracas. White's rhythm on the wood block and Ringo's maracas give the song a Latin flavor. The tenth and final take was used for the finished master.

For the remake of *Love Me Do*, Andy White was once again behind the drums, while Ringo was relegated to tambourine. The group took 18 takes to obtain a satisfactory recording of the song. The main difference between the September 4 recording and the September 11 remake is the tambourine on the later recording.

George Martin probably arrived at the studio while the band was wrapping up *Love Me Do*. After the group finished both songs planned for the single, there was still time to begin work on a third song, *Please Please Me*. Following Martin's advice from the week before, the band per-

formed the song at a quicker pace, but failed to nail it down. This early version is interesting, but suffers in comparison to the remake the group would later record. Conspicuously absent from this version is John's harmonica. John and Paul's harmonies are also not as effective. It is presumed that Andy White played drums on this run through of the song, which made its debut on *Anthology 1*.

After reviewing the completed songs from the two September sessions, George Martin chose the September 4 version of *Love Me Do*, with Ringo on drums, as the A side and *P.S. I Love You* as the B side of the Beatles first single. The disc was released as Parlophone 45-R 4949 on October 5, 1962.

Although the Beatles won the battle to have a record of their own material, Martin was correct in his belief in *How Do You Do It*. He later recorded the song with Gerry and the Pacemakers, who rode the song to the top of the British charts in early 1963. The Beatles version of the song finally made its legitimate debut on *Anthology 1*.

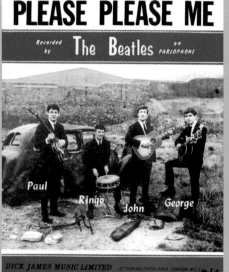

When the group's first album was banded together on February 25, 1963, the September 11 version of *Love Me Do* with Andy White on drums and Ringo on tambourine was used rather than the September 4 version that appeared on the single. On September 6, 1963, approximately one year after the two sessions that produced the two different versions of the songs, *The Beatles Hits* EP was released with the later recorded version with Ringo on tambourine. At some point during the sixties, it was decided to use only the later recording on all releases, including future pressings of the single. To ensure that the original version would not be mistakenly used, the master tape of the September 4 recording was foolishly erased.

The Beatles second single was recorded at a session held at Abbey Road on November 26, 1962. After an hour-long rehearsal, the group began work on a remake of *Please Please Me*. This time the group perfected the song. It was completed in 15 takes, including harmonica overdubs by John. Four days later, George Martin edited the finished master from an unknown number of takes and then mixed the song for mono. *Please Please Me* is an exciting rocker propelled by superb drumming from Ringo. After this recording, George Martin knew there would be no need for a session drummer for the band.

After a break for tea, the band completed the single's B side, *Ask Me Why*, in six takes. The song features John on lead vocals, backed by Paul and George. The group also recorded a few takes of *Tip Of My Tongue*, a mediocre tune written by Paul. When the group realized that the song did not measure up to their standards, it was given to Tommy Quickly, who was also managed by Brian Epstein.

On November 26, 1962, the Beatles recorded their second single, *Please Please Me* and *Ask Me Why*. Producer George Martin was particularly excited by *Please Please Me*. Upon completion of the recording, he reportedly told the group, "Boys, you've got your first number one hit."

Martin knew that no British musical act had ever made it big in America, but he had high hopes that *Please Please Me* would break the mold. He hoped that Capitol, as an EMI subsidiary, would issue the record in the States.

Dave Dexter received the new Beatles single in either late 1962 or early 1963. Upon reviewing the disc for possible release on Capitol, Dexter did not like what he heard. Once again, he was bothered by John's harmonica riffs and informed EMI that Capitol would not be issuing the record.

George Martin was bitterly disappointed by Capitol's decision. He firmly believed that *Please Please Me* was going to be a big hit and could not understand why EMI would not order its American subsidiary to issue the disc in the States. EMI's explanation that Capitol was completely autonomous and knew its market did little to reduce the friction between Martin and EMI.

Paul Marshall recalls being told by EMI's L.G. Wood and/or Roland Rennie that Beatles management was frustrated with Capitol's refusal to issue Beatles records. EMI transferred the rights to the Beatles recordings to Transglobal with instructions to get the new single released in America as quickly as possible to appease Martin and Brian Epstein.

Marshall offered *Please Please Me* to Atlantic Records, which rejected the song. He was told by label head Jerry Wexler's secretary that Atlantic did not like the song because it was derivative and "not pure." Later that year Atlantic signed the Fourmost, a Brian Epstein-managed band, and released the group's recording of Lennon-McCartney's *Hello Little Girl* on its Atco subsidiary on November 15, 1963. After Beatlemania struck America, Atco issued four of the Beatles 1961 Hamburg recordings in mid-1964.

Recalling Vee-Jay's success with Frank Ifield's *I Remember You*, Marshall offered *Please Please Me* to Vee-Jay. As the label had profited from the Frank Ifield deal, Vee-Jay felt it had nothing to lose by issuing the Beatles 45.

Paul Marshall's story is consistent with the affidavit given by Transglobal president Joseph Zerga in a 1964 lawsuit brought by Capitol against Vee-Jay. Mr. Zerga stated:

"The offices of Transglobal were located in the same building adjoining the offices of Mr. Marshall. Mr. Marshall, without my knowledge, made commitments for the placement of The Beatles' master recordings with Vee-Jay directly with Mr. Abner, the then president of Vee-Jay. As Mr. Marshall made the commitment, there was no objection made, although I had knowledge that Mr. Marshall was also the attorney for Vee-Jay."

Under the terms of a January 10, 1963, licensing agreement signed by Ewart Abner and Joseph Zerga, Transglobal leased to Vee-Jay the exclusive rights to use the master recordings of *Please Please Me* and *Ask Me Why* for the purpose of manufacturing and selling phonograph records in the United States. To exercise its rights to these recordings, Vee-Jay was required to manufacture and ship a minimum of 1,000 records within 30 days of receiving the masters. Within 45 days of the end of each quarter, Vee-Jay was required to provide Transglobal with an itemized statement of sales and a royalty payment based upon the number of records sold. The royalty rate was ten percent. The term of the agreement was five years. In the event the agreement was terminated at an earlier time, Vee-Jay had the right to continue selling records made from the masters for a period of six months from the termination date.

Although to Paul Marshall, EMI was obviously a more important client than Vee-Jay, Marshall did look after Vee-Jay's interests in the deal. He added an important addendum to the five-year agreement that gave Vee-Jay the right of first refusal of all recordings by the Beatles, exercisable within 30 days of receipt of the master recordings.

Shortly after signing the licensing agreement with Transglobal, Vee-Jay received a tape from EMI containing *Please Please Me* and *Ask Me Why*. The two songs were entered into the company's Master Book, with *Please Please Me* assigned number 63-2967 and *Ask Me Why* assigned number 63-2968. The record was designated VJ 498.

Vee-Jay sent the tape of the songs to Universal Recording Corporation in Chicago for mastering, a process that involves cutting lacquer discs. On January 18, 1963, Universal sent two lacquers for each side of the record to Audio Matrix in the Bronx, New York, for preparation of the metal parts needed to manufacture the single.

PACKING SLIP

January 18, 1963 19____

SHIPPED BY _____ Universal Recording Corp.
46 E. Walton St

Chicago, Illinois

SOLD TO _____ Audio Matrix _____ Vee Jay W-24474 _____

ITEM	QUANTITY	UNIT	NUMBER	DESCRIPTION
1	2	6'45	63-2967	Please, Please Me
2	2	7"45	63-2968	Ask Me Why
3				
4				
5				please sign and return
6				one copy to Universal
7				
8				*Gus: Received these matrices on 1/24/63,*
9				*covered by your P.O. # 145*
10				
11				*Julio*
12				
13				
14				

CHECKED BY _____ PACKED BY _____ WEIGHT _____
SHIPPED VIA _____ B/L 47-65-19 _____ NUMBER OF PIECES _____

ALL CLAIMS MUST BE PRESENTED WITHIN FIVE DAYS AFTER RECEIPT OF
MERCHANDISE AND MUST BE ACCOMPANIED BY THIS PACKING LIST.

TOPS FORM 3247 LITHO IN U.S.A.

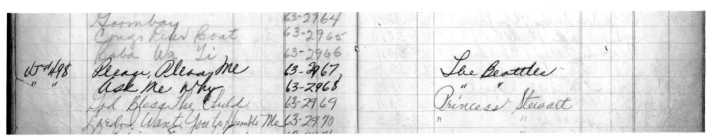

When *Please Please Me* and *Ask Me Why* were entered into the company's Master Book, Vee-Jay misspelled the group's name as The Beattles, demonstrating that both Transglobal and Vee-Jay were uncertain as to the proper spelling of the group's name. Interestingly, this historic Beatles entry was made in a darker ink, causing it to stand out prominently, while the entries for other artists faded away.

Audio Matrix invoices dated January 29, 1963, indicate that the company prepared and shipped metal parts for the Beatles single to the three primary factories used at that time by Vee-Jay to press its records: American Record Pressing Co. (ARP) in Owosso, Michigan; Monarch Records in Los Angeles, California; and Southern Plastics in Nashville, Tennessee.

Meanwhile, Vee-Jay began gathering the information needed to prepare the label copy for the record. Based upon information obtained from Transglobal, Vee-Jay misspelled the group's name as "The Beattles" with two Ts. This error appears on all first pressings of the disc. The songwriters credit is listed as "J. Lennon-P. McCartney." On January 21, 1963, company president Ewart Abner sent a telegram (shown bottom right) to Paul Marshall's law partner, Joe

Vigoda, requesting the name of the American publishing company for the songs.

After learning that the American publisher was Concertone Songs, Vee-Jay sent Concertone a telegram (shown on page 6) informing the company that the record would be released on February 7, 1963.

In England, *Please Please Me* was released four weeks earlier on January 11, 1963, as Parlophone 45-R 4983. Brian Epstein anxiously reviewed the British music weeklies to track the song's progress up the charts.

True or False?

Please Please Me was the first Beatles single to reach number one in England.

True, but...

Although *Please Please Me* was reported at number one by *Melody Maker, New Musical Express* and *Disc*, the *Record Retailer* listing published by *Record Mirror* charted the song at number two. When Apple Records compiled its collection of number one hits, *Beatles 1*, in 2000, it used *Record Retailer* as the benchmark standard for British chart positions. Because *Please Please Me* failed to reach number one on the *Record Retailer* chart, the song does not appear on *Beatles 1*.

In the United States, Vee-Jay's initial release of *Please Please Me* suffered an entirely different fate than Parlophone's British release. For starters, Vee-Jay wasn't quite sure what it had with the Beatles. Was the group pop, R&B or country & western? A Vee-Jay ad appearing in the March 2, 1963, *Cash Box* (shown on the previous page) covered all three chart possibilities. Most early trade magazine advertisements, as well as all initial pressings of the record, misspelled the group's name as THE BEATTLES.

Although the single received minimal attention and failed to chart in any of the major trade magazines, it was not a total flop. Vee-Jay sold approximately 5,650 copies during the first half of 1963. By midyear the record had run its course, selling only two copies during the last six months of 1963. A limited pressing of the single in 1964 added sales of approximately 1,650 units, raising total sales to 7,310 copies. Due to the small number of copies pressed, VJ 498 is relatively scarce and highly collectible.

Ain't that a shame that Vee-Jay couldn't even spell the group's name correctly in this *Billboard* ad in the April 23, 1963, issue. Shame, shame, shame.

Myths

- Vee-Jay employee Barbara Gardner discovered the Beatles while on a talent scouting mission in England.
- The 4 Seasons were responsible for bringing the Beatles to America by making Vee-Jay aware of the group.
- Little Richard discovered the Beatles in England and told Vee-Jay to sign the band.

Fact

New York attorney Paul Marshall, who represented EMI and Vee-Jay, was responsible for Vee-Jay signing a licensing agreement on January 10, 1963, to issue Beatles recordings in the United States.

Billboard reported in its February 16, 1963, issue that Vee-Jay's Barbara Gardner was in London. The story stated that under a deal with EMI, Vee-Jay would release records by the Beatles, a "promising British ... group which has yet to make a large chart impact." This falsely gave the impression that Gardner had discovered the Beatles while in London, a story that was more likely to draw favorable attention to the Beatles than an article titled "New York Lawyer Brings British Band to Vee-Jay after Group Rejected by Capitol and Others."

The 4 Seasons, who recorded for Vee-Jay, were on tour in England during late 1962. The story goes that the group heard the Beatles *Please Please Me* and, upon their return to the States, informed Vee-Jay president Jay Lasker that they wanted to record the song. Vee-Jay expressed no interest in *Please Please Me*, but then went behind the band's back and signed the Beatles, who would go on to replace the 4 Seasons as the dominant group in America. This story is full of holes. *Please Please Me* was not released in England until January 11, 1963, so the 4 Seasons could not have heard the record during their 1962 tour. Furthermore, Vee-Jay entered into its licensing agreement for *Please Please Me* on January 10, 1963. Finally, Jay Lasker was never president of Vee-Jay and did not even begin working for the label until the fall of 1963.

Although Little Richard recorded for Vee-Jay and twice shared the bill with The Beatles in October, 1962, he did not record for Vee-Jay until 1965. Thus, it is highly unlikely that the man who claimed he invented rock 'n' roll had anything to do with Vee-Jay's signing of the Beatles.

Multiple Choice

The first disc jockey to play a Beatles record in America was:

A. Carroll James, WWDC, Washington, D.C.

B. Murray the K, WINS, New York

C. Dave Hull or Bob Eubanks, KRLA, Los Angeles

D. Marcia Shafer, WFRX, West Frankfort, Illinois

E. Dick Biondi, WLS, Chicago

Answer

Carroll James played a copy of the British single *I Want To Hold Your Hand* on December 17, 1963. While he was the first to play the Beatles breakthrough American hit, earlier Beatles records were played prior to that time.

Legendary disc jockey Murray the K reportedly received a copy of *She Loves You* on September 28, 1963, and played it on the radio that evening. *She Loves You* placed third in a listeners' poll of five new singles and received minimal airplay on WINS for the next few weeks. Features such as *On This Day in Rock History* state, "It is believed to be the first Beatles song ever played in the U.S." It wasn't.

KRLA played *From Me To You* in the summer of 1963, but the station was probably not the first to play the song in America.

During the early part of that summer, George Harrison's sister, Louise Caldwell, received a copy of *From Me To You* from her mother. Lou took the British disc to radio station WFRX in West Frankfort, Illinois, where it was aired by Marcia Shafer, a high school student whose father owned the station. Marcia was certainly one of the first to play a Beatles record on the radio in the United States, but she was not the first.

WLS disc jockey Dick Biondi, who frequently got together with Vee-Jay president Ewart Abner, received a copy of the label's first Beatles single, *Please Please Me*, in early February, 1963. Abner endorsed the 45 with his usual "I feel this could be a big record," and Biondi liked what he heard. Biondi believes he may have debuted the single as early as Friday, February 8, 1963, during his 9:00 p.m. to midnight shift. If so, Dick Biondi quietly became the first disc jockey in America to play a Beatles record on the air exactly one year prior to Murray the K's flamboyant *Swingin' Soiree* program featuring the Beatles (see page 146).

WLS
The bright sound of Chicago Radio

SILVER DOLLAR SURVEY

Chicago's Official Radio Record Survey

MARCH 15, 1963

THIS WEEK			WEEKS PLAYED
* 1.	THE END OF THE WORLD	Skeeter Davis — RCA	9
* 2.	HE'S SO FINE	Chiffons — Laurie	4
* 3.	WILD WEEKEND	Rebels — Swan	9
* 4.	RHYTHM OF THE RAIN	Cascades — Valiant	11
* 5.	WALK LIKE A MAN	Four Seasons — Vee Jay	10
6.	RUBY BABY	Dion — Columbia	11
* 7.	SOUTH STREET	Orlons — Cameo	8
* 8.	OUR DAY WILL COME	Ruby & Romantics — Kapp	9
9.	LINDA	Jan & Dean — Liberty	6
10.	OUR WINTER LOVE	Bill Pursell — Columbia	6
*11.	BLAME IT ON THE BOSSA NOVA	Eydie Gorme — Columbia	5
12.	PLEASE DON'T MENTION MY NAME	Shepherd Sisters — Atlantic	5
*13.	SUN ARISE	Rolf Harris — Epic	4
*14.	IN DREAMS	Roy Orbison — Monument	5
*15.	OUT OF MY MIND	Johnny Tillotson — Cadence	6
*16.	DON'T WANNA THINK ABOUT PAUL	Dickey Lee — Smash	5
*17.	ALL I HAVE TO DO IS DREAM	Richard Chamberlain — MGM	5
*18.	I GOT BURNED	Ral Donner — Reprise	6
*19.	DON'T BE AFRAID LITTLE DARLIN	Steve Lawrence — Columbia	6
*20.	ONE BROKEN HEART FOR SALE	Elvis Presley — RCA	6
*21.	HOW CAN I FORGET	Jimmy Holiday — Everest	4
*22.	YOUNG AND IN LOVE	Dick & Dee Dee — WB	7
*23.	BULE	Jack Reno — Fono Graf	6
24.	LOVE FOR SALE	Arthur Lyman — Hi Fi	5
25.	TELL HIM I'M NOT HOME	Chuck Jackson — Wand	4
*26.	DO THE BIRD	Dee Dee Sharp — Cameo	4
*27.	YOUNG LOVERS	Paul & Paula — Philips	5
*28.	YELLOW BANDANA	Faron Young — Mercury	4
*29.	SAX FIFTH AVENUE	Johnny Beecher — WB	6
30.	PIPELINE	Chantays — Dot	4
*31.	CASTAWAY	Hayley Mills — Vista	5
*32.	MR BASS MAN	Johnny Cymbal — Kapp	5
*33.	ON BROADWAY	Drifters — Atlantic	4
*34.	DON'T SAY NOTHIN BAD	Cookies — Dimension	4
*35.	PLEASE PLEASE ME	Beatles — Vee Jay	4
*36.	PIN A MEDAL ON JOEY	James Darren — Colpix	3
*37.	CAN'T GET USED TO LOSING YOU	Andy Williams — Columbia	3
*38.	SANDY	Dion — Laurie	2
*39.	LITTLE STAR	Bobby Callender — Roulette	3
*40.	PUFF	Peter, Paul & Mary — WB	3

FEATURED ALBUMS

THE END OF THE WORLD—SKEETER DAVIS — RCA
I WANNA BE AROUND — TONY BENNETT — COLUMBIA
GOLDEN HITS — VOL. 2 — BROOK BENTON — MERCURY

Don't miss the fun with

Dick Biondi

9 to Midnight — Monday thru Sunday

WLS · DIAL 890 · 24 HOURS-A-DAY

ABC RADIO IN CHICAGO

This survey is compiled each week by WLS Radio/Chicago from reports of all record sales gathered from leading record outlets in the Chicagoland area. Hear Clark Weber play all the SILVER DOLLAR SURVEY hits daily from 3:00 to 6:30 P.M. *Denotes record first heard on WLS.

Please Please Me peaked at number 35 on the March 15, 1963, WLS Silver Dollar Survey (shown above). The number nine song on the chart was Jan & Dean's Linda, which was a number one hit for Buddy Clark in 1947. The song was written by Jack Lawrence for six-year-old Linda Eastman, who later became Paul McCartney's first wife. The number two song was He's So Fine by the Chiffons (see page 179).

LONG PLAYING
TRADE MARK
PARLOPHONE
PMC 1202
PLEASE PLEASE ME
THE BEATLES
mono
PLEASE PLEASE ME ★ THE BEATLES
PARLOPHONE
THE BEATLES
PLEASE PLEASE ME
Photo: Angus McBean

FEBRUARY 11, 1963

On February 11, 1963, exactly one year prior to their first American concert, the Beatles entered EMI Recording Studios on Abbey Road in London to record songs for the group's debut album *Please Please Me*. In what is widely acknowledged to be one of the most productive days ever spent in a recording studio, the Beatles recorded ten high-spirited songs that were standards in their live performances.

When Beatles producer George Martin realized that *Please Please Me* was going to hit it big, it was only natural for him to want to release an album as soon as possible to cash in on the group's success. As Martin observed, "While a single which sells half a million doesn't reap all that great a reward, half a million albums is big business."

Martin briefly considered doing a live remote recording at the Cavern Club in Liverpool, but recalled the chaotic conditions he observed there during a December 9, 1962, concert and realized it would not be practical. Instead, he booked a session at EMI Recording Studios on Abbey Road for February 11, 1963, one of only two days during the month in which the Beatles were not scheduled for a concert appearance. The goal was to record ten songs from the band's stage show and augment the new material with the four songs previously released on the group's first two singles to form a fourteen-track LP (which was the standard number of songs found on a British pop album). The plan worked to perfection as the session yielded ten high quality recordings that formed the basis for the band's first British LP, *Please Please Me*. The same ten songs would later appear on *Introducing The Beatles,* the group's first American album.

By the time the Beatles entered the studio, it was apparent that their grueling schedule and the harsh British winter (one of the coldest on record) were catching up with them. John had a nasty cold that made it hard for him to sing without experiencing pain. He soothed his vocal chords by drinking milk and sucking on Zubes, a British throat lozenge. Despite the adverse conditions, the group's excitement at recording their first album gave them the energy boost needed to get through the day and night.

As was the case with the group's previously recorded singles, the songs were recorded live with minimal overdubs. George Harrison used his Gretsch Duo-Jet electric guitar on most numbers, although he played a Gibson J-160E Jumbo acoustic-electric guitar on some songs. John alternated between his Gibson Jumbo and his Rickenbacker Capri electric guitar. Paul was on his Hofner bass and Ringo was still using his Premier drum kit. The sessions took place in Studio Two during three separate blocks of time that day.

The morning session began at 10:00 a.m. with the recording of *There's A Place*, a Lennon-McCartney tune written primarily by John, who later called the song an "attempt at a sort of Motown black thing." The basic track, with John on lead vocal, was completed in ten takes (including two false starts and one breakdown).

The next song recorded was *I Saw Her Standing There*, which was titled *17* on the recording sheets. The song was written by Paul and John at the McCartney house on Forthlin Road. The rocker had been in the Beatles stage shows since 1962. An early version of the song is on the *Cavern Rehearsal* tape, a crude recording probably made shortly after Ringo joined the band in August, 1962. The song also appears on the *Live At The Star Club* album, which was crudely recorded at the Star Club in Hamburg, Germany, during the 1962 Christmas season.

The Beatles recorded two complete takes of *I Saw Her Standing There* before moving on to an edit piece of the ending and two edit pieces of the instrumental break. None of these edit bits were used. Takes 6, 7 and 8 quickly broke down, while Take 9 was complete. Paul's famous "One, two, three, faaa!" count-in to the song was later lifted from Take 9 and edited to the finished master. The maxi-single *Free As A Bird*, released in 1995 along with *Anthology 1*, contains the full Take 9.

After a break for lunch, recording resumed at 2:30 p.m. with the band running through five takes of *A Taste Of Honey*, a ballad written by Bobby Scott and Ric Marlow for the Broadway show *A Taste Of Honey*. The tune came to the attention of the Beatles through Lenny Welch's recording of the song released on Cadence in September, 1962. This show tune/pop ballad appealed to Paul, who handled the lead vocal.

The next song recorded was *Do You Want To Know A Secret*, a Lennon-McCartney original featuring George on lead vocal. The basic track was completed in six takes. The "do dah do" backing vocals and tapping drum sticks were superimposed onto Take 6, with Track 2, Take 8 selected as the master.

The overdubs continued with Paul double-tracking his vocal on *A Taste Of Honey* to give his voice a fuller sound. The finished master is Track 2, Take 7. John then superimposed his harmonica onto Take 10 of *There's A Place*, with Track 2, Take 13 being selected for the master.

Next the group returned to *I Saw Her Standing There*, at first adding vocals to Take 9. After further review, it was determined that Take 1 was the best performance and that it should be enhanced with hand claps. After one breakdown, Track 2, Take 12 became the finished master.

The last song performed in the afternoon session was *Misery*, which was written by John and Paul for British teen singer Helen Shapiro in late January, 1963. When Shapiro's management passed on the song, it was offered to Kenny Lynch, who became the first artist other than the Beatles to record a Lennon-McCartney song. Lynch released the song as a single in March, 1963. The Beatles recorded their version in 11 takes, with George Martin later adding piano.

The evening session began with the group recording *Hold Me Tight*, a Lennon-McCartney tune written primarily by and sung by Paul. The session sheet indicates that the band ran through 13 takes, including three complete run throughs, six false starts, a breakdown and three edit pieces. The song was neither edited nor mixed, and was not included on the album. The Beatles rerecorded *Hold Me Tight* on September 12, 1963, for their second LP.

The Beatles then knocked out five cover tunes, starting with *Anna*, which was recorded in one take after two false starts. The song was written and originally recorded by Arthur Alexander, a black musician and songwriter from Alabama, whose soulful vocals influenced many soul singers of the sixties. Released on Dot as *Anna (Go To Him)*, Alexander's recording of the song entered the *Billboard Hot 100* on October 27, 1962, and peaked at number 68. It also reached number 10 on *Billboard's Hot R&B Singles* chart. The Beatles recording is memorable for the passionate lead vocal of John, who idolized Alexander. The recording sheet incorrectly lists the song as "*Hannah.*"

The Beatles covered six songs by American artists on their first album. The labels of the American singles that featured these songs are pictured above.

Boys was first recorded by the Shirelles, a group of four black teenage girls from Passaic, New Jersey, that had numerous hits in the early sixties and helped define the "girl group" sound. The Beatles fondness for American girl groups is evidenced by the inclusion on their first album of three songs originally recorded by girl groups. *Boys* was written by Luther Dixon, who produced The Shirelles, and Wes Farrell. Although it was not a hit, the song came to the attention of the Beatles as the flip side of *Will You Still Love Me Tomorrow*, a number one single in the United States on Scepter and a number three British hit on Top Rank in early 1961. Whereas the Shirelles' version of the song has a moderate tempo and sensual R&B groove, the Beatles recorded *Boys* in one explosive take as an all-out rocker with Ringo on lead vocals.

Chains was a number 17 hit for the Cookies that began its 12-week *Billboard* run on November 10, 1962. The song, released on Dimension, was written and produced by the Brill Building songwriting team of Gerry Goffin and Carole King. The Cookies were a trio of black female vocalists from New York that went through numerous lineup changes. The version of the group that recorded for Dimension featured Ethel "Earl-Jean" McCrea on lead vocal. Earl-Jean later recorded *I'm Into Something Good*, which was released on Colpix and reached number 38 in the summer of 1964. Herman's Hermits' cover version of the song became the group's first hit, reaching number one in England and number 13 in the United States in the fall of 1964.

The Beatles recorded *Chains* in four takes, two of which were false starts. Take 1 was deemed the best. George sang the lead vocal, with support from John and Paul.

Baby It's You, written by Burt Bacharach, Hal David and Barney Williams, was recorded by the Shirelles and released on Scepter. The record entered the *Billboard Hot 100* on December 18, 1961, and spent 14 weeks on the charts, peaking at number eight. It was also a number three R&B hit. The record's distinctive percussion, passionate vocals and memorable "sha la la la la" refrain make it one of the best girl group songs ever recorded. John handled the emotional lead vocal on the Beatles version of the song, which closely follows the Shirelles' superb single. The song was recorded in three takes, one being a false start. George Martin later added celesta.

Although the group had been in the studio for 12 hours and John's voice was all but gone, one more song was needed to complete the album. During a break in the studio canteen, it was decided to record one of the more popular rockers from the band's stage show, *Twist And Shout*. The song was written by Phil Medley and Bert Berns, who used the name Bert Russell for his writer's credit on the song. It was originally recorded by the Top Notes and released as a B side on Atlantic in 1961. The song was produced by Phil Spector, who was called in by John to fix the *Get Back/Let It Be* project in 1970. Although Spector would later gain notoriety in the early sixties for his "wall of sound," his handling of the song is weak.

ABOVE TWO PHOTOS - THE COOKIES: The sheet music to *Chains* features a photo of the group. Their release of *Chains* on Dimension 1002 was a number 17 hit in late 1962.

TOP RIGHT TWO PHOTOS - THE SHIRELLES: The cover to the *Baby It's You* LP features a picture of the group with producer Luther Dixon. The album peaked at number 59 in the summer of 1962.

RIGHT: A recording of *Baby It's You* from the Beatles *Live At The BBC* album was released in 1995 on a maxi-single. The disc also includes *Boys,* which, like *Baby It's You,* was originally recorded by the Shirelles and covered by the Beatles.

A tale of two Spectors. *Twist And Shout* was originally recorded by the Top Notes and released on Atlantic 2115 in 1961. The Canadian pressing of the single (left) states that the session was supervised by Phil Spector. Nearly a decade later, the Beatles American single *The Long And Winding Road* (right) bore the infamous legend "Reproduced for disc by PHIL SPECTOR." Although Spector produced many fabulous recordings during his illustrious career, some believe his work on these two records all but ruined two great songs.

Bert Berns' reaction to Spector's production of *Twist And Shout* was similar to McCartney's reaction to Spector's adding strings and a female chorus to *The Long And Winding Road*. Both thought Phil ruined their songs.

Relegated to the flip side of a record that flopped, *Twist And Shout* would have remained unknown but for Bert Berns' belief in the song. When recorded by the Isley Brothers and released on Wand in mid-1962, the song remained on the pop charts for 16 weeks, reaching number 17 in the *Billboard Hot 100* and number two on *Billboard's Hot R&B Singles* chart. It was this version of the song that caught the attention of the Beatles, who quickly added the tune to their stage show. The song appears on *Live At The Star Club*, which was recorded in late December of 1962.

After the canteen break, the group returned to Studio Two. John, shirtless and revived by biscuits and gargling milk, gamely strapped on his guitar, stepped to the mike and belted out the song with an incredible intensity that all but destroyed his vocal chords. With this remarkable single take, the Beatles had recorded one of the greatest rock 'n' roll performances of all time. Although a second take was recorded, it was never considered for the master as John's voice was totally shot from the first rendition.

After the session, the group went upstairs to hear the playback. John doused his throat with a glass of milk. According to Tony Barrow, John's vocal chords were bleeding, as evidenced by the sight of blood mixed with the milk in the glass.

George Martin added overdubs to *Misery* (piano) and *Baby It's You* (celesta) on February 20. The album was mixed in mono and stereo on February 25. The stereo LP contains simulated stereo mixes of *Love Me Do* and *P.S. I Love You*, as well as a different take and edit of *Please Please Me*.

Myth

The Beatles recorded a cover version of Little Eva's *Keep Your Hands Off My Baby* during the February 11, 1963, session.

Fact

Although the February 22, 1963, issue of the *New Musical Express* reported that the Beatles recorded the song during the album session, it is not listed on the recording sheets. The group did record the song for the BBC on January 22, 1963, for broadcast on the January 26 *Saturday Club*. The 1994 album *Live At The BBC* contains this performance, which features John on lead vocal backed by Paul and George.

Martin hired Angus McBean to photograph the group for the album's cover (shown on page 18). The Beatles are pictured looking over the railing of the inside stairwell at EMI's headquarters at 20 Manchester Square, London. The back cover's notes were written by Tony Barrow, who served as press agent for the Beatles and other Brian Epstein-managed acts.

In England, the LP was titled *Please Please Me* to capitalize on the hit single of the same name. The mono version of the album was released as Parlophone PMC 1202 on March 22, 1963. It went straight to the top of the charts where it remained for 30 weeks until being replaced by the group's next album. The stereo LP was released as Parlophone PCS 3042 five weeks later on April 26.

FAST TALK ABOUT HOT Capitol SINGLES ....

FROM THE 'DESK OF *Paul White* NO: 21   WEEK ENDING FEBRUARY 22nd, 1963

CAPITOL SINGLES ARE THE HIT SINGLES!

We've a big list of HOT PROSPECTS this week, but first let me keep you abreast of our
current established hits. The following records are on almost ALL charts:-

         1. YOU'RE THE REASON/Bobby Darin/4897
         2. GREENBACK DOLLAR/The Kingston Trio/4898
         3. LET'S TALK ABOUT LOVE/KEEP AWAY FROM OTHER GIRLS/Helen Shapiro/72062
         4. SING A LITTLE SONG OF HEARTACHE/Rose Maddox/4845

                    THESE ARE THE NEXT SMASH HITS!
         ****

NOTHING GOES UP/NAT COLE/4919 -- This seems to be the side, and initial reaction is
                tremendous. Already a housewives' favourite.

THE WAYWARD WIND/FRANK IFIELD/72077 -- Dealers in Canada seem to be following the pattern
                set in England. They are ordering stock in quantity and
                the disc has only just been released. This is going to
                be No. 3 for Frank!

ETERNALLY/THE CHANTELS/72078 -- Oh Boy -- This R & B side just has to score! The hit-
                making group have come up with their best effort to date --
                it's headed right for the top!

LOVE ME DO/THE BEATLES/72076 -- Give this side a couple of spins and you'll be hooked!
                This is an English record and a recent top 20 disc over
                there. Don't neglect this side!

SUN ARISE/ROLF HARRIS/72059 -- Action a-plenty for the A
                States -- a real chart

I WILL FOLLOW YOU/FRANCK POURCEL/4916 -- What
                "Chariot") is
                been proven
                on Canadia

LAUGH AND THE WORLD LAUGHS WITH YOU/J
                Manit
                the V

JANIE/DANNY COUGHLAN/72068-- Thi
                C

There they are 8 .... I repeat
pace in 1963 with singles.
c-r-a-s-h onto the surveys.

(Red-face Department) -- I

ANDY LAUGHLAND and CHOW-WEL
listed all stations charting
I'm double checking every c

FEBRUARY 22, 1963

While Capitol Records passed on the Beatles first two discs, the company's north of the border subsidiary, Capitol Records of Canada, issued the group's singles from the very start. The Canadian company's *Sizzle Sheet* for the week ending February 22, 1963 (shown left), listed *Love Me Do* by the Beatles as one of Canada's "Next Smash Hits."

The First Decade Of Capitol Records Of Canada

The early history of Capitol Records of Canada is somewhat confusing. In 1947, Hollywood-based Capitol Records explored setting up operations in Canada. Ken Kerr, who previously had served as sales manager for Sparton of Canada, was hired as the company's sole Canadian employee. Before things got going, Capitol abandoned its plans due to restrictions on foreign investment imposed by the Canadian government.

Undeterred by this false start, Kerr soon got together with Johnny Downs and Scotty McLachlan to start a record company with the goal of landing a contract with Capitol to manufacture and distribute its records in Canada. After raising $25,000, the trio started Regal Records in 1948. One year later, in June, 1949, Regal entered into a five year contract to manufacture discs for Capitol. The company's name was changed to Capitol Records of Canada, Ltd. Its first release was Gordon MacRae's *Twenty-Four Hours Of Sunshine*. Less than five years later, the company had pressed over five million records and achieved a 12% market share in Canada.

By the time the five-year pressing agreement between the U.S. and Canadian companies expired in 1954, government restrictions on foreign investment had eased. Capitol Records decided not to renew its contract with the Canadian company and formed a wholly-owned subsidiary in Canada named Capitol Record Distributors of Canada. The new company set up offices in Toronto and contracted with RCA Records in Smiths Falls, Ontario, to press its records. When Capitol Records was purchased by EMI in 1955, the Canadian subsidiary obtained the right of first refusal for the Canadian release of all recordings by EMI's worldwide artists. As the first decade of Capitol's Canadian presence came to an end, the company changed its name to that of the company that started it all, Capitol Records of Canada, Ltd.

Dave Dexter was the man at Capitol Records responsible for reviewing foreign EMI discs for possible release. His scepticism towards British acts and his bias against rock 'n' roll caused him to pass on the Beatles. Dexter's counterpart at Capitol's Canadian subsidiary, Paul White, came from a different background than Dexter and was more willing to experiment with musical talent.

Paul White was a British journalist who moved to Canada in the mid-fifties. His first job there was in the shipping department of Capitol Records. Although loading boxes may seem insignificant to one's development, White viewed his warehouse days as a great experience that taught him which records were the best-sellers. He was soon promoted to the order desk. After serving as the assistant to the company's national promotion manager, White inherited the job when his boss left to work for BMI Canada.

While Dave Dexter was skeptical about British acts, Paul White was from England. When a Capitol sales rep told him of the demand for imported 78 RPM discs recorded by British jazz saxophonist Freddy Gardner, an EMI artist, White brought this to the attention of Harold Smith, who was then serving as company president. Smith told White to compile an album of Gardner's recordings. Although he had no experience in album production, White obtained Gardner's master tapes from EMI, recruited an EMI employee to write liner notes and selected a picture of London's Trafalgar Square for the cover. The resulting album, *Freddy Gardner The Unforgettable* (Capitol of Canada T 6000), was a surprise hit. The record launched both the label's 6000 series and Paul White's career as an album producer. It also made him aware of the market for British acts in Canada.

Although White initially focused on compiling albums aimed at an older audience, he later expanded to pop singles. Unlike its U.S. parent, Capitol of Canada did have some success with British pop artists, beginning in early 1962 with Charlie Drake's *My Boomerang Won't Come Back*. The novelty single flew to the top of Toronto radio station CHUM's *Hit Parade*, remaining on the charts for 12 weeks. Later that year, the label released discs by Frank Ifield

(*I Remember You*) and Helen Shapiro (*I Don't Care*). Both became number four hits. The success of these singles made the company more receptive to recordings by U.K.-based artists than its parent company. By the end of 1964, after Canada had fully embraced the "English sound," the Canadian company's roster of British acts included Cliff Richard, Gerry & the Pacemakers, the Hollies, the Dave Clark Five, the Swinging Blue Jeans, the Animals, Billy J. Kramer & the Dakotas, Herman's Hermits and the Yardbirds. But the key signing occurred nearly two years earlier.

In January, 1963, Paul White received another stack of singles from EMI. Included in the batch was the Beatles first single, *Love Me Do* b/w *P.S. I Love You*, which was released in England on Parlophone 45-R 4949 on October 5, 1962. According to White:

"One evening, as I was getting bored again listening to all these 45s, *Love Me Do* slipped out of its sleeve and plunked down onto the turntable. I thought, 'My God, that's different!' I only thought it was different because, although the guys were definitely singing a simple lyric, they seemed to be happy doing it, compared to the guys on the other 50 records I'd heard that week. So I put them on the 'must listen again' pile. When I listened to it again, I thought, 'I've definitely got to release this record.'"

As was often the practice at that time, White did not bother to obtain the master tape from EMI. Instead, *Love Me Do* and *P.S. I Love You* were dubbed from the Parlophone 45. Thus, when the single was released in mid-February, 1963, on Capitol of Canada, it featured the version of *Love Me Do* with Ringo on drums.

To promote Capitol's singles, Paul White authored a weekly flyer called *The Sizzle Sheet*. In its edition for the week ending February 22, 1963 (shown on page 24), *Love Me Do* was listed along with Frank Ifield's *The Wayward Wind* under the heading "These Are The Next Smash Hits!" White offered the following hype for the Beatles 45: "Give this disc a couple of spins and you'll be hooked! This is an English record and a recent top 20 disc over there. Don't neglect this side!" The March 1 *Sizzle Sheet* claimed that the Beatles disc was starting to gain sales attention. The following week *Love Me Do* was listed as one of the "Choice Up-And-Coming Sure Shots." For the week ending March 15, the Beatles debut was included as one of the "Hot Singles To Watch–And Play."

Paul White eagerly promoted the Beatles single because he "liked the group's fresh new sound." Despite his efforts, Canadian radio stations were not willing to take a chance on programming the song, although the disc received a few spins on CFPL in London, Ontario. Without airplay, the single was doomed and reportedly sold 78 copies (although some accounts list sales at 170 units).

The Beatles next single, *Please Please Me* b/w *Ask Me Why* (Parlophone 45-R 4983) was issued in England on January 11, 1963. Vee Jay issued the same record in the United States on February 7, 1963. Although White probably received a copy of the disc from EMI shortly thereafter, he delayed its release until early April to allow *Love Me Do* a chance to catch on.

The First North American Airplay Of The Beatles?

Toronto, Canada, may well have been home to the first airplay of a Beatles record in North America. Ray Sonin, a jazz reviewer for England's *New Musical Express*, emigrated to Canada in the fifties. He joined Toronto radio station CFRB in 1957. The following year Sonin started and began hosting his radio show *Calling All Britons*, which was broadcast by CFRB on Saturdays, normally between 4:10 p.m. and 5:45 p.m. The show was aimed at the large number of former British residents who had settled in the Toronto area. Ray, assisted by his wife June, discussed British current events and played music from the United Kingdom.

Towards the end of 1962, Ray received a copy of the Beatles first single, *Love Me Do* b/w *P.S. I Love You*. The disc was sent by a Toronto listener who had just returned home from a trip to Liverpool. The accompanying letter told of the Beatles massive popularity in their hometown. Sonin read excerpts from the letter and played *Love Me Do* on his show one late Saturday afternoon in December, 1962. This predates any known broadcast of a Beatles record in either Canada or the United States.

The April 5, 1963, *Sizzle Sheet* proclaimed that *Please Please Me* (Capitol of Canada 72090) was currently number one in England and that a few Canadian stations had reported "great listener reaction." Programmers were warned "Don't lose sight of this one." The following week *The Sizzle Sheet* stated that CFPL in London, Ontario, was listing the song at number 40 and reported "good teen reaction." Despite early positive response, Canada was still not ready for the Beatles. According to White, *Please Please Me* "became a zinc record and sold about 180 copies."

Myth

Capitol Records turned down the Beatles third British single, *From Me To You*, thus forcing EMI to place the record with Vee-Jay.

Fact

Under the terms of the five-year leasing agreement between Vee-Jay and Transglobal, Vee-Jay had a right of first refusal for all EMI masters recorded by the Beatles. Because Vee-Jay exercised its right of first refusal, Capitol was never offered *From Me To You*. However, based upon Dave Dexter's disdain for John Lennon's harmonica playing and his lack of faith in British artists, it is safe to assume that Capitol would have passed on *From Me To You* had the company been offered the song.

The Beatles second U.S. single, *From Me To You* b/w *Thank You Girl*, was issued as VJ 522 on or about May 6, 1963. It duplicated the group's third British single, Parlophone R 5015, which was released about a month earlier on April 11.

From Me To You was written by John and Paul on February 28, 1963, while the Beatles were on a bus heading from York to Shrewsbury as a supporting act on the second leg of Helen Shapiro's winter tour. The idea for the song came from the letters column "From You To Us" that appeared in the *New Musical Express*. According to John, "The first line was mine. Then we took it from there. It was bluesier when we wrote it. We were just fooling about on the guitar. This went on for a while. Then we began to get a good melody line and we really started to work at it. Before the journey was over we'd completed the lyric, everything. We were so pleased."

Less than a week later, on March 5, the Beatles were in Abbey Road's Studio Two recording the song. The track features John and Paul on lead vocals backed by John on his Gibson J-160E "Jumbo" electric-acoustic guitar, George on his Gretsch Duo-Jet electric guitar, Paul on his Hofner bass and Ringo on his Premier drum kit. The first take broke down midway, while Takes 2 through 5 were complete. Take 5 was the first performance to incorporate an instrumental break, which was apparently added by George Martin to lengthen the song. This was followed by a false start and Take 7, which formed the basis for the finished master.

After taking time to record *Thank You Girl*, the Beatles returned to *From Me To You* to add embellishments suggested by George Martin. Track 2, Take 8 added the "da da da da da dun dun dah" vocals over the song's introduction, John's harmonica and George's lead guitar notes to the instrumental break, and John's harmonica over the song's ending. The group then recorded six edit pieces. The first one, which was mistakenly designated Edit Piece 1, Take 8, added John's harmonica to the song's opening instrumental bars.

Later edit pieces experimented with a humming intro and a falsetto intro, neither of which was used.

George Martin edited the song (probably combining Take 8 with one of the first edit pieces serving as the intro) and made mono and stereo mixes on March 14. The mono mix used for the Parlophone and Vee-Jay singles features both the "da da da da da dun dun dah" vocals and John's harmonica during the song's introduction. The stereo mix, apparently made from the unedited Track 2, Take 8, has the "da da da da da dun dun dah" vocals, but no harmonica, over the opening bars.

The single's flip side, *Thank You Girl*, was also written by John and Paul on the Helen Shapiro tour and was also recorded on March 5 with the same instruments as the A side. The Beatles ran through six takes of the song (only four were complete) before stopping to concentrate on the song's ending. Seven edit pieces were recorded before Ringo nailed down the complex drum fills pounded out at the end. The finished master combined Take 6 with the Take 13 ending edit piece.

John returned to Abbey Road on March 13 to overdub harmonica (Takes 14-28). George Martin then edited Takes 6, 13, 17, 20, 21 and 23 to form the finished master. After completing the mono mix used for the single, Martin made a couple of stereo mixes. During the recording and mixing sessions, the song was known as *Thank You Little Girl*.

In England, the single skyrocketed to the number one position, remaining there for six weeks during its 16-week run. It was a totally different story in America. Although *Cash Box* listed *From Me To You* as its "Pick of the Week," the record's poor performance in the States made this prediction look more like a "Pick of the Weak." The Beatles second Vee-Jay single received little, if any, airplay upon its release in early May.

Nearly two months later *From Me To You* would become the first Lennon-McCartney song to hit the U.S. charts; however, it was not the Beatles recording that accomplished this feat. American Del Shannon, who topped the U.S. and U.K. charts in 1961 with *Runaway*, was a big star in Britain, having scored seven top-ten singles there by the spring of 1963. On April 18, he was one of 15 acts to take part in *Swinging Sound '63*, a BBC-sponsored concert broadcast live from London's Royal Albert Hall. Others on the bill included the Springfields (a folk group featuring Dusty Springfield), Kenny Lynch (who recorded *Misery*) and the Beatles, who performed their latest single, *From Me To You*, as one of their four selections. Del liked the song and told John he was going to record it to give the Beatles more exposure in America. Although John was flattered by this gesture, he later expressed concern that a cover version by Shannon would hurt the Beatles chances of scoring a U.S. hit with their own recording of the song.

Del Shannon recorded *From Me To You* in England. His version of the song entered the *Billboard Hot 100* on June 29, 1963, at number 96 and peaked at 77. *Cash Box* also charted the Shannon single, reporting a peak at number 67. This wasn't really a case of program directors choosing the Del Shannon recording over the Beatles version.

Del Shannon's version of *From Me To You,* released on Big Top 3152, became the first Lennon-McCartney original to chart in the U.S., entering the *Billboard Hot 100* on June 29, 1963, at number 96. It peaked at 77 during its four-week run. *Cash Box* first reported the song on July 16, 1963, at 86. It peaked at 67.

By the time the Shannon single was issued, stations had already passed on the Beatles. Radio was merely broadcasting the latest release by Del Shannon, a proven hitmaker.

Vee-Jay tried unsuccessfully to capitalize on the new interest in *From Me To You* generated by Shannon's single. An ad running in the June 22 *Cash Box* touted the Beatles 45 as "The Original Hit Version!" Vee-Jay also distributed additional promotional copies of the single stamped with "THE ORIGINAL HIT." (See images on page 28.)

Ironically, one of Shannon's hottest markets for his cover of *From Me To You* was Chicago, home of Vee-Jay Records. The *Top Tunes of Greater Chicago* survey charted the Shannon 45 for six weeks, showing a peak at number 10. Although WLS had played *Please Please Me* (see page 17 for the story of DJ Dick Biondi's debut of the disc on WLS), the station ignored the Beatles version. The Shannon single entered its *Silver Dollar Survey* on June 21 at number 31 and peaked at 15 during its six-week run.

The reason WLS failed to air the Beatles single was that Dick Biondi was no longer with the station when the 45 was issued in early May. After being fired by WLS on May 2, Biondi relocated to Los Angeles in June and was hired by KRLA. Biondi brought both Beatles singles with him and convinced the program director to add the more recent 45 (VJ 522) to the station's play list. At first, listeners didn't want to hear the Beatles. They were into the Beach Boys. But KRLA stayed with *From Me To You*, charting the Beatles single for six weeks starting on July 14.

Prior to KRLA adding the single to its play list, VJ 522 had sold only 3,900 units by the end of June. Boosted by airplay in Los Angeles, sales for July 1 through September 30, 1963, were 8,775 units, resulting in total sales of 12,675 copies by summer's end. This led to some *Billboard* chart action, with the Beatles version of *From Me To You* entering the *Bubbling Under The Hot 100* listing at number 125

From Me To You In Canada

Because *Love Me Do* and *Please Please Me* both bombed in Canada, Capitol Records of Canada gave no consideration to putting out the Beatles first album. This, however, did not deter Paul White from issuing the group's third single, *From Me To You* b/w *Thank You Girl* as Capitol of Canada 72101 on June 18, 1963.

The June 21 *Sizzle Sheet* gave the following plug: "Until this week it was ENGLAND's No. 1 disc–This group HAS IT and this disc could be a No. 1 in Canada too!" Two weeks later White made reference to Del Shannon's cover version of the song. "We're having a battle with Del Shannon but so far it's anybody's hit." The July 5 *Sizzle Sheet* also proclaimed that *From Me To You* was "easily the best disc by this Group."

During the next several weeks White reported on stations listing the new Beatles record and on the continuing battle with the Del Shannon version. In the July 26 *Sizzle Sheet* he suggested that stations give both versions equal time. White's final words on the disc ran on August 2. "Sales are satisfactory but without more chart listings, we could lose out to Del Shannon. The Beatles are worth the spins–and they'll make it big in Canada yet." White would ultimately be proven right, but not yet. The Beatles version of *From Me To You* could only muster sales of approximately 500 copies.

on August 3, 1963. The single climbed to number 116 the following week before dropping to 124 on August 17 and then sinking without a trace. In 1964, the single sold an additional 9,451 units, raising total sales to 22,126.

MI chigan 2-6465

INVOICE NO.
C09950

INVOICE

Universal Recording Corporation
46 E. Walton St., Chicago 11, Ill.

ALL PROPERTIES LEFT ON OUR PREMISES
ARE STORED AT OWNERS RISK.

S
O   Vee Jay Records, Inc.
L   1449 S. Michigan Ave.
D   Chicago, Illinois
T
O

TERMS: NET CASH

DATE	CUSTOMER ORDER NO.	OUR JOB NO. W-28214	JOB IDENTIFICATION THE BEATLES			UNIT PRICE	AMOUNT
6/22/63			DESCRIPTION				
QUANTITY	UNIT					25.00	50.00
2			Dub Down			15.50	15.50
1			Tape			13.50	27.00
2			Editing			14.00	14.00
1	12X33		Monaural Dub D/F	63-3402	63-3403	21.25	21.25
1	12X33		Stereo Dub D/F	63-3402	63-3403	19.55	39.10
2	12X33		Monaural Masters	63-3402		19.55	39.10
2	12X33		Monaural Masters	63-3402		38.25	76.50
2	12X33		Stereo Masters	63-3402		38.25	76.50
2	12X33		Stereo Masters	63-3402		.65	1.30
			Master Packing			4.35	8.70
			Air Express to Audio				----------
							368.95

UAR

MAGNA GRAPHIC INC.
Formerly the Kentucky Printing Plate Corp.

430 WEST SHORT ST.   LEXINGTON, KY.   Ph. 255-0240

New York Office
50 E. 42nd Street
Oxford 7-5141

COLOR PROCESS FOR LETTERPRESS AND OFFSET
SPECIALISTS IN DOW RAPID ETCH MAGNESIUM

№ 2048

Date   7/9/63

Customer	Vee Jay Records		Cust. Order No.	SD 1062
Address	1449 S. Michigan Avenue		Cust. Job No.	The Beatles
City	Chicago, Illinois	State	Title	

Quantity	DESCRIPTION	Units	Rate	Amount
1	set 4 color process positives			375.00

JUNE 22, 1963

On June 22, 1963, mono and stereo masters were prepared for Vee-Jay's *Introducing The Beatles* album at Universal Recording Corporation in Chicago for a cost of $368.95 (computer recreation of invoice shown left). A few days later the metal parts for pressing the album were manufactured by Audio Matrix in the Bronx, New York, and sent to the three regional factories used by Vee-Jay to press its records.

True or False?

Introducing The Beatles was released by Vee-Jay on or about July 22, 1963.

False

Although nearly all Beatles books and discographies state that *Introducing The Beatles* was issued on July 22, 1963, this is not correct. Early Beatles historians estimated the date based upon the late June date appearing in the record's trail off areas. Vee-Jay had plans to release the record in the summer of 1963; however, due to financial difficulties, as detailed below, Vee-Jay cancelled its summer releases, including the Beatles album. *Introducing The Beatles* was not released until January 10, 1964.

At the time Vee-Jay released its first Beatles record in February, 1963, the company was becoming a significant player in the music business. Its roster of gospel acts included the Staple Singers, the Swan Silvertones, the Harmonizing Four and the Original Blind Boys of Alabama. Its blues artists included Jimmy Reed and John Lee Hooker. Several of the label's black artists, including Jerry Butler, the Impressions, Dee Clark and Gene Chandler, had enjoyed success on the pop charts. Vee-Jay's move into the lucrative pop field was evident with the signing of white artists such as Frank Ifield, who gave the company a number five hit with *I Remember You*, and the Four Seasons.

While the Fab Four's first Vee-Jay release was being ignored, Vee-Jay's other pop foursome was having tremendous success. The Four Seasons' first two Vee-Jay singles, *Sherry* and *Big Girls Don't Cry*, topped the *Billboard Hot 100*, each holding down the number one spot for five weeks and selling over one million copies. Each also topped the *Billboard* R&B singles chart. *Walk Like A Man*, the group's third single (not counting the group's 1962 Christmas 45, *Santa Claus Is Coming To Town*), was number one for three weeks. The Four Seasons became the first group in the history of the *Billboard Hot 100* to have three number one singles in a row, a feat the Beatles would surpass time and time again.

Following the conventional wisdom in the American music industry that hit singles sell hit albums, Vee-Jay titled its first Four Seasons LP *Sherry & 11 Others*. The record gave the company its first hit album, reaching number six on the *Billboard Top LP's* chart. The next album, *Big Girls Don't Cry and Twelve Others*, hit number eight.

The person guiding Vee-Jay during this time was company president Ewart Abner. He was well liked throughout the industry and considered a promotional genius. The Brackens, who still maintained exclusive ownership of the company, awarded Abner a lucrative longtime contract for his efforts. There was talk of the company going public. On the surface, the future looked bright for Vee-Jay; however, huge problems were looming on the horizon.

Although the Four Seasons were selling millions of records, the group was not being paid its full royalties. By the spring of 1963, rumors of Vee-Jay's financial problems were circulating throughout the industry. In addition to owing a half million dollars to factories and being late with royalty payments, Vee-Jay was also facing a huge tax liability. A substantial part of this liability related to the federal excise tax on oil-related products, which applied to vinyl records. The company was also behind in its payroll taxes and was having difficulty paying its printers and pressing plants. Vee-Jay's liabilities and cash flow problems forced the cancellation of several planned releases, including *Introducing The Beatles* (VJLP 1062), *Young Peoples' Introduction to Hebrew Music.... Presented by Cantor Samuel Vigoda and the Oscar Julius Choir* (VJLP 1063), *Frank Ifield Favorites* (VJLP 1064) and *How About Love* by Alma Cogan (VJLP 1068).

The Brackens became increasingly concerned as the company's debt continued to grow despite the golden hits of the Four Seasons and other artists. When pressed for an explanation, Abner reportedly told the Brackens that substantial unreported sums of money had been spent on payments to disc jockeys to get records played. This practice, known as payola, was commonplace in the fifties, but became a criminal offense after Congressional hearings exposed just how prevalent and persuasive it was.

While the payola explanation was disturbing, it wasn't true. Abner later confessed to the Brackens that he had "borrowed" an estimated three to four hundred thousand dollars of company money to cover his gambling losses. Upon learning the truth, the Brackens were crushed. Abner's likable nature made it difficult for the Brackens to press criminal charges, so they decided to keep the incident private. Vee-Jay corporate minutes indicate that the company entered into a settlement under which Abner gave up his long-term contract with Vee-Jay and the company forgave his debt. Those in the industry who knew the truth covered for Abner because they liked him and did not want to see him disgraced. *Billboard* was kept in the dark and innocently reported that Abner left Vee-Jay to start his own company, Dart Record Sales.

There can be no doubt that Ewart Abner was a remarkable man. He was a promotional genius who contributed significantly to Vee-Jay's impressive growth. His likable nature helped cut deals and get records on the radio. To many, including attorney Paul Marshall, "Abner was Vee-Jay." He was active in the record industry and was involved in community causes. He later became president of Motown Records and served as Stevie Wonder's manager. But the fact remains that Abner's gambling problem and use of company funds to pay off his personal gambling debts led to Vee-Jay's eventual downfall.

Vee-Jay's cash flow problems were a direct result of Abner's misdeeds. Without money, Vee-Jay was unable to pay royalties to its artists. Without money, Vee-Jay was unable to pay its printers and pressings plants. Without money, Vee-Jay was unable to release new records. Without money, Vee-Jay's future was bleak.

The Angus McBean photograph that served as the cover of *Introducing The Beatles* was also featured on the cover of the British EP *The Beatles' Hits,* Parlophone GEP 8880, which was released on September 6, 1963. When Parlophone reissued *Love Me Do* in 1982, the same photograph, with its background restored, appeared on the back side of the picture sleeve.

How Records Are Made

The creation of a record begins with a tape of the recorded music being transferred to a lacquer-coated metal disc. This process is known as mastering. It is the last opportunity for the sound of the record to be adjusted. At this stage, the engineer is limited to adjusting the frequencies and the volume of the recorded music. Once these settings have been made from the tape, the engineer places a blank disc, known as a lacquer, on an electronic lathe, which resembles a phonograph turntable, but has a "cutting head" instead of a stylus or needle. As the disc spins on the lathe, grooves are cut into the soft lacquer coating. Once completed, this lacquer disc, which is often referred to as an acetate or reference disc, can be played on a turntable. Because its outer coating is soft, an acetate can only be played a limited number of times before it begins to wear down.

After a satisfactory-sounding lacquer has been produced, it is sent to a factory to create the metal parts. The first of these, the master, is produced by spraying a metal film over the lacquer. The metal master is then separated from the lacquer, which is destroyed by the process. The result is a round metal sheet. Unlike an acetate, it cannot be played on a turntable as its grooves are a mirror image of those of the acetate. Accordingly, it is described as a negative metal part.

Next comes the mother, which is made from the master. It is another round metal sheet that is slightly smaller than the master. The mother is a positive metal part that can be played on a turntable.

The mother is then used to give birth to the final metal part, known as a stamper, which is used to press the records. The stamper is a durable metal disc that is an exact mirror image of the vinyl record to be produced. Like the master, it is a negative metal part. Although stampers were often manufactured at the factory that produced the masters and mothers, some pressing plants manufactured their own stampers from mothers.

The production of the record begins by placing stampers for each side of the record into a pressing machine. A biscuit-shaped glob of vinyl, which has been softened by heat, is covered on top and bottom by the finished labels. The vinyl compound is then fed into the machine and placed between the stampers, which literally press the record by using a combination of steam heat and hydraulic pressure to mold the vinyl into a positive image of the grooves on the stampers. The excess vinyl is shaved off and the record is cooled by water as it comes out of the pressing machine. In the sixties and until the mid-nineties, singles produced in America normally had a 1½" diameter hole punched out of the center of the completed 45 RPM vinyl record.

All of the metal parts used in the manufacturing process have limited useful lives. Each master typically produces four mothers, although each mother must be carefully examined to ensure it has no defects. Until a mother breaks down, it is capable of producing a multitude of stampers. Under ideal circumstances, stampers can make as many as 2,000 singles or 1,000 albums.

AUGUST 8, 1963

On August 8, 1963, EMI's agent in America, Transglobal Music Company, Inc., sent Vee-Jay a telegram (shown left) demanding that Vee-Jay immediately cease manufacture and distribution of records containing performances of Frank Ifield and "THE BEATTLES." This move was prompted by Vee-Jay's failure to pay royalties on the sales of Ifield and Beatles records. Due to the unilateral cancellation of the leasing agreements with Vee-Jay, Capitol now had the opportunity to issue the latest recordings by these EMI artists.

During the summer of 1963, Paul Marshall, who served as counsel for both EMI and Vee-Jay, learned of Vee-Jay's precarious financial situation and the company's dismissal of Ewart Abner. Marshall believed that Abner was a key component of the company's success and was concerned that Vee-Jay would have trouble remaining in business without Abner. Because EMI and Vee-Jay would most likely be at odds over financial matters, Marshall realized that it would be a conflict of interest for him to keep representing both companies. This meant he could retain his association with only one of the companies–either EMI, then the world's largest recording organization, or Vee-Jay, a company on the verge of bankruptcy. The decision was a no-brainer. Marshall tendered his resignation as counsel for Vee-Jay.

Vee-Jay's cash flow problems forced the company to prioritize its obligations. Because neither Frank Ifield nor the Beatles were considered critical to the company's success, Vee-Jay failed to send royalty statements or payments to EMI's agent, Transglobal Music Company, Inc., regarding sales of Ifield or Beatles records. This prompted Transglobal to send Vee-Jay a letter demanding immediate payment of royalties owed. When Vee-Jay failed to respond, Transglobal sent a telegram to Vee-Jay (shown on page 38) demanding that the label "immediately cease manufacture and distribution of any and all records containing performances of Frank Ifield and the Beattles." The telegram,

which was written by Paul Marshall on the direct order of Transglobal, was filed with Western Union on August 8, 1963, and transmitted to Chicago at 11:57 a.m. that day.

Vee-Jay's failure to account for or pay royalties on sales of Ifield and Beatles discs ultimately led to the label losing the Beatles. It was later determined that Vee-Jay owed a total of $7,430 to Transglobal for royalties on sales of Ifield and Beatles discs. The royalties owed on sales of Beatles records represented a mere $859.

Transglobal considered the August 8, 1963, telegram a unilateral termination of its licensing agreements with Vee-Jay for Frank Ifield and Beatles recordings. This action was most likely taken due to EMI's fear that Vee-Jay would either be out of business or ineffective. EMI wanted to be sure that Ifield and Beatles records would be available for leasing to a company capable of manufacturing and promoting their songs.

The termination of the licensing agreements with Vee-Jay once again gave Capitol Records the right of first refusal for Ifield and Beatles recordings. Around this time, Capitol president Alan Livingston started getting calls from London about the Beatles success. He also began reading about them in the British music press. This prompted him to discuss the Beatles with Dave Dexter at a weekly staff meeting at the Capitol Tower. Livingston recalls:

"So at one meeting, I said, 'Dex, what about the Beatles? I read a lot about them, they're doing well in London.' He said, 'Alan, they're a bunch of long-haired kids. They're nothing. Forget it.' I said 'OK.' I trusted Dexter. And I had no interest in British product at that point. And so a few weeks went by and I began to get nervous because of the British press, I could tell they were doing really well, so I said, 'Dex, what about the Beatles?' And he said, 'Alan, forget it, they're nothing.' I said, 'OK.' And so we turned them down."

Dexter's actions appear humorous when one examines the facts surrounding his decision to pass on the Beatles in the summer of 1963. After Transglobal terminated the license agreements with Vee-Jay, Dexter was sent copies of the two latest British singles by each artist–*I'm Confessin'* by Frank Ifield and *She Loves You* by the Beatles (see page 38). After listening to both 45s, Dexter had faith in one of the songs and arranged for Capitol to place a full-page ad in *Billboard* promoting his "sure-bet" hit (see page 43). Amazingly, Dexter chose *I'm Confessin'* and recommended that Capitol pass on the Beatles for a third time. Dexter's dislike of Lennon's harmonica playing on *Love Me Do* and *Please Please Me* influenced his decision to turn those records down. But *She Loves You* had no harmonica. And, ironically, *I'm Confessin'* did have harmonica. Perhaps Dexter didn't like all that "yeah, yeah, yeah" stuff sung by John and Paul.

When Capitol rejected *She Loves You*, George Martin was furious. He remembers getting a curt reply from the company that they did not think the Beatles would do anything in America. The party line out of Capitol was that the Beatles music "wasn't suitable for the American market."

Dexter's rejection of *She Loves You* in August, 1963, highlights how out of touch he was. At the very time Dexter was sitting in his office at the Capitol Tower in Hollywood, California, judging the Beatles unsuitable for the American market, the group's previous disc, *From Me To You* (VJ 522), was a top forty hit in his own backyard, Los Angeles! The 45 made its debut on the July 14, 1963, KRLA *TUNE-DEX* at number 46. *From Me To You* remained on the charts through the end of August, peaking at number 32 on August 11 (chart shown left) during its six-week run.

After Capitol refused to issue *She Loves You*, Transglobal was once again directed by EMI to find a company to release a new Beatles single. Alan Livingston and EMI attorney Paul Marshall confirm that Transglobal tried unsuccessfully to place the Beatles with several companies. According to Livingston, "they sent them to Decca, RCA-Victor, Columbia Records, A&M and every record company they could get to, they got to them all, and everyone of them turned them down."

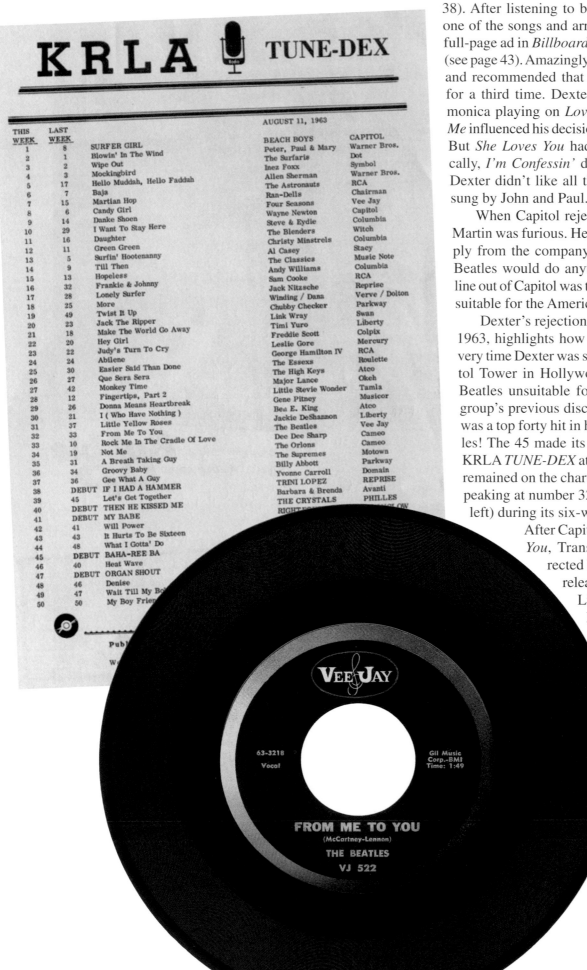

George Harrison's Reconnaissance Mission

The day after *She Loves You* was issued in America, George Harrison visited his sister, Louise "Lou" Caldwell in Benton, Illinois. George and his brother Peter arrived at Lambert Airport in St. Louis on Tuesday, September 17, 1963. His vacation, which marked the first time a Beatle went to America, took place during a rare two-week break for the band, during which time John and his wife Cynthia visited Paris, and Paul and Ringo traveled to Greece. Two days earlier, the Beatles had received top billing at a Sunday afternoon concert at London's Royal Albert Hall that featured 11 other acts, including the Rolling Stones.

According to Lou, the plans originally called for Ringo to come to the States with George. Lou thinks Ringo changed his mind when he learned that she wanted to get local media coverage for the pair of Beatles. George was also against media attention, telling Lou he wanted a real vacation where he could see the ordinary side of America.

Prior to George's visit, Lou had attempted to get her brother's records played on the radio. In July, she sent a copy of the Beatles latest British single, *From Me To You*, to St. Louis radio station KXOK. In a letter dated July 31, 1963, station program director Bud Connell told Lou, "It would be difficult for us to change to the Beatles version because we have been playing the Del Shannon record [of *From Me To You*] for quite a long time, and it is formerly established in the market." Connell added that it was unfortunate the Beatles version did not receive promotion in the United States. He concluded with words of encouragement: "Perhaps the next release will become Number 1 in the nation.... We hope so!" Although the next record, *She Loves You*, initially bombed, it later topped the charts.

Lou was able to get WFRX, a small station in West Frankfort, Illinois, to play the Beatles version of *From Me To You*. During the summer of 1963, Marcia Shafer, a 17-year-old high school student whose father owned the station, occasionally played the record, and perhaps *Love Me Do* and *Please Please Me*, on her *Saturday Session* teen-oriented radio show.

Although Marcia was not the first disc jockey to play a Beatles record in the United States, she was the first to interview a Beatle on the air. According to Lou, George wanted to meet Marcia to thank her for playing his group's records. Lou's husband drove her, George and Peter to the station, where Marcia interviewed George for about 15 to 20 minutes. Unfortunately, no one thought to record the interview. In her high school newspaper, Marcia wrote, "Their music is wild and uninhibited and outsells the world's greatest recording artists, although not one of the Beatles can read music."

George got his wish to see the ordinary side of America when he went to a drive-in picture show. He saw two films at the Marion Drive-In: *The Nutty Professor* starring Jerry Lewis and *Wonderful To Be Young* with British singer Cliff Richard. By the time George saw the film, Richard had scored 22 top ten hits in the U.K., including six that topped the charts. In America, Cliff Richard did not hold the same celebrity status. Seeing the British star relegated to second billing at a drive-in reminded George that success in England was no guarantee for success in America.

During his stay in Benton, George spent time with a fellow musician whose last name was similar to Beatles bass player Paul McCartney. Lou introduced George to Gabe McCarty who, like Paul, played bass guitar left handed. Gabe played in a local band, the Four Vests (shown right). He took George on shopping trips for records and a guitar.

George purchased several albums while in Benton. In the sixties, many furniture and appliance stores had record departments. In small towns, these stores were the only place one could buy records. George went to Barton and Collins Furniture Store, where he bought between 20 and 30 albums. One of those LPs was *If You Gotta Make A Fool Of Somebody* by James Ray. Harrison bought the album due to his fondness for the title track, which reached number 22 in early 1962. But he also grew to appreciate and later record one of the other songs on the record, *Got My Mind Set On You*, which was written by Rudy Clark. When released as a single from Harrison's *Cloud Nine* album in October, 1987, *Got My Mind Set On You* became a surprise number one hit the following January.

George also purchased a Rickenbacker 425 electric guitar from Fenton Music Store in nearby Mt. Vernon. The guitar was fire glow red; however, at George's request, the guitar was sanded down and refinished black. Harrison paid approximately $400 cash for the Rickenbacker.

On Saturday, September 28, 1963, George went to see Gabe's band, the Four Vests, at the VFW (Veterans of Foreign Wars) Hall in Eldorado. In addition to Gabe McCarty on bass, the group consisted of Kenny Welch on lead guitar, Vernon Mandrell on rhythm guitar and Burleigh Bowlin on drums. After the first set, George was invited by McCarty to join the group on-stage. With a little encouragement, Harrison agreed and was handed Welch's Rickenbacker. Although no one remembers the exact set of songs played by George, those present remember Harrison leading the band through Hank Williams' *Your Cheatin' Heart* and rockers from the Beatles repertoire such as Chuck Berry's *Roll Over Beethoven* and *Johnny B. Goode* and Carl Perkins' *Everybody's Trying To Be My Baby* and *Matchbox*.

According to Lou, "You could feel the electricity in the room the moment George began to play. The people were banging their fists on the tables and stomping their feet." In addition to his musical ability, those in the audience certainly noticed Harrison's British accent and long hair. One person told McCarty, "That new kid that's trying out for your band— you'd be crazy if you didn't take him on." Another told George, "You know, son, with the right kind of backing, you could go places."

It is believed that 75 to 100 people were present that evening, which was the first time Lou saw her brother perform. She thought, "If one Beatle can cause that much excitement, imagine what it must be like with all four." Four months later, Lou would see her brother reprise his U.S. performance of *Roll Over Beethoven* before eight thousand screaming fans when the Beatles opened with the song at their first American concert.

George and Peter began their journey home on September 30, flying from St. Louis to New York. According to Lou, before heading for London, they attended the Broadway show *Stop The World, I Want To Get Off*. Upon his return to England, George joked that he had been on a reconnaissance mission to determine the Beatles chances of success in America. His assessment as reported to Derek Taylor: "I think we can make it; I don't think there's a lot of competition."

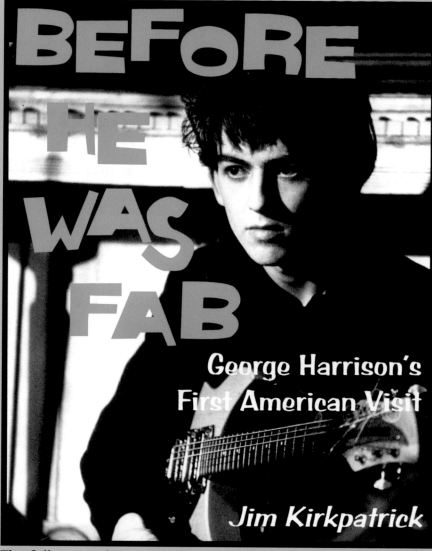

The full story of George's first American visit is detailed in Jim Kirkpatrick's book *Before He Was Fab*.

The Four Vests, 1963

In his autobiography *A Cellarful of Noise*, Brian Epstein summed up the importance of America to the Beatles. "We knew that America would make us or break us as world stars." In his mind, the United States was the heart and soul of popular music. If the Beatles could conquer America, they would rule pop music. And Brian thought it would happen. He was telling anyone who would listen that the Beatles would one day be bigger than Elvis.

Those around Brian did not share his optimism. While they were in awe over how well things were going in the U.K. for the Beatles and Brian's other acts, America was a different world. No British music act had ever made a lasting impression there. But Brian believed in his boys.

Operation U.S.A. began on November 5, 1963, with Epstein's visit to New York. Brian wanted to give the impression he was important, so he opted to stay at the prestigious and costly Regency Hotel. His primary purpose was to promote Billy J. Kramer, who made the trip with Brian. The 20-year-old Kramer was managed by Epstein and signed to Liberty Records in America. Although his first two singles were big hits in England (see box below),

Kramer's Liberty releases had been ignored. Brian hoped that introducing Kramer to the folks at Liberty would prompt the label to give the singer's records a push and lead to stardom in the States.

According to former Beatles publicist Tony Barrow, Epstein desperately wanted a solo artist star in America. He thought Kramer had the potential to develop into a successful cabaret crooner capable of headlining shows in New York and Las Vegas. Billy J. recalls that Brian "thought I had the kind of appeal that was right for the American market. I didn't have this mop-top hairdo and I was smart and I had the boy-next-door image, and he thought maybe I was the one that was going to do it." Kramer, who was insecure about his career, didn't share Brian's confidence, but wasn't about to turn down a free trip to New York.

The other purpose of Brian's visit was to explore why the Beatles hadn't "happened" in America, and, more important, perhaps do something about it. A story in the October 22, 1963, *Daily Mirror* mentioned Brian's upcoming trip and quoted him as saying he intended to "start spreading the gospel of the Beatles in the U.S.A."

Billy J. Kramer

Billy J. Kramer, whose real name was William Howard Ashton, was born on August 19, 1943, in Bootle, Liverpool. In 1959 he formed the Phantoms and served as the group's rhythm guitarist. When the band's singer left, he took over as lead vocalist and quit playing guitar when his instrument was stolen and he was unable to afford a replacement. When Billy put together another band known as the Coasters (not the American R&B group), he changed his name to Billy Kramer. The "J" was later added at the insistence of John Lennon, who thought it would improve the name. Lennon told the singer the "J" stood for Julian (John's first son).

In a 1962 reader's poll conducted by *Mersey Beat*, Billy Kramer & the Coasters placed third behind the Beatles and Gerry & the Pacemakers. Shortly thereafter, he signed a management contract with Brian Epstein. When the Coasters indicated they did not want to be full-time musicians, Brian paired him with a Manchester band, the Dakotas. Although the Dakotas were not particularly keen on backing Kramer, they agreed when promised by Brian that they could also record on their own. (The group had a top 20 British hit in the summer of 1963 with the instrumental *Cruel Sea*.)

Billy J. Kramer and the Dakotas were quickly signed to Parlophone Records. This gave the group access to a steady flow of Lennon-McCartney tunes and to George Martin. The first single was recorded on March 21, 1963, and paired *Do You Want To Know A Secret* (which the Beatles recorded for their first LP) with *I'll Be On My Way* (which the Beatles recorded for a BBC radio session). When released in England on April 26, 1963, Kramer's *Do You Want To Know A Secret* worked its way

up to number two on the U.K. charts, unable to dislodge the Beatles *From Me To You*. In America, Dave Dexter and Capitol passed on Kramer's recording. It was shopped to other labels and eventually leased to Liberty Records, which issued the single in June, 1963. With virtually no promotion behind it, the 45 sank without a trace.

Kramer's next single was recorded on June 27, 1963. It followed the same formula of pairing Lennon-McCartney originals, *Bad To Me* (which the Beatles never recorded) and *I Call Your Name* (which the group later recorded for an EP). The single was issued in the U.K. in July, 1963, and topped the charts. Liberty's American release of the 45 failed to chart.

The A side to his third single, Lennon-McCartney's *I'll Keep You Satisfied*, was recorded at Abbey Road on October 14, 1963. When Kramer was unable to get a satisfactory take of Lennon-McCartney's *I'm In Love*, the record was issued with *I Know*, a song co-written by George Martin and Bob Wooler, the Cavern's disc jockey. The single was released in England in November, 1963, and in the U.S. later that month on Liberty. The disc was a number four hit in England, but predictably failed to attract any attention in the States despite Kramer's promotional visit to New York in early November, 1963.

After the Beatles opened up the floodgates for British bands, Kramer did have some moderate U.S. success when his recordings were transferred to the Imperial label. His biggest American hit, *Little Children*, peaked at number seven in the spring of 1964. Billy J. returned to New York for an appearance on the June 7, 1964, *Ed Sullivan Show*.

The Beatles in the British Press

Although the British music weeklies were writing about the Beatles in early 1963, the group did not receive any coverage in Britain's daily national newspapers until mid-spring. The May 9, 1963, *Daily Mirror* reported that Liverpool had become the gateway to the hit charts, with the Beatles firmly entrenched at the top. The paper gave the following explanation: "Liverpool abounds in talent. It has youngsters who can play instruments well, sing well—and write songs that are melodic and palatable throughout the land. It borrows its sound mainly from America. But it interprets them in its own natural Lancashire way....Keep your eye and ear on Liverpool."

The May 17 *Daily Mail* contained a reference to Jane Asher and a story involving Paul McCartney, who had been denied entry to the lunch room on the set of a BBC special program. The article stated that experts had called the Beatles "one of the best groups in the world."

The May 24 *Daily Mail* Pops column ran a piece on Liverpool groups titled "The Sound of Scouse." The article downplayed the so-called "Liverpollan sound" and "Mersey beat," stating that the only thing the groups had in common was a "fiercer approach to singing and guitar playing than their gentler Southern rivals."

The June 26 *Daily Sketch* contained an article on how British acts were, for the first time in a lifetime, replacing American artists at the top of the British charts. It ran pictures of Cliff Richard, the Shadows and the Beatles. The July 4 *Daily Herald* briefly mentioned John Lennon's appearance on the popular TV program *Juke Box Jury*.

In one of the first articles referring to fans pursuing the boys, the July 16 *Daily Mirror* ran a piece titled "Police join in Beatle chase." Paul was pulled over for speeding as the boys headed home after a concert at a New Brighton ballroom. According to Paul, "People were following us in a van, so to escape, I exceeded the speed limit."

The July 25 *Daily Mirror* ran an article on Brian's latest discovery, Tommy Quickly, which called the Beatles "one of the biggest disc properties in Britain." That same day, the *Daily Herald* referred to the Beatles in an article on beat groups. The August 8 *Daily Mirror* had a picture of the Beatles dressed in Roaring Twenties bathing suits.

The September 9 *Daily Herald* ran a story on the rapid chart success of *She Loves You* titled "The Beatles Catch Up with Elvis." The article called the group a "cult" that had become the "highest paid property in British show business." Their sound was described as "extrovert and virile," to which John replied "I think people are a bit fed up with all the smooth stuff, don't you?"

The September 10 *Daily Mirror* ran a feature on the Beatles titled "Four frenzied Little Lord Fauntleroys who are making £5,000 every week." The article told of shrieking and foot-stamping fans at their concert at the Odeon Theatre, which resonated with "the whistling banshee of the 2,000-strong audience like a screaming power-dive from twelve o'clock high." Writer Donald Zec called the group: "Four cheeky-looking kids with stone-age hair styles, Chelsea boots, three electric guitars, and one set of drums, who know their amps and ohms if not their Beethoven." He described John as the "dry-witted one" and George as the "quiet one." He called Paul the group's unofficial spokesman who looked like "a young David Tomlinson in search of a barber." He stated that Ringo had a formidable nose and resembled "the 'heavy' in a teenage Western." The tags for John and George stuck.

Fans took exception to some of Zec's remarks. Their comments appeared in the September 14 *Daily Mirror*. A duo calling themselves "Two Very Angry Fans" wrote "the four Fab Beatles are handsome Mod boys who deserve every penny they get." Another pair wrote that the Beatles had "enlivened the pop scene which was previously getting a little tiring" and "Not only have they created a new sound, but a wonderful new craze in suits, jackets and haircuts." Babs from Sheffield called the group fantastic and stated that "they could look like monkeys, and dress like tramps, but their fans wouldn't care. It's the music that counts." Zec replied, "It's tough enough having to listen to them—don't tell me I have to love 'em as well."

On September 16, the day *She Loves You* was released and ignored in America, the *Daily Mirror* ran an article titled "6,000 Fans—The Beatles Just Fled." The story told of girls who "swept out of their seats and tried to rush the stage" at the band's Royal Albert Hall concert.

The Beatles were gaining coverage in the widely-read working class and middle-brow daily newspapers. The group was also receiving tremendous radio and television exposure. In Brian's mind, the Beatles were still "just an increasingly important group in the entertainment realm." A widely-watched and well-publicized television appearance, observed by London reporters, propelled the Beatles to an unprecedented level of media coverage.

Val Parnell's Sunday Night At The London Palladium, which was televised throughout the U.K. during prime-time Sunday evening, was the British equivalent of *The Ed Sullivan Show*. The Beatles headlined the October 13, 1963, *Palladium* show, which was seen by over 15 million people, and performed *From Me To You*, *I'll Get You*, *She Loves You* and *Twist And Shout*. The bedlam caused by the group both inside and outside the theater caught the attention of British news editors, who elevated the Beatles from a successful entertainment act to a national news phenomenon. The *Daily Herald* heralded the coming of "Beatle Fever!" The *Daily Mirror* mirrored these sentiments describing the mass hysteria as "Beatlemania!" The latter term became part of the British vocabulary and would soon be heard throughout the world. *The Times* ran its first story on the group on October 28, 1963.

Brian's contacts in New York were Geoffrey Ellis and Walter Hofer. Ellis was an Oxford University graduate who had studied law. He became friends with Brian while living in Liverpool. Ellis was relocated to New York in 1958. He and Brian kept in touch, and Brian wrote Ellis in the fall of 1963 to let him know about his trip to New York. During his visit, Brian spent several evenings with Geoffrey going to restaurants, night clubs and taking in the sights.

New York entertainment attorney Walter Hofer met Brian through Dick James, who was the Beatles music publisher and Hofer's friend and client. During a 1963 trip to Paris, Hofer saw James, who was vacationing in Belgium and wanted to see Hofer to discuss an important matter. In an interview with David Klein, Hofer told of the meeting:

"I took one of those lovely French trains to Belgium on a lousy, miserable day, and Dick and I went walking on the beach and he said to me, 'There's a group out of Liverpool, the manager's name is Brian Epstein. He came to me and needs help. You'd be doing me a real personal favor if you would be so kind as to help him because he's never been in the entertainment business before.' So when I went back to London, I went to visit Brian and that's how it started."

Although Hofer did his best to help Brian, not all of his efforts were successful. His attempt to set up Epstein in a social setting with the right people was a miserable failure. Hofer recalled, "I had a cocktail party for Brian at my house [on Saturday, November 9], invited a slew of people, and very few showed up because who wants an English group and who's interested in an English manager? It was funny because Dick Glasser, who at the time was the...head of A&R for Liberty, flew in all the way from the [West Coast] for the party, and the people around him didn't show up."

Billy J. Kramer remembers Brian's disappointment with Liberty Records' lack of interest. He also remembers exercising at a gym near his hotel, sight seeing and buying lots of records. On November 12, Billy J. appeared on Joe Franklin's mid-day entertainment show on WOR-TV to lip sync *Do You Want To Know A Secret*. Kramer admits he was intimidated by it all, and when asked by Brian what he thought of New York, he replied, "I think I should get on the next plane out of here."

Billy J. further remembers he and Brian getting together with British composer Lionel Bart, who wrote the Broadway hit musical *Oliver!* Although no one knew it at that time, three months later the cast of *Oliver!* would share the stage of *The Ed Sullivan Show* with the Beatles.

Brian's most important meetings took place at the Delmonico Hotel, where Ed Sullivan lived. Sullivan was the host of a popular variety show that aired on the CBS television network on Sunday night (see pages 150-152). The seeds for the meetings were planted in the summer of 1963.

George Harrison's sister, Louise Caldwell, was living in the States and spending time promoting her brother's band (see page 48). She wrote letters to Brian suggesting ways to get American exposure for the Beatles. One of her recommendations was to have the group appear on *The Ed Sullivan Show*. Lou recalled, "That show was watched by everyone back then." Brian also heard about the importance of Sullivan's show from London's theatrical agents.

Jack Babb, who was the talent coordinator for *The Ed Sullivan Show*, spent his summers in Europe checking out potential acts for the program. Assisting Babb with his scouting was Peter Prichard, a theatrical agent based in London working for impresarios Lew and Leslie Grade. Prichard was also employed by Ed Sullivan as his European talent coordinator. Through his work for the show, Prichard became good friends with Sullivan and Babb. He also knew Brian. The Beatles manager had met Prichard when he moved to London and sometimes called him for advice.

During the summer of 1963, Prichard took Babb to see the Beatles on at least one occasion. Although the Beatles were developing a large following on the British concert circuit and had two huge hit singles with *Please Please Me* and *From Me To You*, the group had yet to become part of the national consciousness. Because no British pop act had ever achieved prolonged success in America, neither Prichard nor Babb gave any consideration to booking the Beatles on *The Ed Sullivan Show* at that time.

On Thursday, October 31, 1963, Ed Sullivan and his wife were at London Airport. It was an unusually busy day at the airport with the Prime Minister due to fly out and contestants for the Miss World contest (being held that year in London) arriving. Although the city was experiencing a heavy rainstorm that Halloween day, over 1,500 youngsters lined the rooftop gardens of the Queen's Building and others congregated on the ground. Ed Sullivan asked what all the commotion was about and was informed that it was for the Beatles, who were returning to England after a tour in Sweden. He replied, "Who the hell are the Beatles?" Sullivan was told that the Beatles were a well known pop group. His curiosity was aroused, but he wasn't ready to book an unknown-in-America British band at that time.

The enthusiastic airport reception for the group was reported in the British papers. The story was even picked up by *The New York Times*, which ran a brief account of the event in its November 4, 1963, edition. The article, which drew little notice at the time, stated that the screams of fans drowned out the whine of taxiing jets.

At the same time some Americans were first hearing about the Beatles through their brief mention in *The New York Times*, the group was playing before British high society at the annual *Royal Command Performance*, also known as the *Royal Variety Show*. Their presence on November 4, 1963, at London's Prince of Wales Theatre drew more attention than the arrival of the Royal Family, with the by-then-usual swarm of screaming fans being held back by rows of linked-at-the-arms police. The Beatles, who were seventh on the bill of 19 acts, impressed the upscale crowd with their humor and performances of *She Loves You, Till There Was You, From Me To You* and *Twist And Shout*.

Paul drew laughs when he introduced the ballad *Till There Was You* by joking that the song had been recorded by their "favorite American group, Sophie Tucker." Known as the "last of the red-hot mamas," Sophie Tucker was a Russian-born immigrant to America who had several vaudeville hits from 1910 through 1930. Sophie's large size prompted Paul to refer to her as a group unto herself. John's introduction to *Twist And Shout* was even more memorable.

Prior to ripping into the rocker, John said, "For our last number I'd like to ask your help. Would the people in the cheaper seats clap your hands? And the rest of you, if you'll just rattle your jewelry." While Brian viewed Lennon's remarks as being a bit risqué, he was relieved that the crowd seemed charmed by John's cheeky humor. Before the show, John had joked to Brian that he was going to ask the Royals to rattle their "fookin' jewelry."

The next morning Brian, along with Billy J. Kramer, headed to London Airport for the trip to New York. A few days earlier, Brian had been contacted by Peter Prichard, who had learned of Brian's plans to visit the States. Prichard mentioned that Brian should try to get the Beatles on *The Ed Sullivan Show* and offered to negotiate a deal. When Brian stated that he would rather handle the negotiations himself, Prichard told Brian to call him when he got to New York so that he could set up a meeting with Ed Sullivan.

As Brian's plane was heading to New York, Prichard began working out his pitch to Sullivan for the Beatles. He later called Sullivan to give him a report on the *Royal Variety Show*. Prichard mentioned the tremendous response the Beatles received and recommended that Sullivan book the Beatles for his show. Sullivan, remembering the large crowd at London Airport, was interested, but needed an angle to promote the group, which at that time was still unknown in America. Prichard informed Sullivan that the Beatles were the first "long-haired boys" to be invited to appear before the Queen of England. That convinced Sullivan to seriously consider the group for his show. (Although the Queen customarily attended the *Royal Variety Show*, she missed the 1963 gala. The Queen Mother and Princess Margaret were in the audience representing the Royal Family.) Prichard told Sullivan that Brian would probably be satisfied if the *Sullivan Show* covered travel and lodging expenses, so he recommended that the Beatles be paid union scale pay for the performances.

Brian's 1963 appointment book indicates that he met with Sullivan at his suite at the Delmonico Hotel on Monday, November 11. This was followed by a 5:00 p.m. dinner meeting the next day at the Delmonico Hotel's restaurant.

The initial meeting was apparently attended only by Brian and Ed Sullivan. They agreed that the Beatles would appear on Sullivan's February 9, 1964, show live from New York. The group would make a second live appearance the following week on a special remote show broadcast from the Deauville Hotel in Miami Beach. This show, which would feature Mitzi Gaynor, had already been scheduled. The double play arrangement appealed to Brian as it would give his boys a trip to New York for the first show followed by a bit of a vacation in sunny Florida for the second show. When Brian demanded that the Beatles headline both shows, Sullivan balked. While the television host knew of the group's phenomenal popularity in England, he was understandably reluctant to headline a British act that was virtually unknown in America.

Bob Precht, Sullivan's son-in-law and producer of the show, was asked to attend the second meeting during which the deal was finalized. Upon his arrival at the Delmonico, Precht was introduced to Brian and told by Sullivan that

the manager had a great group of youngsters who were going to be "really big." Precht immediately sensed that Ed had already made a decision to book the band on the show. This bothered him as he did not like Ed committing to acts without his prior approval.

Although Sullivan often paid up to $10,000 for a single performance, he offered Brian only $3,500 for each show. He agreed to pay the group's transportation and lodging expenses. Realizing the importance of having his boys on *The Ed Sullivan Show*, Brian agreed to the deal provided the Beatles receive top billing. Although Brian claims Sullivan gave in to this demand, it is unlikely that Sullivan did more than agree to consider top billing for the group. By the time the first show aired three months later, Sullivan eagerly promoted the Beatles as the headline act. However, Mitzi Gaynor received top billing for the Miami show.

Bob Precht suggested that in addition to the two live programs, the Beatles should tape a performance for later broadcast. The parties agreed on a payment of $3,000 for the taped segment, thus bringing the total for the three shows to $10,000. As was often the case with Brian's negotiations, the deal was then sealed with a handshake.

After leaving the meeting, Precht began having second thoughts about featuring the unknown British band on the show and called Sullivan at his suite to voice his concerns. Sullivan assured him that he felt it was worth the investment. And that ended the matter. The decision had been made. Sullivan later told *The New York Times*, "I made up my mind that this was the same sort of mass hit hysteria that had characterized the Elvis Presley days."

Brian's 1963 appointment book indicates that during his stay in New York he contacted representatives of *Billboard*, *Cash Box*, the William Morris Agency, Shroeder Publishing, Liberty Records, Atlantic Records, Vee-Jay Records and Laurie Records (U.S. label for Gerry & the Pacemakers). He met with Gloria Stavers, editor of *16* magazine. His connection with the Armed Forced Radio Network later led to an interview with Paul (see page 189).

Some accounts state that Brian met with Capitol's Director of Eastern Operations, Brown Meggs, and that Brian secured a deal with the company to release the Beatles future recordings. This does not appear to be the case. Brian's 1963 appointment book contains no references to either Brown Meggs or Capitol, thus casting doubt on reports that Brian met with Meggs during the visit. Even if they did meet, Meggs did not have the authority to commit Capitol to signing the group. That would not happen until late November, 1963, when Capitol entered into a licensing agreement with EMI for the Beatles.

As Brian headed back to London on November 14, 1963, he had much to think about. He had failed to get Liberty Records or anyone else excited about Billy J. Kramer, but had booked the Beatles for three appearances on *The Ed Sullivan Show*. That alone made the trip a success. Operation U.S.A. was definitely gaining momentum. And proof of America taking notice of the Beatles was on the newsstands the week he headed home. The current issues of *Time* and *Newsweek* magazines contained articles in their music sections on the Beatles.

That fine old man is Sir Winston—89

In the bow tie and the siren suit he made famous during World War II, Sir Winston Churchill celebrated his 89th birthday by waving to well-wishers from the window of his London home. When President John Kennedy was born, Churchill was a 43-year-old political has been trying to fight his way back He did, and became a world her who saw—and made—more his tory than most men will ever read

The Sister sings and strums to fame

A bespectacled Belgian nun singing a song she made up by herself and playing a guitar that isn't even electric. Run this combination up the Tin Pan Alley flagpole and who salutes? Just the whole U.S., that's who. By last week Sister Luc-Gabrielle's hauntingly lovely recording, *Dominique*, had sold 750,000 copies, making it the top tune in the country by a runaway.

Princess Margaret meets the red-hot Beatles

Even Princess Margaret was snapping her fingers. After the Royal Variety Show performance, she greeted the mop-haired Beatles, whose thunderous rock and roll and irreverent humor has British teen-agers in a frenzy. She was lucky to get to them. Screaming fans caused such a ruckus that police were forced to lock the Beatles in the theater 13 hours—until the crowd finally went home.

CONTINUED ON PAGE 4

The first significant mainstream coverage of the Beatles in America appeared in the November 15, 1963, issue of *Time* magazine in a story titled "The New Madness." *Time* observed: "Though Americans might find the Beatles achingly familiar (their songs consist mainly of 'Yeah!' screamed to the accompaniment of three guitars and a thunderous drum), they are apparently irresistible to the English." The group was described as a "wild rhythm-and-blues quartet" that had sold 2,500,000 records. The story reported that "crowds stampede for a chance to touch the hem of the collarless coats sported on stage by all four of them."

Time informed the American public that: "Although no Beatle can read music, two of them dream up half the Beatles' repertory. The raucous, big-beat sound they achieve by electric amplification of all their instruments makes a Beatles performance slightly orgiastic. But the boys are the very spirit of good clean fun. They look like shaggy Peter Pan, with their mushroom haircuts and high white shirt collars, and on stage they clown around endlessly–twisting, cracking jokes, gently laughing at the riotous response they get from their audience. The precise nature of their charm remains mysterious even to their manager."

Newsweek's first Beatles story, titled "Beatlemania," appeared in its November 18, 1963, issue. The magazine reported that the Beatles "wear sheepdog bangs, collarless jackets, and drainpipe trousers" and that "all four sing ... and sing ... and sing." After stating that the "sound of their music is one of the most persistent noises heard over England since the air-raid sirens were dismantled," *Newsweek* described the music and performances as follows:

"Beatle music is high-pitched, loud beyond reason, and stupefyingly repetitive. Like rock 'n' roll, to which it is closely allied, it is even more effective to watch than to hear. They prance, skip, and turn in circles; Beatles have even been known to kiss their guitars. The style, certainly, is their own. 'They don't gyrate like Elvis,' says one young girl. 'They stamp about and shake and, oh dearie me, they just send the joy out to you.'"

By November, 1963, *The New York Times* was starting to pick up stories on the Beatles. Its November 4th edition ran a short piece on the crowd that greeted the group at London Airport upon their return from Sweden on October 31. A November 24 article on British films contains a few paragraphs about the group. Writer Stephen Watts calls the Beatles a "social phenomenon ... wearing floor-mop haircuts which remind one of nothing so much as an adolescent version of the Three Stooges." This leads into his report that Walter Shenson would be producing a Beatles film.

The first extensive coverage in the *Times* appeared in its Sunday, December 1, 1963, *New York Times Magazine*. Writer Frederick Lewis' three-page article "Britons Succumb to 'Beatlemania'" was supplemented with a cartoon and three pictures. The article begins with descriptions of skirmishes and battles between fans and the police, all caused by a "phenomenon called the Beatles." According to Lewis, "To see a Beatle is joy, to touch one paradise on earth, and for just the simplest opportunity of this privilege, people will fight like mad things and with dedication for a Great Cause, like natural survival."

The article states that for months the Beatles have been the preoccupation of the British, eclipsing government and even football (soccer). It gives examples of the hysteria caused by the group during the first ten days of November. In Carlisle, 400 school girls fought police while waiting to get tickets. In Dublin, "young limbs snapped like twigs in a tremendous free-for-all." In London, a female reporter had her hand kissed repeatedly after it brushed a Beatle. In Birmingham, they disguised themselves as police to get by the crowd. Capitol later used a similar listing of examples of Beatlemania on the liner notes to its *Meet The Beatles!* LP.

Lewis writes that "Their music is basically rock 'n' roll, but less formalized, slightly more inventive." He calls their act both hilarious and outrageous. Although he states their appeal is strongest to females ages 10 to 30, he recognizes that "Beatlemania ... affects all social classes and all levels of intelligence." He notes that at the *Royal Variety Show*, the Queen Mother was seen clapping on the off beat and Princess Margaret snapped her fingers.

As for the group's success, Lewis points to their working class background, Northern England attitude and Liverpool roots. Their success enables the Beatles to "act as spokesmen for the new, noisy, anti-establishment generation.... We admire their freshness and innocence so much that it's almost like giving birth." He notes that the rise of the Beatles marks the end of American dominance of the popular music scene in England.

The article ends with a quote from John. "We're having a fab time. But it can't last long. Anyway, I'd hate to be old. Just imagine it. Who would want to listen to an 80-year-old Beatle?"

The December 13, 1963, issue of *Life* ran a short piece on the group in its "Newsfronts of the World" section, which featured a picture of Princess Margaret meeting the "red-hot Beatles" (shown left). Readers were told, "Even Princess Margaret was snapping her fingers. After the *Royal Variety Show* performance, she greeted the mop-haired Beatles, whose thunderous rock and roll and irreverent humor has British teenagers in a frenzy. She was lucky to get to them. Screaming fans caused such a ruckus that police were forced to lock the Beatles in the theater 13 hours – until the crowd finally went home."

The same page contained two other features that provided interesting contrasts and parallels. Sir Winston Churchill, wearing the bow tie and siren suit he made famous during World War II, is seen celebrating his 89th birthday by waving to well-wishers from his London home. The legendary Churchill, who served as British Prime Minister during its finest hour, was known throughout the world. The Beatles, wearing stylish suits and boots, would soon surpass Churchill in terms of worldwide recognition.

The other picture shows Sister Luc-Gabrielle, a Belgian nun, strumming her nylon-string acoustic guitar and singing *Dominique*. Credited to "The Singing Nun," the song topped the *Billboard Hot 100* for four straight weeks in December, 1963. One month later the Beatles would hold the number one spot for 14 consecutive weeks. Her album, *The Singing Nun*, topped the *Billboard* album chart for ten straight weeks before being replaced by *Meet The Beatles!*

PARLOPHONE

with the beatles

stereo

Newsweek

DECEMBER 2, 1963   25c

JOHN
FITZGERALD
KENNEDY

1917-1963

NOVEMBER 22, 1963

During the early evening hours of Friday, November 22, 1963, teenagers in England were listening to the Beatles second album, *With The Beatles*. The record, which was released that day, had advance orders of over 270,000 units. While British fans were enjoying great new Beatles songs such as *It Won't Be Long* and *All My Loving*, President Kennedy's motorcade was making its way through the streets of Dallas....

With The Beatles was issued in England on November 22, 1963, to coincide with the holiday shopping season. Although the band had recorded the 10 songs needed to flesh out its first album in one incredible session held on February 11, 1963, the Beatles needed six days in the studio to complete the 14 tracks for the second LP. The band's hectic touring schedule caused the recording sessions to be spread over two days in July (18 and 30), two consecutive days in September(11 and 12) and two touch-up days in October (3 and 23).

The group knocked out six cover tunes in July: *You Really Got A Hold On Me, Money (That's What I Want), Devil In Her Heart, Till There Was You, Please Mister Postman* and *Roll Over Beethoven*, as well as two Lennon-McCartney originals, *It Won't Be Long* and *All My Loving*. When the Beatles returned to the studio in September, they recorded five more Lennon-McCartney songs, *All I've Got To Do, Not A Second Time, I Wanna Be Your Man, Little Child* and *Hold Me Tight*. They also recorded George's first solo composition, *Don't Bother Me*. Three of the songs required additional work in October.

Advance orders for the album topped 270,000; however, it is not known how many copies were sold in stores the first day of the record's release. In 1963, few young-sters in England could afford to purchase LPs, but certainly some fans were able to persuade their parents to buy the new Beatles album for them that Friday afternoon. Those lucky enough to obtain a copy were treated to a well-crafted mixture of group compositions and cover tunes.

In America, a different story was unfolding. That morning, CBS News had broadcast a story titled "The Beatles: New Phenomena In Britain" (see pages 60-61). It was now lunch time on the East Coast. Walter Cronkite was standing by the United Press ticker in the CBS newsroom when the machine began ringing and printing out a bulletin. Cronkite pulled the paper from the ticker and, after reading the first few words, shouted, "Let's get on the air."

Those watching the soap opera *As The World Turns* saw their program replaced on the screen with the words *"CBS NEWS BULLETIN."* Stunned viewers heard Cronkite's familiar voice inform them that, "In Dallas, Texas, three shots were fired at President Kennedy's motorcade in downtown Dallas. The first reports say that President Kennedy has been seriously wounded by this shooting.... Mrs. Kennedy jumped up and grabbed Mr. Kennedy. She called out, 'Oh, no!' Then the motorcade sped on. United Press says the wounds for President Kennedy could perhaps be fatal."

Myth

The assassination of President Kennedy played a key role in the Beatles success in the United States. The youth of America, despondent over the death of the President, were looking for something to lift them out of their doldrums. The Beatles provided the needed tonic.

Fact

The connection between the death of President Kennedy and the explosion of Beatlemania in America has been blown out of proportion by those looking for an explanation as to why America's youngsters embraced the group.

Explanation

I was part of the youth of America in the sixties and can speak firsthand on this matter. Although I was only eight and a half years old in November, 1963, I will never forget where I was and how I learned about the assassination. On that Friday afternoon, my third grade teacher was called out of the classroom by an assistant to the principal. About ten or fifteen minutes later she returned to the room looking shook up. Without saying a word, she went to the blackboard and wrote, "The President is dead. Class dismissed." She then sat down at her desk, lowered her head and cried. I remember going to my cousin's house and watching television coverage of the assassination that afternoon and evening. I remember hearing about Oswald's death at Sunday School. I remember seeing highlights of the funeral procession on television. I remember the President's son saluting the horse-drawn casket. I was shocked and saddened by President Kennedy's tragic death, but by the holiday season of 1963, I was over it.

In early January, 1964, I heard *I Want To Hold Your Hand* on the school bus radio. The excitement of the music and quality of the singing immediately grabbed me. I was hooked. *She Loves You, Please Please Me, I Saw Her Standing There, All My Loving* and others had the same effect. The fact that they were British, had long hair and were cool was certainly part of it, but the main reason I embraced the Beatles is the same reason people do 40 years later–the quality of the music. In all due respect to President Kennedy, his death did not cause me to become a Beatles fan.

I have discussed the alleged connection between the Kennedy assassination and the popularity of the Beatles with many first generation American Beatles fans. None of these individuals believes that President Kennedy's death played any part in his or her attraction to the group. Admittedly, this is by no means a scientific survey, but I have yet to find any evidence to support the connection, which has been written as gospel in countless books, magazines and newspapers.

When one looks beyond the United States, the connection becomes even more tenuous. The Beatles were extremely popular in England, Japan, Germany, France, Italy, Australia, Denmark, Sweden, the Netherlands, Canada and several other countries. None of these nations was suffering the trauma of having its head of state assassinated, yet the youth of these countries embraced the Beatles.

CBS then returned to regular programming, but was soon back on the air live from the newsroom with Cronkite seated at his desk delivering details of the developing story. "We've just had a report from our correspondent Dan Rather in Dallas that he has confirmed that President Kennedy is dead. There is still no official confirmation of this, however...." As Cronkite discussed concerns and fears people had expressed regarding the reception Kennedy would get in Texas, he was handed a sheet of paper. Cronkite placed his reading glasses on and announced, "From Dallas, Texas, the flash apparently official, President Kennedy died at one p.m. Central Standard Time, two o'clock Eastern Standard Time, some 38 minutes ago."

The Monday evening after the assassination, CBS broadcast a special titled *The Four Dark Days*. In the program, Dan Rather reported on the innocent start of Friday, November 22, 1963. "Long before Mr. Kennedy and the presidential party took off from Fort Worth for the brief flight to Love Field in Dallas, thousands gathered at the steel fence to greet them. The crowd was excited and the President seemed to be.... The crowd, many of them in their late teens, seemed particularly charmed with Mrs. Kennedy." The reporter described the motorcade drive through Dallas, informing the viewers that "the people were on the sidewalks, 14 and 15 lines deep."

Exactly 11 weeks later, the Beatles would receive an even more enthusiastic reception than that given to the President when their plane landed in New York and their motorcade took them to the Plaza Hotel near Central Park. By that time, New York's Idlewild Airport had been renamed Kennedy International Airport in honor of the slain President.

Although the death of President Kennedy did not cause Americans to fall for the Beatles, it may have indirectly contributed to the group's success in the United States. The saturation coverage of the Beatles by the American press in early 1964 closely parallels the conduct of the British press a few months earlier.

During the summer of 1963, England was rocked by a series of sex scandals involving government officials and judges. The most serious involved John Profumo, a Cabinet Minister who served as Secretary of State for War. Profumo was caught having a sexual affair with a 22-year-old model who had also bedded the naval attaché at the Russian Embassy. The possibility of Profumo sharing bedtime secrets with a woman who was also sleeping with a Russian representative was indeed provocative during the height of the Cold War. Although Profumo first denied the affair, he later resigned in disgrace. Sexual indiscretions involving other members of the British government and judges also surfaced. The sex scandal was quickly followed by the Great Train Robbery, which left Scotland Yard scouring the countryside for criminals who had disappeared with 2.5 million pounds. The political fallout generated by the sex scandal led to a reevaluation of Prime Minister Harold Macmillan, who resigned as criticism of his government grew. All of these stories were reported in lurid detail by the British newspapers and tabloids, which were concentrated on London's Fleet Street.

Philip Norman, in his Beatles biography *Shout!*, theorizes that the massive coverage of the Beatles by the British press was in response to months of reporting somber events. "By the end of September, every editor on Fleet Street was looking for a diversion from this incessant heavy news – something light; something unconnected with the aristocratic classes; something harmless, blameless and, above all, cheerful." Beatlemania proved to be the perfect escape.

Similarly, the American press had grown weary of reporting on the assassination and other depressing events. The Beatles provided a break from over two months of somber news. In the February 11, 1964, *New York Daily News*, Anthony Burton observed, "It's a relief from Cyprus and Malaysia and Viet Nam and racial demonstrations and Khrushchev. Beset by troubles all around the globe, America has turned to the four young men with the ridiculous haircuts for a bit of light entertainment."

Beatlemania was fun to cover regardless of how one felt about the four young lads from Liverpool. Members of the press who found the group charming enjoyed reporting on the mass hysteria created by the band. Those who hated the Beatles or failed to understand their popularity took great pleasure in mocking the group and its fans. Their negative and condescending comments served only to strengthen the resolve of the group's devoted followers. By keeping the Beatles in the news, the press helped fuel Beatlemania in America.

Thus, while President Kennedy's assassination did not cause the youth of America to embrace the Beatles, it may have led the press to give more coverage to the Beatles, which in turn helped spread Beatlemania throughout the United States.

T 6051

BEATLEMANIA!

HIGH FIDELITY
THE "6000" SERIES
Capitol
RECORDS

WITH THE BEATLES

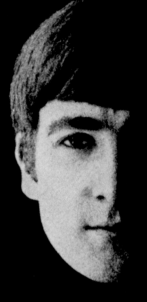

THE NEWSPAPERS SAY . . .
A NEW DISEASE IS SWEEPING THROUGH BRITAIN . . . AND DOCTORS ARE
POWERLESS TO STOP IT . . . IT'S BEATLEMANIA! THIS LIVERPOOL GROUP
PLAY TO PACKED HOUSES WHEREVER THEY GO . . .

        SANDY GARDINER

THE BEATLES HAVE CREATED A TEEN-AGE CULT MORE FRENETIC THAN
ANYTHING THE BOBBYSOXERS DREAMED OF IN THE HEYDAY OF FRANK
SINATRA . . . FOUR POP IDOLS FOR THE PRICE OF ONE . . .

        ALAN HARVEY

AT THE ROYAL VARIETY PERFORMANCE SHOW . . . THE QUEEN MOTHER
BEAMED . . .
A RAUCOUS, BIG BEAT SOUND . . . GOOD CLEAN FUN . . . "BEATLEMANIA"
. . . WAS STRIKING EVERYWHERE . . .

        TIME MAGAZINE

THEIR THEATRE APPEARANCES DRAW SCREAMING FANS . . . THE QUEEN
MOTHER FOUND THEM "SO YOUNG, FRESH AND VITAL" . . . THEY STAMP
ABOUT AND SHAKE . . . PRANCE . . . SKIP . . .

        NEWSWEEK MAGAZINE

NOVEMBER 25, 1963

The first Beatles album released in North America was *Beatlemania! With The Beatles*, which was issued by Capitol of Canada on November 25, 1963. The record entered the Top 5 album chart published by Toronto radio station CHUM at number five on December 16, 1963. Four weeks later on January 13, 1964, the disc topped the chart. It remained the number one album for five weeks before being replaced by the Beatles next Canadian LP, *Twist And Shout*.

Special BEATLES Issue

NATIONAL RECORD NEWS

"Beatlemania" SWEEPS U. S.

How It All Started

They wore black leather jackets, their hair was untidy and the only way one could tell them apart from characters in a Marlon Brando movie was that they had no motorcycles.

They were the Beatles, but no one knew it. In those days they called themselves a variety of things—The Quarrymen, Moon Dogs or The Moonshiners. It was early 1958, and they spent most of their time playing in the cellar of a friend's home in Liverpool for kicks.

CELLAR CLUB

If there was a turning point for the four young men, introducing men.

THE BEATLES, four young Englishmen, have become, in just one year, the

What Britain Says

The Beatlemania phenomenon that began in England last year and is now sweeping the United States, has created a wave of controversy so extensive that psychologists and sociologists are taking a hard clinical look at it. Many adults regard Beatlemania with horror, distaste, and even fear and find it easy to blame the Beatles for what they, the adults, feel is a lack of taste and control and a dangerous mass h y s t e r i a among young people.

CORBETT SAYS

Anthony Corbett, a noted English psychologist praised the Beatles as having provided "a desperately needed re-English inhibitions the Beatles as having prov-ed "a desperately needed re-

Lewis of that paper's London bureau, examined the socio-logical implications of Beatle-mania and came up with other theories.

"They (the Beatles) are working class and their roots and attitudes are firmly of the north of England. Be-cause of their success, they can act as spokesmen for the new, noisy, anti-establishment generation which is becoming a force in British life," Lewis wrote.

"The Beatles are part of a strong-flowing reaction against the soft, middle-class south of England, which has controlled popular culture for so long."

Beatlemania has touched so long."

Beatlemania has touched

Moonshiners. It was early 1958, and they spent most of their time playing in the cellar of a friend's home in Liverpool for kicks.

CELLAR CLUB

If there was a turning point for the four young men

THE BEATLES, four young Englishman, have become, in just one year, the

ed "a desperately needed re-

Beatlemania has touched

If there was a turning point for the four young men

THE BEATLES, four young Englishman, have become, in just one year, the

ed "a desperately needed re-

so long."

Beatlemania has touched

December 4, 1963

NEW ENGLISH MADNESS TO SPREAD TO U.S.;

BEATLEMANIA WILL BE IMPORTED HERE

HOLLYWOOD -- Beatlemania, the totally unprecedented musical phenom-enon that has turned England topsy-turvy this past year will spread to the United States in 1964. Alan W. Livingston, president of Capitol Records, Inc., announced today that his company has concluded negotiations with Electric & Musical Industries (EMI), Ltd., for exclusive U.S. rights to re-cordings by The Beatles, the sole cause of the mania.

In making the announcement, Livingston said: "With their popularity in England and the promotion we're going to put behind them here, I have every reason to believe The Beatles will be just as successful in the United States."

(more)

DECEMBER 4, 1963

On December 4, 1963, Capitol Records issued a press release (computer re-creation shown above) stating that the company had obtained the exclusive U.S. rights to recordings by the Beatles. Capitol president Alan Livingston boldly predicted that the group's popularity in England combined with Capitol's promotion would make the Beatles just as successful in the United States.

The December 4, 1963, Capitol press release (shown on the preceding page) led to the first major story on the Beatles in *Billboard*. Although over a dozen references to the Beatles appeared during the year (primarily in the international section), the group did not receive any significant coverage until the magazine's December 14, 1963, issue. In a page-three article titled "Capitol Has New Beatles Bashes," *Billboard* reported that the label had completed negotiations with EMI for exclusive distribution of future recordings by the band and planned to release the group's *I Want To Hold Your Hand* single in mid-January. The article stated that the disc had over one million pre-release orders when it was issued in England on November 29, 1963. The article did not tell the convoluted story of how Capitol had repeatedly turned the group down before finally agreeing to release its recordings.

As detailed earlier in this book, Capitol's Dave Dexter passed on the Beatles first two singles, *Love Me Do* and *Please Please Me*. In order to appease George Martin and Brian Epstein, EMI (through its agent Transglobal) entered into a leasing agreement with Vee-Jay to issue *Please Please Me* in the States. Under the terms of the agreement, Vee-Jay had a right of first refusal for all Beatles recordings for a five-year period. Vee-Jay released *Please Please Me* and *From Me To You*, but failed to render royalty statements on sales of their Beatles records, prompting Transglobal to unilaterally terminate the licensing agreement. This gave Capitol the opportunity to issue *She Loves You*; however, Dexter recommended that the label turn down the song because he found it unsuitable for the American market. Transglobal then placed *She Loves You* with Swan, a small label based in Philadelphia. The record bombed. In mid-October, 1963, Transglobal transferred its rights in the Beatles back to EMI, which believed the facilities and resources of a large record company were needed to properly exploit the Beatles in the U.S. EMI once again went to Capitol, hoping to persuade the company to issue the group's upcoming single, *I Want To Hold Your Hand*. Incredibly, Dexter failed to hear the single's potential and recommended that Capitol pass on the Beatles for a *fourth* time!

Brian Epstein was totally frustrated with Capitol's refusal to release the band's recordings. He decided to take matters into his own hands and no longer rely on EMI. During his visit to New York in November of 1963, he may have met with Brown Meggs, who was stationed in New York and served as Director of Eastern Operations for Capitol. Although some accounts state that the 32-year-old Meggs was responsible for Capitol's signing of the Beatles, this is unlikely as Meggs had no involvement with the signing of artists aimed at the teen market. Decisions regarding the release of recordings by foreign artists were made by Dave Dexter, who worked out of the Capitol Tower in Hollywood. And when it came to the Beatles, Dexter viewed the group as "a bunch of long-haired kids." Brian realized that his best shot of getting his boys on Capitol was to take his cause to the president of the company. Capitol president Alan Livingston recalls:

"I'm sitting in my office one day and I got a call from London from a man named Brian Epstein, who I didn't know.

I took the call. And he said, 'I am the personal manager of the Beatles and I don't understand why you won't release them.' And I said, 'well, frankly, Mr. Epstein, I haven't heard them.' And he said, 'Would you please listen and call me back.' And I said, 'OK,' and I called Dexter and said, 'Let me have some Beatles records.' He sent up a few and I listened. I liked them. I thought they were something different. I can't tell you in all honesty I knew how big they'd be, but I thought this is worth a shot. So I called Epstein back and said, 'OK, I'll put them out.' Smart man, Epstein, he said, 'Just a minute, I'm not gonna let you have them unless you spend $40,000,' (that was a pound translation) 'to promote their first single.' You didn't spend $40,000 to promote a single in those days, it was unheard of. For whatever reason, I said 'OK, we'll do it,' and the deal was made [in late November, 1963]."

Anxious to get feedback on the label's new signing, Livingston sought the opinion of his wife, Nancy Olson: "I brought the record home and played it for my wife Nancy, who has an excellent ear and followed the popular scene very carefully. I said, 'I want you to listen to this, I think it's gonna change the music business.' And she said, '*I Wanna Hold Your Haaaaand*, are you kidding?' So I thought, maybe I made a mistake. We put the record out. I never got through the $40,000. The record exploded. And the rest is history."

Alan Livingston's commitment for Capitol to spend $40,000 promoting the Beatles first single may sound insignificant today, but in 1963 dollars that was a considerable sum. It was also without precedent. Promotion in the early sixties consisted primarily of running advertisements in music industry magazines such as *Billboard* and *Cash Box*. Record companies did not advertise singles and albums in teen-oriented or music-related magazines. There was no *Rolling Stone*. There were no music chain store publications. No thought was given to placing ads in comic books. With no MTV, promotional films were rare. Advertising and promotional expenditures were not aimed directly at record buyers. Money was spent to get the songs on the radio and the records into stores. The strategy was simple: get radio airplay and distribution; the sales will follow.

Capitol's $40,000 promotional budget for the Beatles gave the company the ability to expand beyond traditional marketing. It also inspired creative thinking. While Livingston doesn't believe Capitol spent the full $40,000, no one really knows how much money Capitol actually spent on promoting the Beatles first single and album. Most newspaper and magazine stories place the sum at $50,000, while others go as high as $100,000. What matters is how the money was spent.

Although Brown Meggs' title at Capitol was Director of Eastern Operations, his responsibilities included the coordination of corporate public relations. Thus, Meggs was in charge of overseeing what became known as "the Beatles Campaign." He was assisted by Fred Martin, Jr., whose title was press relations manager. Although Fred worked out of the Capitol Tower, he reported directly to Meggs and took a very active role in the campaign. According to Meggs, "No Capitol employee did more for the Beatles than Freddy Martin."

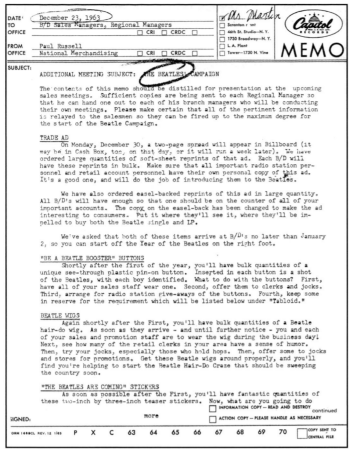
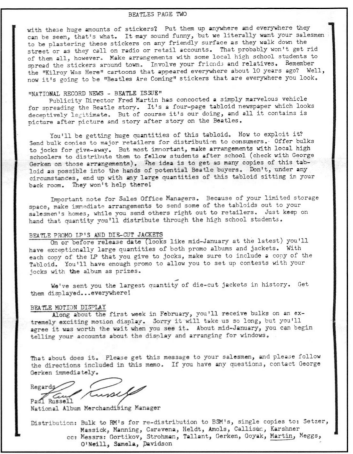

A December 23, 1963, memo from Paul Russell, National Album Merchandiser Manager, detailed the Beatles Campaign to Capitol employees. Pictured above is the copy of the memo sent to Capitol Press Relations Manager Fred Martin.

The details of the Beatles Campaign were outlined in a December 23, 1963, Capitol memo (shown above) prepared by Paul Russell, National Album Merchandising Manager. The memo was distributed in bulk to regional managers for distribution to branch managers, with instructions that all pertinent information be "relayed to the salesmen so they can be fired up to the maximum degree for the start of the Beatles Campaign." While most of the nation was preparing for the Christmas and New Year's holidays, Capitol was readying its mighty sales force to make 1964 the "Year of the Beatles."

The Capitol memo describes one of the more ingenious promotional tools created for the campaign:

"Publicity Director Fred Martin has concocted a simply marvelous vehicle for spreading the Beatle story. It's a four-page tabloid newspaper which looks deceptively legitimate. But of course it's our doing, and all it contains is picture after picture and story after story on the Beatles."

The *Special Beatles Issue* of the *National Record News* tabloid (shown on page 70) was sent in mass quantities to Capitol's sales force. The memo gave the following instructions on how to exploit the tabloid: (1) send bulk copies to major retailers for distribution to customers; (2) offer bulk copies to disc jockeys for giveaways; and (3) most important, make arrangements with local high school students to distribute them to fellow students after school. The goal was "to get as many copies of this tabloid as possible into the hands of potential Beatle buyers."

The *National Record News* was put together entirely by Fred Martin. In addition to pictures and stories on the group, it contains tales of Beatlemania and fashion news regarding the Beatle hairdo, described as the "distinctive, mushroom-shaped coiffure which has become the group's visual trademark." The tabloid has biographies of John, Paul, George and Ringo (see pages 170-173), as well as manager Brian Epstein, who is called the "fifth Beatle." The group is quoted as saying, "We'd have been nowhere but for Brian. Still in Liverpool clubs, pounding it out." While clever, entertaining and informative, the tabloid contains an embarrassing error. Page three has solo pictures of each of the Beatles. Unfortunately, Paul is identified as John, George as Paul and John as George. Only Ringo is correctly identified. Still, the newspaper was not only a great promotional item for Capitol, but also a wonderful and educational souvenir for America's novice Beatles fans.

The Capitol memo contains information about a two-page advertisement (shown on the following two pages) that was scheduled to appear in *Billboard* and *Cash Box*. Capitol ordered large quantities of soft-sheet reprints of the ad and instructed its employees to make sure that all important radio station and retail account personnel were given their own copy of the ad/poster. The memo correctly observed that the advertisement was "a good one, and will do the job of introducing them to the Beatles."

Capitol got additional mileage out of the trade advertisement by ordering easel-backed reprints containing minor text modifications to make the ad more suitable for record store customers. Salesmen were instructed to obtain counter space in all important accounts for the easel-backed standee (shown on page 122).

Alan Livingston
From Bozo To The Beatles With Sinatra Thrown In For Good Measure

Alan Livingston began his career in the music business by leading his own orchestra while a student at the University of Pennsylvania. He went on to receive a B.S. degree in economics from the Wharton School of Finance and Commerce. After serving as a lieutenant in the Army, he worked in Public Relations for Calvert's Whiskey.

Livingston started working for Capitol Records in 1946. His initial assignment for Capitol was to develop a catalog of children's records. Livingston's first creation was Bozo the Clown, a character who would later become a television star and part of American culture. Bozo made his debut in September of 1946 on the Capitol album *Bozo At The Circus*, which was written and produced by Livingston. The album was an immediate hit, selling over 100,000 copies in its first month and later becoming a million seller. This was followed by several other successful Bozo albums, including *Bozo Sings*, *Bozo And His Rocket Ship* and *Bozo Under The Sea*.

Under Livingston's direction, Capitol dominated the children's records market. When the *Best-Selling Children's Records* chart made its debut in the June 12, 1948, issue of *Billboard*, eight of the top ten albums were Capitol releases, including the chart-topping *Bozo At The Circus*, the fantasy *Bozo And His Rocket Ship* (#7) and two other Livingston creations, *Sparky's Magic Piano* (#6) and *Rusty in Orchestraville* (#9). During 1949, there were many weeks when Bozo had four records in the top ten. Bozo's amazing chart domination would be surpassed approximately fifteen years later when the Beatles held the top five spots in the *Billboard Hot 100* during the week of April 4, 1964. Livingston wrote and produced many of Capitol's children's records, including albums featuring Woody Woodpecker, Walt Disney properties and Warner Brothers cartoon characters such as Bugs Bunny. He created the "Record-Reader," a book and album combination (a packaging concept copied many times over). He also co-wrote the pop novelty tune *I Taut I Taw A Puddy Tat*, which was recorded by Mel Blanc. The song was a number nine pop hit in 1951.

After becoming vice-president of the label, Livingston received a call from Sammy Weisbourg, president of the William Morris Agency, who informed Livingston that the agency had recently signed Frank Sinatra. At the time, Sinatra's career was at an all time low. Weisbourg asked whether Capitol would consider signing Sinatra. When Livingston said yes, the shocked Weisbourg replied "You would?" On March 14, 1953, Frank Sinatra signed a seven-year contract with Capitol Records. The agreement was executed at Lucey's Restaurant, where Johnny Mercer, Glenn Wallich and Buddy DeSylva first met to formulate their plans to launch Capitol Records in 1941.

Livingston told Sinatra that he wanted him to work with arranger Nelson Riddle; however, Sinatra was reluctant to do so out of his loyalty to Axel Stordahl, with whom he had worked for most of his career. Because the first Sinatra-Stordahl recordings for Capitol, *I'm Walking Behind You* and *Lean Baby*, didn't have the magic Livingston and producer Voyle Gilmore were looking for, Sinatra reluctantly agreed to try a session with Nelson Riddle on April 30, 1953. The impact on the music was immediate, producing the classic *I've Got The World On A String*. However, it was *Young-At-Heart* that became the defining moment in Frank Sinatra's comeback, peaking at number two during its 22-week run on the charts in spring, 1954.

After ten years with Capitol, Livingston left the music business to work for the National Broadcasting Company in 1956. While at NBC, he produced the pilot for the western series *Bonanza*, which became the television network's most successful series up to that time.

In 1961, Capitol persuaded Livingston to return to Capitol as its president. During his tenure, the company signed the Beach Boys, the Beatles, the Band and many other successful rock artists.

He left Capitol in 1968 to establish his own production company, Mediarts, Inc., which was involved with film,

©2003 www.popsiephotos.com

On February 10, 1964, the Beatles were presented with gold record awards for *I Want To Hold Your Hand* and *Meet The Beatles!* by Capitol president Alan Livingston at the Plaza Hotel (see pages 162-163).

records and music publishing. Two of the company's successful projects were the film *Downhill Racer*, starring Robert Redford and Gene Hackman, and Don McLean's song *American Pie*, which was transferred to United Artists and became a number one hit in 1972. After selling his interest in the company to United Artists, he was involved with various film projects. Although he was not directly involved in the production of *Star Wars*,

Livingston was senior vice president and president of the Entertainment Group of 20th Century Fox during the time *Star Wars* was developed. In 1988, Livingston published the novel *Ronnie Finkelhof, Superstar*, which tells the story of a Harvard prelaw student who becomes an overnight success as a rock musician. Livingston is married to actress Nancy Olson, whose film credits include *Sunset Blvd.* and *The Absent Minded Professor*.

Alan Livingston wrote the lyrics to the novelty hit *I Taut I Taw A Puddy Tat* (left). In 1953, he brought Frank Sinatra to Capitol, and paired him with Nelson Riddle (at left with Sinatra in middle picture). *Young-At-Heart* (right), arranged by Nelson Riddle, left no doubt that the "Chairman of the Board" was back.

DECEMBER 26, 1963

Capitol Records had planned on issuing its first Beatles record, *I Want To Hold Your Hand*, on January 13, 1964. When disc jockeys in three major markets began playing the song from the British 45, demand for the single caused the company to begin distributing the record the day after Christmas. Within weeks, *I Want To Hold Your Hand* topped the national and local charts throughout America.

WWDC disc jockey Carroll James (shown above with the Beatles) played the British 45 *I Want To Hold Your Hand* (Parlophone R 5084) prior to the release of the Capitol single.

As 1963 drew to a close, Beatlemania was about to invade the United States. For most Americans, it arrived on AM radio with *I Want To Hold Your Hand*. Although the song was not the first Beatles record released in the United States, it was the one that made America take notice of the group. As detailed earlier in this book, the first three U.S. Beatles singles, *Please Please Me*, *From Me To You* and *She Loves You*, had little impact when originally issued in 1963. *I Want To Hold Your Hand* changed everything. It gave the Beatles their coveted American hit and opened the floodgates for other Beatles songs, as well as recordings by other British acts.

Capitol originally scheduled *I Want To Hold Your Hand* for release on January 13, 1964, but Walter Cronkite, a 15-year-old girl living near the nation's capital and a DJ set in motion a chain of events that led the label to begin distributing the single three weeks earlier on December 26, 1963.

On the evening of December 10, 1963, Marsha Albert and her family, who lived in Silver Spring, Maryland, were watching the *CBS Evening News with Walter Cronkite*. Towards the end of the broadcast, the network ran a story about a curious musical phenomenon taking place in England known as Beatlemania. The report included a clip of the Beatles performing *She Loves You*. Marsha liked what she saw and heard. According to WWDC disc jockey Carroll James, she wrote a letter to the station referring to the Beatles appearance on the news and asked, "Why can't we have this music in America?" Because WWDC had a policy of doing anything for its listeners, James arranged to have a copy of the Beatles latest British single, *I Want To Hold Your Hand*, delivered to him by British Overseas Airways Corporation (as in "Flew in from Miami Beach B.O.A.C.").

On December 17, 1963, Carroll James had Marsha Albert come down to the station to introduce the song on his radio show. WWDC wisely taped the proceedings for posterity. The tape begins with James introducing Marsha to the listeners. "So Marsha Albert, of Dublin Drive, of Silver Spring, has the honor of introducing something brand new, an exclusive, here at WWDC. Marsha, the microphone on the Carroll James show is yours." The fifteen-year-old then does the honors. "Ladies and gentlemen, for the first time on the air in the United States, here are the Beatles singing *I Want To Hold Your Hand*."

After the song ended, James requested that listeners write in to let him know what they thought of the Beatles. But most couldn't wait and began calling the station immediately. According to James, the station's switchboard lit up like a Christmas tree with eager listeners phoning in to praise the song. *I Want To Hold Your Hand* was immediately added to WWDC's playlist and placed in heavy rotation.

It didn't take long for Capitol to learn that a Washington, D.C., station had jumped the gun by playing *I Want To Hold Your Hand* four weeks prior to its scheduled release date. Capitol telephoned WWDC and requested that the song be pulled off the air, but the station refused. Alan Livingston then called New York attorney Walter Hofer, who represented Brian Epstein, the Beatles and the song's publisher, Duchess Music Corporation (a subsidiary of MCA). The Capitol president requested that Hofer get James to stop playing the record. Hofer called James and sent him a telegram demanding that WWDC "cease and desist" playing the song, but the disc jockey refused. According to Hofer, James told him, "Look, you can't stop me from playing it. The record is a hit. It's a major thing."

Myth

WWDC disc jockey Carroll James received his copy of the British pressing of *I Want To Hold Your Hand* from his girlfriend, who was a stewardess with British Overseas Airways Corporation (B.O.A.C.).

Fact

Although Carroll James arranged for B.O.A.C. to bring him a copy of the Beatles latest British single, the flight attendant who delivered the record to him was not his girlfriend.

Discussions with Walter Hofer and the head of MCA publishing convinced Livingston that neither Capitol nor MCA would be able to stop WWDC from playing the record. As Livingston believed this was an isolated situation that would not spread elsewhere, he decided to press a few thousand copies of *I Want To Hold Your Hand* to send to the Washington area.

This strategy might have worked had James not made a tape copy of the song for a disc jockey buddy of his in Chicago, who then played it on his show. Listeners in the Windy City also reacted favorably towards the song. When a St. Louis disc jockey with KXOK played a tape of the Beatles new song, his station was hit with tons of listener requests for the song.

With Christmas less than a week away, stations in three major markets were playing *I Want To Hold Your Hand.* In addition, tapes of the song were circulating among the nation's disc jockeys. Capitol quickly realized that the genie was out of the bottle. The company also remembered that radio airplay was essential for sales. Capitol's job was to get stations to play the Beatles so it made no sense to try to halt airplay just because the record's scheduled release was weeks away.

Although record companies traditionally did not issue any new product during the holiday season, Capitol was beginning to realize that there was nothing traditional about the Beatles. The company pushed up the single's release date to the day after Christmas. Capitol also realized that its initial factory requisite of 200,000 units would be insufficient to meet demand. Word went out to Capitol's factories in Scranton and Los Angeles to step up production by having all pressing machines exclusively manufacture the Beatles 45. Capitol also subcontracted with other companies, such as RCA and Decca, to press additional copies of the single.

In England, *I Want To Hold Your Hand* had been released on Parlophone R 5084 on November 29, 1963, with *This Boy* on the B side. With advance orders of over one million copies, the record leaped to the top of all of the British charts.

For its first Beatles release, Capitol issued what it considered to be the two best songs available. Apparently, Capitol's A&R staff wanted rockers on both sides, so *I Saw Her Standing There* replaced the ballad *This Boy* on the flip side of *I Want To Hold Your Hand.* Capitol was not aware that Vee-Jay would soon be releasing its *Introducing The Beatles* album, which opened with *I Saw Her Standing There.*

Capitol's first Beatles 45 made its debut in the *Billboard Hot 100* at an impressive number 45 on January 18, 1964. *Billboard* described the A side as a "driving rocker with surf on the Thames sound and strong vocal work from the group." The following week it exploded to the number three spot before reaching the top in its third week on February 1, 1964, replacing Bobby Vinton's *There! I've Said It Again* and holding off Lesley Gore's *You Don't Own Me* and the Marketts' wonderful instrumental *Out Of Limits*. It spent seven weeks at number one before passing the torch

𝕸𝖞𝖙𝖍
Before the Beatles took America by storm, rock music was dead in the United States.

Fact
During the weeks prior to the release of *I Want To Hold Your Hand*, the number one songs in America were *Dominique* by the Singing Nun and Bobby Vinton's *There! I've Said It Again*. While this supports the view that rock was dead prior to the Beatles invasion of America, a more careful look at the *Billboard* charts reveals otherwise. During December, 1963, and January, 1964, the garage band classic *Louie Louie* by the Kingsmen spent six weeks at number two. In addition, *Surfin' Bird* by the Trashmen was in the top ten for five weeks. Although the Beatles impact on American music can not be overstated, one should not conclude that the pre-Beatles sixties era was devoid of exciting music.

to *She Loves You.* In all, *I Want To Hold Your Hand* spent 15 weeks in the *Hot 100*, including a dozen in the top ten.

Cash Box and *Record World* also reported the song at number one. In fact, it was *Cash Box* that first reported *I Want To Hold Your Hand* at number one in its January 25, 1964, issue, touching off a celebration involving the group, Brian Epstein and George Martin in Paris, France.

The single's flip side, *I Saw Her Standing There*, entered the *Billboard Hot 100* on February 8, 1964, remaining in the *Hot 100* for 11 weeks, peaking at number 14. Although the song received considerable airplay, *Cash Box* gave it little recognition, charting the song for one week at 100. *Record World* ignored it altogether.

Boosted by saturation programming, Capitol's first Beatles record was an instant best seller with over 250,000 copies sold in its first three days of release. By January 10, 1964, the 45 had sold over 1,000,000 units, enabling Capitol to obtain RIAA (Record Industry Association of America) certification in time to present the band with a gold record award ceremony held at the Plaza Hotel one month later on February 10. By mid-January, the single was selling 10,000 copies an hour in New York City. The March 28, 1964, *Billboard* reported Capitol's claim that the record had sold 3,400,000 units. The record went on to sell over 5,000,000 copies.

I Want To Hold Your Hand was written by John and Paul as the group's fifth British single. The Beatles recorded the song, along with its British flip side *This Boy*, at a session on October 17, 1963, at Abbey Road's Studio Two. The session marked the first time the group used a four-track recorder. The song was completed in 17 takes. Although no outtakes of the song have been released, a few bits of false starts are included in a "medley" of outtakes on Volume 2 of the *Anthology* video.

I Saw Her Standing There was recorded at the February 11, 1963, session during which ten songs were completed for the group's first British album, *Please Please Me*. The song is an exciting Paul McCartney rocker that was selected to open the *Please Please Me* album, as well as Vee-Jay's *Introducing The Beatles*. Capitol also placed the song on its *Meet The Beatles!* album.

Capitol packaged the single in an attractive picture sleeve featuring a classic black and white Dezo Hoffmann portrait of the group dressed in their collarless Pierre Cardin suits. Ringo is seated in a wooden chair, surrounded by his fellow band mates. Paul, looking very suave, holds a lit cigarette between the top and second fingers of his right hand. When Capitol issued a twentieth anniversary reissue of the single and its sleeve in 1984, Paul's cigarette was airbrushed out of the picture. For its thirtieth anniversary sleeve, the cigarette was left alone.

The picture sleeves for *I Want To Hold Your Hand* were prepared by two different printers: Queens Litho in New York and Bert-Co Enterprises of Los Angeles. The East Coast sleeve has a straight-cut top. The West Coast sleeve has a tab-cut top. Its photograph is cropped tighter (the top of George's head is cut off) and is darker than the picture on the East Coast version. Approximately 80% of the sleeves were printed by Queens Litho.

The orange and yellow swirl labels for the original single were printed by two different printers: Keystone Printed Specialties Co., Inc. of Scranton, Pennsylvania, and Bert-Co. The East Coast labels have larger record numbers than their West Coast counterparts. There are also type size and spacing differences between the two label variations.

The first pressings of the record are identified by the "Walter Hofer" publishing credit on the *I Saw Her Standing There* side of the disc. The second label variation lists the publisher for *I Saw Her Standing There* as "George Pincus & Sons Music Corp." After a limited number of labels were printed with the Pincus credit, the labels on the B side were changed for the final time to identify the song's publisher as "Gil Music Corp." Although the Pincus labels are the rarest of the three variations, the first-issue Hofer labels have the greatest value. The Gil labels are the most common and least valuable.

East Coast

CAP 5112.PS1A   CAP 5112.01A

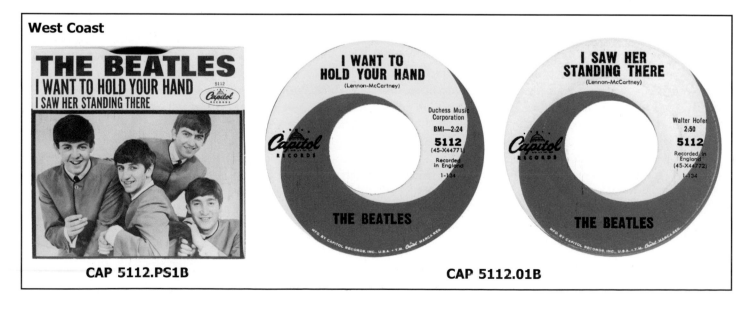

West Coast

CAP 5112.PS1B   CAP 5112.01B

BEATLES AWARD

To Radio Station

WMCA

in recognition of

Outstanding Promotion, Programming, and
Merchandising of the Beatles during

BEATLE YEAR I

1964

Joe O'Brien   Harry Harrison   Jack Spector   Dan Daniel   B.Mitchel Reed   Johnny Dark

wmca good guys

radio 57-first on your dial

Radio station WMCA in New York added *I Want To Hold Your Hand* to its play list on December 26, 1963, the day the single was released. In appreciation, Capitol prepared a custom picture sleeve with a picture of the WMCA Good Guys on one side (above) and the standard *I Want To Hold Your Hand* picture and information on the other. The 1,000 WMCA sleeves were paired with copies of the Capitol single and given to listeners as prizes in the station's Beatles wig contest. Contestants were instructed to take photos of their friends or from newspapers and to draw Beatles wigs on them. The two most original entries were also awarded $57 from Radio 57, WMCA. Capitol later presented the station with a special Beatles award (upper left) complete with fake signatures of the group.

The WMCA Good Guys, shown above in Beatles wigs, reviewed 86,000 entries to their station's wig contest. First prize went to Roberta Corrigan, who prepared a book of several pictures, complete with humorous captions. Roberta's Winston Churchill (lower right) is quoted, "Since the Beatles left for America, I find England 67% more peaceful, Barber Shop revenues up 72%, and laryngitis down 125%!" Second place went to Kay B. Smith for putting a Beatles wig on the Mona Lisa.

JANUARY 3, 1964

The first entertainment show broadcast of the Beatles on American television took place on the evening of Friday, January 3, 1964, when a taped performance of the Beatles singing *She Loves You* was shown on *The Jack Paar Program*. Within days, Vee-Jay and Swan put out their own Beatles singles to capitalize on the excitement generated by Capitol's *I Want To Hold Your Hand*. By month's end, MGM released *My Bonnie*, a song recorded in Hamburg, Germany, in 1961 by singer Tony Sheridan backed by the Beatles.

Furthermore, Vee-Jay felt it could capitalize on *Please Please Me* being the Beatles first big hit in England.

Within days of the band's *Jack Paar Program* appearance, Vee-Jay prepared a special title sleeve for promotional copies of its "new" Beatles single, *Please Please Me*. The blue and white sleeve proudly describes the release as "THE RECORD THAT STARTED BEATLEMANIA." It states that "England's sensations" just did the *Jack Paar Show* on January 3, and coming up would be *Ed Sullivan* on February 9 and 16. The sleeve also refers to the group being featured in *Time*, *Life* and *Newsweek* magazines.

While *Please Please Me* went virtually unnoticed when first issued in February, 1963, it was an entirely different story this time around. Paul's introduction to the song at the group's February 11, 1964, Washington Coliseum concert said it all:

"We would like to sing a song ... that was our first hit in England. This song was released in America; it didn't do anything. It was released again. And, uh, well it's doing something. [Chuckles from John and George.] You know, so ... yeah it is. The song we'd like to play for you now, a song called *Please Please Me*."

Vee-Jay royalty statements indicate that a distributor ordered 1,000 copies of VJ 581 at the end of 1963. During the first 15 days of the new year, 55,510 stock copies and 506 DJ promotional copies were sent to distributors. As detailed in a subsequent chapter, Capitol Records then obtained a temporary injunction prohibiting Vee-Jay from pressing or distributing any Beatles product. When the injunction was lifted a few weeks later, Vee-Jay distributed 1,068,882 copies of the record, including 101 promotional copies, during the month of February. An additional 75,460 units, including 101 promotional copies, were shipped in March. The record continued to sell throughout the year. It is estimated that Vee-Jay sold 1,185,725 copies of the single, including 6,000 sent to foreign markets.

Please Please Me entered the *Billboard Hot 100* on February 1, 1964, at number 68. Although distribution problems brought on by the temporary injunction slowed the song's upward movement, by the time the March 14, 1964, issue of *Billboard* hit the streets, *Please Please Me* had reached the number three spot behind Capitol's *I Want To Hold Your Hand* and Swan's reissue of *She Loves You*. It remained there for one more week before being knocked back to number four by *Twist And Shout*, which was released on Tollie, a Vee-Jay subsidiary. On the *Billboard Hot 100* chart for April 4, 1964 (shown right), *Please Please Me* dropped to number five on a chart that featured Beatles songs in the top five positions. All told, the Vee-Jay single spent 13 weeks on the *Billboard* chart. *Cash Box* and *Record World* also reported the song at number three.

The single's flip side, *From Me To You*, had been a number one hit in England and surely would have been at least a top five record had it remained a separately issued A side. Vee-Jay's decision to place the song on the B side of *Please Please Me* backfired as *From Me To You* was essentially wasted. Two of the major trade magazines charted the song separately. *Billboard* reported the song at number 41, while *Cash Box* showed a peak at 46.

Encouraged by the success of Capitol's *I Want To Hold Your Hand* and the general buzz about the Beatles, Swan reissued its *She Loves You* single in mid-January, 1964. This time the song exploded. The single entered the *Billboard Hot 100* on January 25 at number 69. It entered the top ten at number 7 during its third week on the charts and moved up to the second slot behind *I Want To Hold Your Hand* on February 22. After four weeks at number two, the Swan 45 hit the number one spot for its first of two weeks at the top on March 21. *Billboard* charted the song for 15 weeks. *Cash Box* and *Record World* also reported the song at number one. The single sold over two and a half million copies.

Although *I Want To Hold Your Hand* was the first Beatles hit in the United States, *She Loves You* is the song that best conjures up images of Beatlemania. From Ringo's thundering drum opening to the final "yeah, yeah, yeah, yeah," *She Loves You* is two minutes and 18 seconds of pure excitement. When the Beatles made their February 9, 1964, American debut on *The Ed Sullivan Show*, 73 million people watched as the band followed its performance of *All My Loving* and the ballad *Till There Was You* with a rocking version of *She Loves You* that left no doubt as to what the big beat sound was all about. Teenage girls screamed each time the boys shook their heads as they shouted "Oooo" leading into the chorus. When the Beatles were filmed in front of hundreds of screaming fans at the Scala Theatre for the frenzied concert scene at the end of *A Hard Day's Night*, the song chosen to conclude the madness and define Beatlemania was *She Loves You*.

For the week ending April 4, 1964, the Beatles held the top five spots in the *Billboard Hot 100*, plus seven more spots with *I Saw Her Standing There* (#31); *From Me To You*, VJ 581 (#41); *Do You Want To Know A Secret*, VJ 587 (#46 in its second week); *All My Loving*, Capitol of Canada 72114 (#58); *You Can't Do That* (#65); *Roll Over Beethoven*, Capitol of Canada 72133 (#68); and *Thank You Girl*, VJ 587 (#79). The next week, *There's A Place* and *Love Me Do* joined them, giving the Beatles a record 14 songs in the *Hot 100*. The group also had the top two LPs with *Meet The Beatles!* and *Introducing The Beatles*.

MGM Records joined the Beatles sweepstakes in mid-January by entering into a five-year leasing agreement with Deutsche Grammophon for the American rights to four songs recorded by the Beatles in Hamburg, Germany, in 1961. Three of the songs, *My Bonnie (My Bonnie Lies Over The Ocean)*, *The Saints (When The Saints Go Marching In)* and *Why*, feature Tony Sheridan on lead vocals backed by the Beatles. The remaining track, *Cry For A Shadow*, is an instrumental written by John Lennon and George Harrison.

The first two songs, credited to "Tony Sheridan and the Beat Brothers," had previously been issued (and ignored) in America by Decca Records in April, 1962. When MGM released *My Bonnie* and *The Saints* on January 27, 1964, the single was credited to "THE BEATLES with Tony Sheridan." The record entered the *Billboard Hot 100* on February 15 at number 67 and peaked at 26. *Cash Box* reported the song at 29 and *Record World* at 31. MGM also released a compilation LP containing all four "Beatles" songs and a 45 pairing the other two songs.

While television and film later provided the unforgettable images of the Beatles and the mass hysteria they created, it was radio that first gave the group mass exposure in America. To fully appreciate the power of radio in the sixties, one must realize how different things were then. For America's youth, there were few entertainment options. Television provided limited choices. There was no MTV. Nor were there video games. Home computers were not even dreamed of, so there was no Internet to surf. This was a time when after-school activities had not grown into the mind boggling number of football, baseball, basketball, swimming and soccer practices that now dominate afternoons, evenings and weekends. After-school hours were normally spent doing homework, talking on the phone and listening to the radio (though not necessarily in that order).

According to Capitol's Brown Meggs, between the time the label issued *I Want To Hold Your Hand* on December 26, 1963, and the boys arrived in New York on February 7, 1964, the Beatles had become instant stars in America, thanks to the efforts of several New York disc jockeys who

were constantly playing the group's records and taped interviews with the band. Radio stations were battling to out-Beatle each other. The WMCA Good Guys sponsored a Beatles wig contest (see page 85). WABC was receiving 3,000 letters a day from Beatles fans. WINS aired exclusive interviews with the Beatles obtained by station owner Group W's foreign correspondents in London and Paris.

While Capitol was delighted that some of the nation's most influential radio stations were broadcasting interviews with the Beatles, the label realized that most stations did not have the clout to obtain interviews with the group. To accommodate these stations, Capitol prepared hundreds of special open-end interview records that enabled a disc jockey to give the impression that he was personally conducting an in-station interview with the band. The illusion was created by combining a script of statements and questions to ask the group with a record containing gaps of silence to insert the disc jockey's reading of the script along with the prerecorded responses of the boys. Capitol hoped that radio personalities would be anxious to air a "personal" interview with the Beatles. It was a win, win, win situation as Capitol got publicity and airtime for the Beatles, disc jockeys got to impress their listeners by appearing to have an exclusive interview with the group and listeners all over the country got to hear the boys and their British accents.

As part of its Beatles Campaign, Capitol sent copies of the interview record to broadcasters in early 1964. It was titled *The Beatles Open-End Interview.* The interview record was produced by Jack Wagner, who prepared the script and edited comments from the group to form a brief interview leading up to the playing of the Capitol hit single *I Want To Hold Your Hand*. The Beatles comments were recorded at Abbey Road during the first week of January, 1964. Side one of the disc has the interview and the single, while the second side contains two songs from Capitol's *Meet The Beatles!* album, *This Boy* and *It Won't Be Long*. The record was distributed in a picture sleeve (shown above) that features the cover of the album on one side and the open-end interview script on the other.

A Sampling of Early 1964 American Beatles Singles

Vee-Jay Promo
VJ 581.PS2

Vee-Jay Oval Colorband
VJ 581.01B

Vee-Jay Brackets Colorband
VJ 581.02A

Vee-Jay Silver Bars
VJ 581.03

Vee-Jay Black Oval
VJ 581.04

Vee-Jay Block Letters
VJ 581.05

**Vee-Jay Yellow Label
VJ 581.07**

**Vee-Jay White Label
VJ 581.08B**

**Vee-Jay Purple Brackets
VJ 581.10**

**Swan 1964 Reissue
SWAN 4152.02A**

**MGM Promo
MGM 13213.DJ1A**

**MGM Stock Copy
MGM 13213.01B**

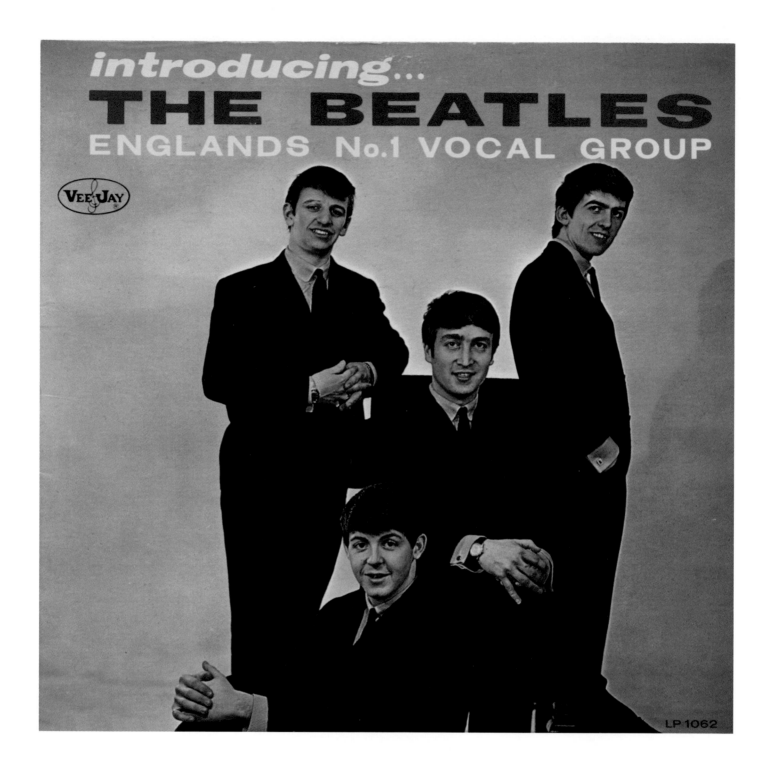

JANUARY 10, 1964

Exactly one year after signing an exclusive licensing agreement to release Beatles recordings in the United States, Vee-Jay issued its *Introducing The Beatles* LP on January 10, 1964. The record was the first Beatles album released in the United States. While the disc faced stiff competition from Capitol's *Meet The Beatles!* album, it still sold over 1.3 million copies.

Although Beatles discographies have long listed July 22, 1963, as the release date for *Introducing The Beatles*, the album did not come out at that time. Vee-Jay had planned on issuing the album in the summer of 1963; however, financial difficulties caused the company to cancel the release of most of the records on its summer schedule, including *Introducing The Beatles* (see pages 32-36). Shortly thereafter, Vee-Jay president Ewart Abner was dismissed by the company when owners Vivian and Jimmy Bracken learned that Abner had taken a few hundred thousand dollars of company money to pay off his personal gambling debts. When Vee-Jay ignored requests by EMI's agent, Transglobal, to provide royalty statements and payments for Ifield and Beatles records, Transglobal terminated its licensing agreement with Vee-Jay for Ifield and Beatles masters on August 8, 1963 (see pages 38-40).

Abner's replacement, Randy Wood, attempted to get Vee-Jay back on track. The company's revised release schedule for fall, 1963, included five new albums, but left out *Introducing The Beatles*. This omission shows that Vee-Jay had totally abandoned its plans to issue the Beatles LP.

On December 4, 1963, Vee-Jay's Board of Directors met to discuss what could be done to improve the company's precarious financial situation. The minutes from the meeting contain discussions about the importance of product and the need "to give the public what they want ... and sell it at a profit." There are, however, no references to the Beatles. At that time, Vee-Jay had no idea Beatlemania was about to invade America or that it could profit from the release of Beatles records. Vee-Jay had totally forgotten about the band. Ironically, Capitol Records issued a press release the same day which would start a chain of events that would reintroduce the Beatles to Vee-Jay.

Details from the Capitol press release appeared in the December 14, 1963, *Billboard*. Word quickly spread through the music industry that Capitol was planning an extensive publicity campaign to launch the Beatles in America. This alerted Vee-Jay to the group's potential. After all, Capitol wouldn't be spending a ton of money to promote the Beatles unless the label believed it would pay off in sales.

Vee-Jay employees remembered that their company had released two Beatles singles and that preliminary steps had been taken during the past summer to release an album by the group. In fact, the metal parts needed to press the album were still sitting at the three primary factories used by Vee-Jay to press its records. In addition, 6,000 front cover slicks had been printed. It was certainly time for Vee-Jay to consider doing something with the Beatles.

By the time Vee Jay's Board of Directors met again on January 7, 1964, the Beatles were due to arrive in America exactly one month later. In contrast to the previous month's meeting, the Beatles were the dominant topic. The minutes contain the following entry:

"Jay Lasker brought up the Beatles recordings — Walter Hofer says there is one thing we can release and one thing we have no right to release according to R. Renee. We have an LP that could be huge — at least 30,000 LP's could be gotten out. Vivian Bracken asked where we stand legally on this matter.

"Randy Wood said it looked like we have the same identical LP as Capitol has. The Beatles are a calculated risk — we have an agreement with them but can't find it. They gave us masters and on this assumption it would seem they are aware of the agreement we have. Mark Sands said we have to take the calculated risk in our present position even if we have to pay in a year or two if we loose [sic].

"For the month of December we lost cash money based on sales volume — for January we are hard pressed to come up with $300,000 — we constantly have to contend with the liabilities we inherited — we won't have cash in February to make up for the credits coming up in the next few months — so we have to take a chance on the Beatles."

The minutes show that executive vice-president Jay Lasker had discussed Vee-Jay's rights to its Beatles masters with attorney Walter Hofer, who would soon defend Vee-Jay in court. Hofer apparently discussed the Vee-Jay Beatles masters with Roland Rennie, who was then serving as president of Transglobal. Under the terms of the licensing agreement, Vee-Jay had the rights to the songs previously released on VJ 498 and VJ 522, but did not have the rights to the songs on the unreleased album because the company failed to timely exercise its right of first refusal. Lasker recognized the potential sales a Beatles album would generate and reported that they could have 30,000 albums shipped by Friday, January 10, 1964.

Randy Wood mistakenly believed that Vee-Jay's *Introducing The Beatles* was the same album as Capitol's upcoming *Meet The Beatles!* In fact, the only overlap between the two albums was *I Saw Her Standing There*. A further indication of the low priority Vee-Jay had placed on the Beatles prior to December of 1963 is Wood's comment that they could not locate a copy of the company's licensing agreement with Transglobal for Beatles masters. Both he and comptroller Mark Sands recognized that releasing Beatles records was a calculated risk. Not a risk from a sales standpoint, but rather a legal risk as Vee-Jay knew they probably did not have the right to release a Beatles album of previously unreleased masters. Because the company needed the cash a Beatles album would undoubtedly generate, Vee-Jay was willing to take the risk even if it meant getting sued by Capitol Records and having to pay up in a year or two if it lost its legal battles with Capitol. Thus, Vee-Jay's decision to release *Introducing The Beatles* came with an attitude of "damn the torpedoes, full speed ahead!"

Vee-Jay summary sheets of distributors' orders show that the first orders for the album were taken on January 8, 1964, the day after the Board meeting. On January 10, Randy Wood sent a telegram to Vee-Jay's distributors pushing the new Beatles album, LP-1062, which was described as a "monster." Distributors were told, "lithos and information enroute" and warned, "Don't wait–tie up big users. This is best seller since Presley days."

When *Introducing The Beatles* went on sale in January, 1964, there were three different back cover variations. Vee-Jay originally intended on using an edited version of Tony Barrow's back liner notes from the *Please Please Me* LP; however, no back liners were printed in the summer of 1963, and the company was unable to locate the information.

Front Cover

Ad Back

Blank Back

Titles on Back

Realizing that EMI and Capitol would not be pleased by its plans to issue the Beatles album, Vee-Jay could not request liner notes information from EMI.

In order to avoid delays and issue the LP as soon as possible, Vee-Jay decided to construct the initial batch of covers with glossy back slicks printed from the film used for the company's colorful inner album sleeve, which promoted 25 Vee-Jay albums. Because these back slicks advertise other Vee-Jay LPs, this cover variation is known as the "Ad Back" cover. The covers to these rare and highly collectible first-issue albums have "Printed in U.S.A." running vertically along the lower left front cover slick. The stereo version of this cover is one of the most valuable and sought after Beatles album variations.

A second cover variation, known as the "Blank Back," has a blank white back liner. In all likelihood, the Blank Backs were a limited transition run substituted after all Ad Back slicks had been used, but prior to receipt of the new back liners that would be used on future production runs. Blank Back covers have been documented with and without "Printed in U.S.A." front cover slicks.

Vee-Jay ultimately decided to rush out a simple back liner that merely contained the album's title and its song titles listed in two columns. This version is known as the "Titles On Back" or "Column Back" variation. Although Ad Backs were manufactured first, all three cover variations were assembled within days of each other and were issued at the same time in January, 1964.

To get *Introducing The Beatles* to its distributors as quickly as possible, Vee-Jay placed large orders with its three primary pressing plants: ARP in Owosso, Michigan; Monarch in Los Angeles; and Southern Plastics in Nashville. These factories had been sent metal parts for the album during the summer of 1963. Vee-Jay also had new metal parts prepared for a fourth factory, Allentown Record Co., Inc. (ARC) in Allentown, Pennsylvania. By January 15, 1964, Vee-Jay had shipped 79,169 mono and 2,202 stereo copies of *Introducing The Beatles* to distributors.

The shipment of over 80,000 copies of its Beatles album in less than a week was encouraging for Vee-Jay, but January 15, 1964, would not be a day of celebration. As detailed in the next chapter, Vee-Jay was hit that day with a preliminary injunction prohibiting the company from manufacturing or distributing any Beatles records. During the next few months, the injunction would be lifted and reinstated over and over again, thus undermining the company's ability to get its Beatles records in the stores.

The next day, January 16, brought additional legal problems. A judge issued a restraining order prohibiting Vee-Jay from manufacturing or distributing *Introducing The Beatles* because the album contained two songs that Vee-Jay did not have publishing clearance to issue. Capitol's subsidiary, Beechwood Music Corporation, owned the publishing rights to *Love Me Do* and *P.S. I Love You* and refused to grant Vee-Jay permission to issue the songs. To get around this hurdle, Vee-Jay removed the two songs from the record and replaced them with *Please Please Me* and *Ask Me Why*. Universal Recording Corporation in Chicago prepared lacquers for the reconfigured album on or about January 22, 1964. The masters, mothers and stampers needed to press the record were manufactured as early as January 24, with additional metal parts prepared in early February.

Copies of *Introducing The Beatles* containing *Love Me Do* and *P.S. I Love You* are referred to as "Version One" LPs. The reconfigured album with *Please Please Me* and *Ask Me Why* is known as "Version Two." The album's labels, as well as its Titles On Back slick, were modified to reflect the change in the lineup. Vee-Jay began issuing copies of Version Two of *Introducing The Beatles* on or about February 10, 1964.

Introducing The Beatles made its debut in the *Billboard Top LP's* chart at number 59 on February 8, 1964. The next week it moved up to number 22 and by its third week it was number three. On February 29, the album began its first of nine straight weeks at number two, unable to surpass Capitol's *Meet The Beatles!* LP. All told, *Introducing The Beatles* spent 49 weeks on the charts, including 15 weeks in the top ten and 21 weeks in the top twenty. The album also held down the second spot for several weeks in *Cash Box* and was reported at number one by *Record World*.

Introducing The Beatles had net sales of approximately 1,304,316 mono and 41,910 stereo units. Because Vee-Jay did not allow the RIAA to audit its sales figures, *Introducing The Beatles* was never certified gold by the RIAA. Vee-Jay president Randy Wood presented the Beatles with an in-house gold record award for the album on August 23, 1964, at a ceremony held backstage at the Hollywood Bowl before the group's concert appearance.

There are several cover variations for Version Two of *Introducing The Beatles*. While most of the back liners list *Please, Please Me* with a comma, some do not have the comma. Some albums have a 4" x 2¼" sticker affixed to the front cover. The sticker has a crimson border with the word "Featuring" in crimson and "Twist and Shout" and "Please, Please Me" in purple. Some mono covers were converted for use as stereo covers with the placement of "Stereophonic" or "Stereo" stickers (at least three confirmed variations) or with "Stereophonic" and "SR 1062" machine stamped in black print at the top of the cover.

There are a mind-boggling number of label and typesetting variations for *Introducing The Beatles*. This resulted from Vee-Jay's use of several pressing plants and the rush to get records on the market to keep up with demand. For Version Two, Vee-Jay also used Columbia Records factories in Terre Haute, Indiana, and Bridgeport as well as H.W. Waddell Co. in Burbank, California. When printers ran out of Vee-Jay oval or brackets colorband label backdrops, they did not wait to be resupplied. Instead, they used generic black labels and overprinted a Vee-Jay logo in silver ink. Some copies of the album were printed with 45-size labels. Samples of the numerous label variations appear on the following two pages. The first four variations are Version One labels and the remaining variations are Version Two.

  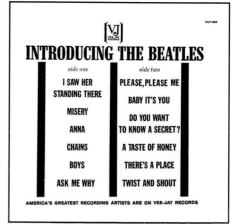

The lacquer acetates for Version Two of *Introducing the Beatles* were mastered by Universal Recording Corporation in Chicago. Even though the Beatles were a household name by January of 1964 when the album was reconfigured, the label still misspelled the group's name as "BEATTLES." New back liners were prepared to reflect the new song lineup.

Stereo Oval Colorband
VJ 1062(1).SR1A
ARP (Rare)

Stereo Oval Colorband
VJ 1062(1).SR1B(i)
Monarch (Rare)

Mono Oval Colorband
VJ 1062(1).MR1C
Southern Plastics

Mono Brackets Colorband
VJ 1062(1).MR3
ARC

Mono Oval Colorband
VJ 1062(2).MR1A
ARP

Stereo Brackets Colorband
VJ 1062(2).SR2A
ARP

**Stereo Brackets Colorband
VJ 1062(2).SR2B(i)
Monarch**

**Stereo Brackets Colorband
VJ 1062(2).SR2C
ARC**

**Mono Brackets 45-size Label
VJ 1062(2).MR3
ARP**

**Stereo Black VJ
VJ 1062(2).SR4A
Columbia**

**Mono Black Oval
VJ 1062(2).MR5
Columbia (Rare)**

**Mono Black Small Brackets
VJ 1062(2).MR6
Southern Plastics (Ex. Rare)**

Consumer Alert!

Introducing The Beatles is probably the most counterfeited album of all time. While many of the counterfeits are obviously bogus, some look like the real thing. These impressive-looking counterfeits are often purchased by unsuspecting collectors and fans as original issues. During the sixties, seventies and eighties, counterfeit Vee-Jay albums were frequently sold in department stores and other locations serviced by job rackers.

Thus, the fact that a record was purchased from a legitimate store does not mean that the record is a genuine album from 1964. This is particularly true of copies of *Introducing The Beatles* bought in stores after 1965.

The counterfeits manufactured on the East Coast were reportedly pressed for companies with ties to organized crime. A former Vee-Jay employee was responsible for the West Coast counterfeits.

The first counterfeits of *Introducing The Beatles* are Version Two albums that were manufactured in the mid-sixties. They are easy to spot due to the poor quality of the cover, which is blurry and has washed-out colors (left). The bogus disc in many ways appears to be genuine, but the colorband is missing the color green (middle). Another counterfeit Version Two disc features a large white brackets logo on a black label (right). Although Vee-Jay used a similar label on several of its albums, no Beatles albums were pressed by Vee-Jay with this label style.

Most of the counterfeits of *Introducing The Beatles* are Version One albums that were manufactured in the late sixties, seventies and eighties. Unfortunately, the bulk of the bogus albums have covers that closely resemble the real thing. An exception is the brown border cover (left), which is an obvious counterfeit. The good news is that most counterfeit records can easily be spotted by one simple rule. If "The Beatles" appears below the center spindle hole, the disc is counterfeit. (Bogus examples are shown middle and right.) These discs have many other flaws, but you need not look any further if "The Beatles" is below the center hole. Note: If a disc is counterfeit, chances are the cover is also counterfeit.

There are two tests that can be used to spot bogus Version One stereo covers. The "flap test" requires inspection of the inside of the cardboard jacket. Legitimate Version One covers have ¼" flaps at the top and bottom of the inside jacket. Illegitimate covers have no flaps, ½" flaps at the top and bottom or a ¼" flap only at the bottom. The "Honey test" requires inspection of

the back cover. Many of the counterfeit covers have back slicks with the same imperfections. The most noticeable flaw appears in the word **HONEY** in the song *A Taste Of Honey*. Both the **H** and the **E** are missing ink in the upper left part of the letter. While this test does not always work, it is often useful in weeding out albums still in the shrink wrap.

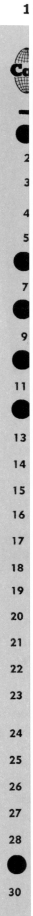

JANUARY 20, 1964

Although Capitol initially planned to issue its first Beatles album in mid-February, the company pushed its release date forward to January 20, 1964, due to demand for Beatles product. By the time the group arrived in America on February 7, 1964, *Meet The Beatles!* was poised to take over the number one spot on the charts. The album sold over three and a half million copies within two months of its release.

After determining that *I Want To Hold Your Hand* and *I Saw Her Standing There* would be its first Beatles single, Capitol was faced with preparing an album to introduce the Beatles to the United States. The company decided to go with the group's most recent LP, *With The Beatles*; however, as discussed below, some alterations would be made.

While Capitol wisely decided to use the same striking front cover photo as the British album, the company thought the title *With The Beatles* lacked impact. As it had no way of knowing Vee-Jay's plans to resurrect and issue its *Introducing The Beatles* album, Capitol probably considered naming its album *Introducing The Beatles*. Imagine the confusion that would have caused. But, as fate would have it, Capitol chose *Meet The Beatles!*

The album was mastered on December 19, 1963. The acetate's labels (shown center) misspell the group's name as "THE BEATTLES." This is the same spelling error that appears on the group's first U.S. release, VJ 498 (see page 6).

Original plans called for the album to be released in mid-February, 1964, but, as was the case with its single, *I Want To Hold Your Hand*, Capitol moved the release date forward due to growing demand for Beatles product. In the December 28, 1963, issue of *Cash Box*, Director of East Coast Operations, Brown Meggs, announced that Capitol would release its Beatles album in January. According to a January 13, 1964, Capitol press release, *Meet The Beatles!* had advance orders of 240,000 units.

Meet The Beatles! was released on January 20, 1964; however, it appears some stores received copies a week earlier. In an ad appearing in the January 12, 1964, *New York Times*, Liberty Music Shops told customers to "come in today and ask to see the album that's sure to make '1964... The Year of the Beatles.'" The album debuted in *Billboard*'s February 1, 1964, *Top LP's* chart at number 92, making it the first Beatles album to chart in the U.S. The February 8th issue of *Billboard* tracked the LP at number three. By the February 15th issue, Capitol's debut Beatles LP had replaced *The Singing Nun* as the top album, fending off Vee-Jay's *Introducing The Beatles* and remaining number one for 11 weeks before being replaced by *The Beatles' Second Album* on May 2. *Billboard* charted *Meet The Beatles!* for 71 weeks, including 17 weeks in the top five and 21 in the top ten. *Cash Box* and *Record World* also charted the LP at number one.

Testimony to the phenomenal sales of Capitol's two Beatles records, *I Want To Hold Your Hand* and *Meet The Beatles!,* appeared in the March 5, 1964, affidavit of Capitol vice president Voyle Gilmore in the New York litigation between Capitol and Vee-Jay Records. Gilmore claimed that Capitol was selling approximately 500,000 Beatles records a week and had already sold over 6,000,000 copies of their

two Beatles releases. The March 28, 1964, *Billboard* reported sales of *Meet The Beatles!* at 3,650,000 units and *I Want To Hold Your Hand* at 3,400,000 units.

The fact that the Capitol LP was outselling the single caught everyone off guard. Prior to the Beatles, rock albums were normally not big sellers. Selling a few hundred thousand LPs was considered a tremendous success. A few of Elvis Presley's albums had sold in excess of a million units, but these were either Christmas, greatest hits, sacred or movie soundtrack LPs. Neither of the King's first two rock 'n' roll albums hit sales of a million. None of Capitol's first three Beach Boys' albums sold a million. The phenomenal sales of *Meet The Beatles!*, which went on to sell over five million copies, taught the record industry that huge profits could be generated by well-crafted rock albums.

Although *With The Beatles* was a proven best-seller in England, Capitol decided to alter the British disc. Changes were made for marketing and financial reasons.

In America, the conventional wisdom was that hit singles made hit albums. As *With The Beatles* did not contain either *I Want To Hold Your Hand* or *I Saw Her Standing There*, some songs from the British LP would be deleted to make room for these songs.

Economics also entered into the formula. While British pop albums typically had 14 tracks, American LPs normally had 12 songs. The disparity resulted from the different method of calculating song publishing royalties between the two countries. In the U.S., publishers are paid a mechanical license fee for each song that appears on a record. Under this system, each song represents an additional cost. In England, song publishers receive a share of the total royalties paid on each album sold. For example, if an LP contains 14 songs, the publishing royalty owed on each song is a fourteenth of the total publishing royalty due from the sale of the album. Because the number of songs included on the disc has no direct cost effect, British record companies can afford to provide a more generous number of songs per album. Thus, for financial reasons, Capitol decided to limit its first Beatles album to the American standard of a dozen selections.

Although Capitol is often criticized for the way it tore apart the Beatles British albums and issued its own reconfigured records, such criticism is unfounded when aimed at *Meet The Beatles!* Capitol's selection of songs formed the perfect disc for Americans to meet the Beatles.

Recognizing that hit singles sell albums, Capitol placed both sides of its single, *I Want To Hold Your Hand* and *I Saw Her Standing There*, as the album's opening tracks. The next song is *This Boy*, the B side to the British single *I Want To Hold Your Hand*. Following the opening rockers with *This Boy* was brilliant programming as the ballad effectively slows down the pace of the album and showcases the beautiful vocal harmonies of John, Paul and George. The last three songs on the first side are the first three songs from side one of *With The Beatles*, namely *It Won't Be Long*, *All I've Got To Do* and *All My Loving*. All songs on side one are Lennon-McCartney originals.

Side two opens with the next three songs from *With The Beatles*, namely George Harrison's *Don't Bother Me*, Lennon-McCartney's *Little Child* and the Broadway show tune *Till There Was You*. The final three songs on the Capitol album are the remaining Lennon-McCartney originals from the British LP: *Hold Me Tight, I Wanna Be Your Man* and *Not A Second Time*.

With the exception of *Till There Was You*, all of the album's songs were written by members of the group. This enabled Capitol to exploit the band's songwriting abilities.

The five selections from *With The Beatles* not included on Capitol's first Beatles album were cover versions of songs originally recorded by American artists. Capitol probably reasoned that American record buyers would not be interested in hearing a British band perform American tunes. After all, who needs the Beatles version of Chuck Berry's

It Won't Be Long was the first Lennon-McCartney original recorded for *With The Beatles*. After ten takes during the morning session of July 30, 1963, the group returned to the song that evening. The released master is an edit of Takes 17 and 21. The rocker opens with an energetic chorus full of trademark "yeah's" before moving to a catchy guitar riff and passionate lead vocals by John on the verses and bridge. Paul and George supply backing vocals. George Martin thought the song was worthy of being the potboiler opener for the Beatles all-important second British album. Had it been released as a single, it would have been a huge hit.

John takes the spotlight again on *All I've Got To Do*, which was recorded in 15 takes on September 11, 1963. The moderate-paced song opens with a strummed guitar setting the stage for John's lead vocal. Highlights include a catchy melody, great singing and Ringo's distinctive drumming with effective use of his high-hat.

All My Loving was recorded on July 30. The song opens with Paul's lead vocal and quickly adds its exciting, fast-paced instrumental backing, dominated by John's high-speed churning rhythm guitar. George plays a rockabilly-

Roll Over Beethoven when Chuck Berry's version is available? This view changed when the Canadian single of the Beatles *Roll Over Beethoven* was imported from Canada and began receiving heavy airplay on U.S. radio stations and selling enough copies to chart. Capitol responded by giving serious consideration to issuing the Beatles version of the Chuck Berry rocker as its follow-up to *I Want To Hold Your Hand*. Although George Martin convinced the label to release *Can't Buy Me Love* instead, *Roll Over Beethoven* was prominently listed as a featured selection on the cover of *The Beatles' Second Album*, which also contained the other four cover versions from *With The Beatles*.

The recording histories of *I Want To Hold Your Hand* and *I Saw Her Standing There* are covered earlier in this book. The beautiful ballad *This Boy*, with its striking three-part harmony, was recorded at the same October 17, 1963, session as *I Want To Hold Your Hand*. The song was perfected in 15 takes, with two more takes for overdubs. The *Free As A Bird* maxi-single from 1995 contains Takes 12 and 13, which break down prior to completion due to the boys flubbing the lyrics. The laughter at the end of each take shows how much fun the group had in the studio in the early days.

style guitar solo during the instrumental break. Paul overdubbed a harmony vocal for the third verse. In live performances, Paul and George sang the last verse together. Another high-quality song that could have been a hit single.

George's *Don't Bother Me* was his first solo composition recorded by the Beatles. The group first attempted the song on September 11, 1963, but was not satisfied with the result. Returning to the song the next day, the Beatles started from scratch, with the remake designated Take 10. A finished master was completed in ten takes, including overdubs. George's voice was double-tracked and other overdubs included John on tambourine, Paul on claves and Ringo on a loose-skinned Arabian bongo drum. The band's initial attempt at the remake, Take 10, is an excellent live-in-the-studio performance. Towards the end of the song George can be heard singing "Oh yeah, rock 'n' roll now."

John's *Little Child* was also started on September 11 and completed the following day. The infectious rocker has many of the ingredients of past hits, including "come on's, "oh yeah's" and John's wailing harmonica. Paul contributed a piano part to overdub Take 15, which was edited with Take 18 to form the finished master.

Buddy Young.

Revised: 2-4-64

From: Brown Meggs
        Capitol Records, Inc.
        Sperry Rand Bldg.
        1290 Avenue of the Americas
        Plaza 7-7470

AMERICAN ITINERARY: THE BEATLES

Friday, Feb. 7   Beatles arrive Kennedy International Airport
                    at 1:40 P.M. from London via Pan American
                    Flight #101 (International Arrivals Bldg.).

                    Beatles party (8) will consist of:

                    The Beatles (Messrs. George Harrison, John Lennon,
                    Paul McCartney, Ringo Starr); Mrs. John Lennon;
                    Mr. Brian Epstein (personal manager); 2 road
                    managers.

                    Capitol Records will officially greet the Beatles
                    in the International Arrivals Building and conduct
                    them into the airport press facility for an arrival
                    press conference.

                    ...tographers and cameramen _only_ will
                    ...cover The

![Photograph of the four Beatles walking on a London street]

Capitol RECORDS

PHOTO

The four young Beatles (left to right--John Lennon, Ringo
Starr, Paul McCartney and George Harrison) are shown during
one of the few moments they've had this past year without
thousands of fans mobbing them. Most of the time it requires
a police guard before the talented quartet can venture out
onto the streets in London. The group arrives in the U.S.
early in February for various appearances including the
Ed Sullivan Show and Carnegie Hall.

1/64
Photo # 10631-4

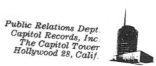

Public Relations Dept.
Capitol Records, Inc.
The Capitol Tower
Hollywood 28, Calif.

FEBRUARY 4, 1964

On February 4, 1964, Capitol's Brown Meggs issued an internal memorandum titled "AMERICAN ITINERARY: THE BEATLES." With the group's arrival just days away, Capitol was getting ready to change its battle cry from "The Beatles Are Coming!" to "The Beatles Are Here!"

𝔐𝔶𝔱𝔥

"For all Capitol and CBS cared, the Beatles were just going to walk off the plane and go to their hotel. Nobody would have known they were in America."

— Beatles merchandiser Nicky Byrne

Fact

Although some accounts state that Capitol was hopeless and doing nothing to publicize the Beatles arrival, nothing could be further from the truth. As detailed below, Capitol was working hard to ensure that the group's arrival would be a well-attended media event.

Two and a half weeks prior to the Beatles arrival in America, Capitol attended a round robin meeting with CBS TV, Ed Sullivan's representatives and United Artists. Although United Artists had yet to begin filming its Beatles movie, the company wanted to take advantage of the media attention that would be focused on the group in New York to promote the upcoming film. Details of the meeting were summarized by Mike Hunter and Gabe Sumner of the United Artists publicity department in a January 23, 1964, memo titled "The care and handling of 'THE BEATLES' During Their American Stay." The memo demonstrates that Capitol, CBS and UA intended to pool their resources to maximize publicity for the Beatles as well as their separate interests (Capitol–record sales, CBS–television ratings and UA–movie buzz). The memo also shows that some plans were changed relatively late in the game.

The entry for February 7 indicates that the Beatles were scheduled to arrive at Kennedy Airport on B.O.A.C. Flight #505 at 3:40 p.m.. The flight had been booked by Brian Epstein's assistant Alistair Taylor, who was later told to switch to Pan American Airways because *The Ed Sullivan Show* had a tradeout deal with the airline in exchange for promotional consideration. Capitol Records was to arrange a short press conference at the airport's VIP Lounge or press room and provide limousines to transport the Beatles to the Plaza Hotel. The memo states that UA would "work closely with Capitol Records handling the arrival at Kennedy Airport" and, "Because of the expected mob welcome," all UA contact men would be involved. February 8 and 9 were allocated to CBS for rehearsals and performances on *The Ed Sullivan Show*.

Monday, February 10, was reserved for media interviews. UA was to handle an 11:00 a.m. press conference for newspaper reporters, magazines, fan magazines and trade reporters. Capitol was assigned the task of organizing a 4:00 p.m. disc jockey mass interview. All parties were to try setting up private interviews for Bill Glover of the Associated Press, Ed Kalish of *Variety*, *The New York Post*, Paul Gardner of *The New York Times* and a few others.

The next two days were listed as rehearsals and concerts at Carnegie Hall. Thus, as of January 22, the Washington Coliseum show had not been booked. The entry for

February 13 states that the Beatles were to travel to Miami for a short vacation, but that there was a possibility that the group would first do a concert in Philadelphia. The remainder of the itinerary covers the Miami visit and the scheduled return to New York on February 17 and to London the following day. There would be no Philadelphia show, and the Beatles would later extend their stay in Miami.

An important part of the strategy involved Capitol exploiting radio stations to get the word out that the Beatles were coming. The memo reported: "Capitol Records is trying to arrange with all disc jockeys to keep plugging their arrival and telling listeners to meet the Beatles at the Airport." A follow-up meeting involving Capitol, CBS and UA was scheduled for January 27.

On January 29, 1964, the public relations department of Capitol Records issued a press release titled "What's Happening in Beatleland..." The document falsely claims that *I Want To Hold Your Hand* was number one after one week and boasts of the group's impressive record sales, noting that "all this is happening without the group ever having set foot in the United States." The press release then details the group's scheduled arrival, the *Ed Sullivan Show* appearances, the concerts at the Washington Coliseum and Carnegie Hall (with news of the recording of an album to be titled *The Beatles At Carnegie Hall*), magazine coverage and merchandising. The complete text of the document is reproduced on the following page.

On February 4, 1964, Brown Meggs distributed a revised Beatles American itinerary to key Capitol employees (see page 130). The entry for Friday, February 7, states that the Beatles would arrive on Pan American Flight #101 and would be accompanied by John's wife Cynthia, manager Brian Epstein and two road managers. Capitol was to officially greet the Beatles in the International Arrivals Building and lead them to the airport press facility for a press conference. Only accredited photographers and cameramen would be permitted on the field to cover the Beatles deplaning. No other press would be given access to the Beatles until the group cleared customs and entered the press room. Capitol was to transport the Beatles to the Plaza, arrange for preregistration of the group and escort them directly to their rooms.

CBS was given the responsibility for Saturday and Sunday. Photographers ("still only, no flash") would be permitted to cover the *Sullivan* dress rehearsal.

Monday, February 10, was a day of press conferences, interviews by appointment and a disc jockey reception. Capitol assigned Fred Martin to oversee all press functions.

Travel plans for the Beatles February 11 trip to Washington, D.C., were the responsibility of Norman Weiss and Jerry Perenchio of GAC. Harry Lynn was listed as the contact for the Washington Coliseum concert.

The entry for February 12 indicates that the Carnegie Hall concerts were promoted by Sid Bernstein and Walter Hyman. The listing also states that the event would be recorded by Capitol. The remaining entries cover the Miami leg of the trip, which was largely the responsibility of the CBS Television Network.

FROM THE PUBLIC RELATIONS DEPARTMENT/HOLLYWOOD & VINE/HOLLYWOOD 28, CALIFORNIA/HOLLYWOOD 2-6252

NEWS

January 29, 1964

WHAT'S HAPPENING IN BEATLELAND . . .

Like 'em or not, The Beatles have become the biggest thing in pop music since Elvis Presley turned up a decade ago.

The Beatles' first American single, "I Want To Hold Your Hand," was released by Capitol Dec. 30. One week later it was the No. 1 record in the country on three of the four record tradepaper charts. The following week, it was tops on all listings. Early in its third week of release it passed the million mark in sales, a fact which is at this writing being certified in an audit by the Record Industry Association of America.

Capitol issued its album "Meet The Beatles," on Jan. 20. By Jan. 27, it had passed 400,000 in sales. The LP, too, appeared on the charts after a week on the market. As far as can be determined, nobody, not even Presley, has achieved such rapid volume with a single or an LP.

It should be noted, too, that all this is happening without the group ever having set foot in the United States. That, however, will be remedied Friday afternoon Feb. 7 when the group arrives at New York's John F. Kennedy Airport for appearances on the Ed Sullivan Show, the first of which will be aired Feb. 9.

BEATLES AT CARNEGIE

Last week it was disclosed that The Beatles will give three concerts during their U.S. trip. The first is scheduled the night of Feb. 11 at the Coliseum in Washington, D.C.

The following night, The Beatles will give two concerts at, of all places, Carnegie Hall. The first begins at 7:30, the second at 10:00 and the New York Police Department is still wondering how it will get one crowd out and the other in.

First public announcement of the Beatles' Carnegie appearances was made in the New York papers last Sunday (1/26). The advertisement stated that tickets would be available only at the Carnegie Hall box office, which would open at 9:00 a.m. Monday. By 3:00 p.m. Jan. 27, the concerts -- 2700 seats for each performance -- were completely sold out.

Voyle Gilmore, Artists & Repertoire Vice President for Capitol said he would fly to New York and personally record the Carnegie Hall concerts. The resulting album -- to be titled "The Beatles at Carnegie Hall" -- will probably be issued in April.

MAGAZINE COVERAGE

Meanwhile, it is safe to say that, before the Beatles arrive, there will not be a major American periodical which will not at least have a Beatles article in the works.

Among those already out with sizable pieces chronicling Beatlemania are: Life, Time, Newsweek, Saturday Review, New Yorker, McCall's, Mademoiselle, Vogue, New York Times Magazine, and ad infinitum. Wire services have moved thousands of words about the phenomenally successful English group, and the jam-up of media requesting interviews with The Beatles is quickly getting out of control.

In the past few weeks, Beatlemania has done a lot more than sell a lot of records.

A Beatle-cut hairdo was created by Hollywood hair stylist Gene Shacove and among his customers now sporting the new coiffure are Janet Leigh and the Mmes. Milton Berle and Steve McQueen. A record store in New York has tied-in with a neighboring barber shop, the latter offering a free Beatles haircut with every copy of Capitol's "Meet the Beatles," and vice-versa.

BEATLE ICE CREAM

Beatle fan clubs are sprouting like crabgrass, and Beatle wigs are the rage on high school campuses. United Artists has announced that a Beatles movie, as yet untitled and without a finished script, will begin shooting in March in England.

Beatle buttons, Beatle sweatshirts, and even Beatlenut ice cream are being readied for the marketplace. Where it will all end is an absolute mystery. All that is known is that Beatlemania is off to a more riotous start than anybody, including the Beatles, ever dreamed.

CBS mounted sound equipment and a camera on top of a station wagon to capture the sounds and images of the Beatles arrival for broadcast on the *CBS Evening News with Walter Cronkite*. Rows of fans lined the airport's upper arcade in anticipation of seeing the group set foot on American concrete (top photo). Hundreds of fans stationed themselves outside the International Arrivals Building at Kennedy Airport in hopes of seeing the Beatles pass by (bottom photo).

𝔐𝔶𝔱𝔥

"Each fan was given a free T-shirt, a dollar and a bus ride to the airport. And that's how Beatlemania started in America." — Photographer Dezo Hoffmann

Fact

While some fans received free T-shirts and bus rides to Kennedy Airport, the significance of this has been over-played. The plan to give away T-shirts was not devised by Beatles management or their press agent. It was put together by Nicky Byrne, who was the head of Seltaeb (Beatles spelled backwards), a merchandising company holding the rights to license Beatles items. He ordered T-shirts printed with the Dezo Hoffmann picture of the Beatles used on the *I Want To Hold Your Hand* sleeve. Radio stations reportedly told listeners they would receive a free T-shirt if they went to see the Beatles arrive at Kennedy Airport.

While some of the youngsters had been given free Beatles T-shirts, it was not the T-shirt that caused thousands of fans to play hooky from school and go to the airport. They wanted to see the Beatles. The T-shirt was just a bonus. Few, if any, teenagers would have cut school and flocked to the airport to greet either the Singing Nun or Bobby Vinton for a free T-shirt even though each had recently enjoyed a month at the top of the charts with *Dominique* and *There! I've Said It Again*. The only inducement youngsters needed was the knowledge of when and where the Beatles were arriving, and New York radio made sure its listeners knew the particulars. Radio was responsible for the reception at the airport. Capitol's plan to have disc jockeys plug the Beatles arrival worked to perfection.

On Wednesday, February 12, WNBC-TV reported that police had accused Beatles publicity men of busing youngsters to the Plaza. While some student busing may have occurred, only a small percentage of the humongous crowd outside the Plaza could have fit in the buses. The others drove, walked or took the subway to be there.

Furthermore, the large crowds that would soon greet the Beatles in Washington, D.C., and Miami demonstrated that youngsters did not need to be bribed or bused to see the Beatles.

Photographers, reporters and disc jockeys jockeyed for position to get close to the Beatles during the group's first American press conference, which took place at Kennedy Airport.

Photograph by Bill Eppridge ©2003

FEBRUARY 7, 1964 (EVENING)

The Beatles spent their first evening in America relaxing in the relatively calm setting of their suite at the Plaza Hotel. They were filmed by the Maysles Brothers, photographed by the press and interviewed by Brian Matthew of the BBC and New York disc jockey Murray the K.

Photograph by Bill Eppridge ©2003

"And that's the way it is, Friday, February 7, 1964."

The Beatles had just finished watching themselves on the *CBS Evening News* and heard Walter Cronkite give his traditional sign-off. It was now 7:00 p.m. in New York and time for a prearranged telephone interview with Brian Matthew, host of *Saturday Club*, a popular BBC radio program. After Ringo switches the TV to WNBC for *The Huntley-Brinkley Report*, he picks up a ringing telephone, but it isn't Matthew. He quickly tells the caller, "We're waiting for a very important call from London which you're blocking the line on." After Ringo hangs up, Paul asks who the caller was, and Ringo informs him it was Maureen Cleave, a British reporter who accompanied the group to America.

A few minutes later Matthew's call is put through. Paul is the first on the line, greeting him with "Hello, Brian Bathtubes." McCartney describes the tremendous New York reception. "They were all just sort of hanging all over the airport ... thousands of pressmen, and thousands of New York cops and things ... it was ridiculous, y'know!" He tells of an earlier visit to their suite by the Ronettes, who were brought in by a DJ (Murray the K), who thinks he can arrange a meeting with the Miracles. Paul adds that they hope to see the Isley Brothers perform. John then gives his first impression of America. "They're sort of, they're wild. They're all wild.... Maybe it's just the first impression, yeah, they just seemed all out of their minds."

During his interview with Ringo, Matthew asks the inevitable questions about reaction to their hair, leading to the following exchange:

Brian: You proved that you don't wear wigs, I hope.
Ringo: Yeah.
Brian: What did you do?
Ringo: We took them off.

George is the last to talk to Matthew, telling him that the Beatles have six songs in the top 100: "*I Want To Hold Your Hand, She Loves You, Please Please Me, From Me To You, My Bonnie*, which is a laugh, and *I Saw Her Standing There*." Harrison adds that in New York, "three records are number one."

Brian Matthew's interview was recorded by BBC engineers in London and by BBC reporter Malcolm Davis, who was in New York with the group. Davis sent his tape of the Beatles responses to London on a high quality phone line. Matthew later edited the Beatles responses with fresh dubs of him re-asking the questions to create a better sounding interview. Davis also filed his own report with the BBC, which included on-the-scene descriptions of the group's arrival at Kennedy Airport and the Plaza Hotel, as well as interviews with fans and Murray the K. The interview with Brian Matthew and Davis' report ran the following morning (February 8) on *Saturday Club*.

Murray the K

Murray Kaufman, better known as Murray the K, was an influential disc jockey for WINS in New York. In addition to being one of the city's top radio personalities, he presented concerts in New York and compiled oldies LPs, including *Murray the K's 1962 Boss Golden Gassers* (shown right). The record contains two songs covered by the Beatles on their first LP: *Twist And Shout* by the Isley Brothers and *Baby It's You* by the Shirelles. The liner notes brag that "Murray's talents lie not only in the aggressive teen-appealing manner in which he runs his shows but in ascertaining the material that more than whets the appetites of his clan as well." His tag line was telling people he liked, "You're what's happening, baby."

Murray was a big supporter of the girl groups of the early sixties, particularly those from the New York area. The Shirelles (shown above with Kaufman) benefitted from his constant spinning of their discs. His reputation and large listening audience enabled him to make stars out of newcomers and reenergize fading veterans' careers.

Murray the K first heard Beatles music through the efforts of independent promotion man Bud Helliwell, who brought the DJ a copy of Swan's *She Loves You* single. Murray reportedly played the record on September 28, 1963, as one of five singles making its WINS debut. The disc placed third in a listener response contest and received minimal airplay for the next week or so before being dropped. (Kaufman later recalled the Beatles single being outvoted by *Coney Island Baby* by the Excellents and a disc by the Four Seasons; however, this is unlikely. *Coney Island Baby* made its radio debut nearly a year earlier, entering the *Billboard Hot 100* on November 24, 1962, and peaking at 51. The Four Seasons did not issue a new single in September or October of 1963.)

While Murray was vacationing in Miami in early 1964, *I Want To Hold Your Hand* began racing up the charts. WINS program director Joel Chaseman called Kaufman and told him to get back to New York because the Beatles were coming. Murray reportedly told his boss, "Get yourself an exterminator," but changed his tune when he realized that the Beatles were "what's happening."

Upon his return, Murray jumped on the Beatles bandwagon in a big way. He gave his listeners details of the group's itinerary, helping create the massive crowd of youngsters that greeted the band at Kennedy Airport. During the Beatles first American press conference, he managed to push his way to the front, temporarily taking charge and conducting his own interview. This caused one reporter to yell, "Hey, will you tell Murray the K to cut that crap out?" The Beatles played along, with Ringo and John yelling "Cut that crap out!"

Murray's boldness continued later that day when he dropped by the Plaza shortly after the Beatles had finished eating an early dinner in their suite. To ensure he would be welcome, he brought along the Ronettes.

Kaufman taped an interview for WINS. John mentioned the group's upcoming shows. When asked why they had turned down other offers, John said, "Our manager doesn't want to over expose us ... so that we can come back." As for playing Carnegie Hall rather than Madison Square Garden, John explained that "Carnegie Hall was already arranged ... and then when all the other offers started coming in, well we would have been overworked." George then discussed the group's film project.

Murray had trouble with John's Liverpool accent and joked, "for foreigners, you speak English very well."

When Murray brought up marriage, George told him, "I haven't got enough money for meself yet, never mind a wife." After an evasive discussion about the group's finances, he asked Paul what his main purpose was. Paul said he was "hoping to become a tramp some day" and that he was saving up because he wanted to be a rich hobo. Kaufman, realizing his serious question had given way to humor, responded, "That's the best kind, baby. Rich or poor, it's always good to have money."

Shortly after the interview ended, Murray left with the Ronettes to prepare for his evening radio show. During the next two weeks he would serve as the group's tour guide, taking them to night clubs and traveling with the band to Washington, D.C., and Miami.

Photograph by Bill Eppridge ©2003

The Beatles, with press agent Brian Sommerville looking on, sit around the tape recorder that was later used to record their BBC telephone interview. The microphone is on the same table as the phone.

True or False?

All three American television networks showed film of the Beatles arrival on their evening news programs.

False

Although NBC was the first U.S. network to broadcast a story on the Beatles, the transcript from the February 7, 1964, *Huntley-Brinkley Report* ends with Chet Huntley telling viewers: "The Beatles arrived in New York today. The four English musical stars–with their pudding bowl haircuts–were greeted by about four thousand shrieking teenagers at Kennedy Airport and mobbed by another large group of juveniles when they got to the Plaza Hotel. All day long some local disc jockeys had been encouraging truancy with repeated announcement of the Beatles travel plans, flight number and estimated time of arrival. British journalists tell us that the record company had sixteen press agents handling the arrival, but we wouldn't know about that. However, like a good little news organization, we sent three camera crews to stand among the shrieking youngsters and record the sights and sounds for posterity. Our film crews acquitted themselves with customary skill and ingenuity and the pictures are very good–but someone asked what the fuss was about and we found we couldn't answer. So... good night for NBC News..."

As the evening wore on, photographers snapped away and the Maysles Brothers continued filming. George, who had earlier told Murray the K that he had "been up for days, hacking," was coming down with a throat infection. He would soon call the hotel doctor. Paul let everyone know his watch was still on English time. Although it was late back home, it was early in New York.

John: If we go to bed now we'll...
Ringo: Be up at three.
John: That's what I mean. Aren't we going out?
Ringo: Yes. Later.
John: Later.
Ringo: Well it's only early. It's America, you know.
John: Oh I know it's America here. I noticed.

Although the group was anxious to sample the New York night life, they were getting tired and chose not to venture out. The next morning, Paul told reporters that the group got lazy and listened to the radio and watched TV.

The Beatles were fascinated by American radio. Paul was filmed several times during the New York visit listening to a transistor radio. That evening, the boys sampled New York stations, including Murray the K on WINS.

Television in the sixties was limited to a handful of choices. Because New York was a major market, it had eight stations. While it is not known what the Beatles watched that Friday night, there were several quality programs to choose from, including *That Was The Week That Was*, *The Twilight Zone*, *Alfred Hitchcock Presents*, *The Jack Paar Program* with guests Bill Cosby and Nancy Wilson and *The Tonight Show* with guest Sam Cooke.

Photograph by Bill Eppridge ©2003

Paul and Ringo catch up with the news of the day, including the lead story of Castro cutting off water to America's military base at Guantanamo Bay, Cuba.

The Ronettes

The Ronettes were a trio of young black female singers from New York whose *Be My Baby* was a number two hit in America and a number four hit in England during the fall of 1963. The Beatles met the Ronettes, along with producer Phil Spector, at the London home of Decca promotion manager Tony Hall a week before coming to America (photo shown left).

The Ronettes scored subsequent hits with *Baby I Love You* (#24) and *Walking In The Rain* (#23). Spector became infatuated with and later married the group's lead singer, Veronica "Ronnie" Bennett. The Ronettes were one of the opening acts on the Beatles 1966 tour of America, but Ronnie's place was taken by her cousin, Elaine. In 1971, Ronnie Spector recorded George Harrison's *Try Some, Buy Some*, which was released as a single on Apple.

FEBRUARY 8, 1964

The Beatles spent their second day in America posing for the press in Central Park (shown top left on a horse-drawn carriage) and rehearsing for their *Ed Sullivan Show* appearance. George, who had a throat infection, spent most of the day resting in bed. By mid-afternoon, he was feeling well enough to check out the set at CBS Studio 50, where he was greeted by a relieved Sullivan and a horde of photographers.

The Beatles second day in America got off to an early start with the group having breakfast in their hotel suite. Murray the K and Ed Rudy, a former DJ turned syndicated radio reporter, dropped by for interviews. Both later issued records containing their conversations with the boys.

George remained in bed. Dr. Jules Gordon, the resident physician at the Plaza Hotel, had examined George the night before. He reportedly requested an autographed picture of the group before beginning his examination, which revealed that Harrison had strep throat and a fever of 104 degrees. Dr. Gordon prescribed some drugs and ordered George to rest in bed. The doctor considered getting a nurse to administer his medicine each hour, but then realized this could be accomplished by Harrison's sister, Lou, who had flown to New York to be with her brother. Dr. Gordon reasoned that George's sister was probably the only female in New York who wasn't crazy over him and thus capable of functioning normally in his presence. George remained in bed. Later that morning, Dr. Gordon minimized the severity of George's condition in a statement to the press. "It's just the transition from London weather to New York weather."

Although the Beatles and their entourage were disappointed and mildly concerned over Harrison's health, the saturation coverage of the group's arrival in the local newspapers provided a boost. Paul Gardner of *The New York Times* began his article with: "Multiply Elvis Presley by four, subtract six years from his age, add British accents and a sharp sense of humor. The answer: It's the Beatles (Yeah, Yeah, Yeah)." New York's *Daily News* featured the Beatles on the front page of its February 7 final edition.

Because it was Saturday, the group's young fans were out of school and free to stake out strategic positions for Beatles encounters. Hundreds gathered outside the Plaza, whistling, screaming and chanting, "We want the Beatles! We want the Beatles!" Fifty policemen, reinforced by private detectives, stood guard. Some patrolled the streets on horseback. Barricades surrounded the hotel's perimeter. Determined fans hovered nearby, taking over the fountain near the hotel. New York's finest were engaged in military-style tactics to keep the crowd at bay. United Press reported, "The Plaza has been turned into virtually an armed camp since the Beatles arrived." This was quite a contrast from the hotel's reputation as a place of Old World charm, with impeccable service and a formal yet relaxed atmosphere.

Although the Beatles reservations were made under their own names, the Plaza was soon told that these were the Beatles. The Beatles management, Capitol and CBS thought it best to warn the Plaza of what to expect from the group's fans. Although the Plaza's general manager joked that he called the Waldorf and offered to trade the Beatles for Mr. Khrushchev (premier of the Soviet Union), he told a reporter, "We've had a little bit of excitement outside our door, but on the whole we've had a lot of fun with the Beatles...They've conducted themselves well and they are a credit to England."

Shortly before noon, John, Paul and Ringo left the safety of their suite and headed down to the lobby. In hopes of fooling the mass of youngsters gathered at the hotel's entrance, the boys avoided the decoy limousines parked in front and quickly piled into a small red car belonging to one of the guards. Their cover was blown when the police car leading the way turned on its siren and red lights. The mini-entourage headed to Central Park, where the three took part in a photo session with journalists from all over the world. Because George remained behind, only John, Paul and Ringo are in the Central Park photos that would later appear in numerous teen magazines and on several Beatles bubble-gum trading cards. The trio took a horse and buggy ride, posed on rocks by a lake and had lunch at the boathouse. They ordered a typical American meal of cheeseburgers and malted milks. The Park proceedings were filmed by newsreel cameras and the Maysles Brothers.

At the conclusion of the photo session, John, Paul and Ringo were picked up by a black Cadillac limousine and driven through the Park and then to CBS Studio 50 for their first *Ed Sullivan Show* rehearsal. During the ride, Paul continued to show his fascination with American radio by listening to WINS on his Pepsi transistor radio. Over 500 fans were waiting for the group outside the CBS studio. When the limo briefly stopped a block from the entrance, several girls approached the car and began hitting the windows. After a quick "Hi, girls" and wave from Paul, the car, now escorted by patrolmen on horses, drove to an area in the next block secured by the police. The group then exited the limo and headed inside. (The drive from Central Park to the studio appears in *The First U.S. Visit*, but is edited out of sequence, giving the impression that the footage was shot during the previous day's ride from the airport to the Plaza Hotel.)

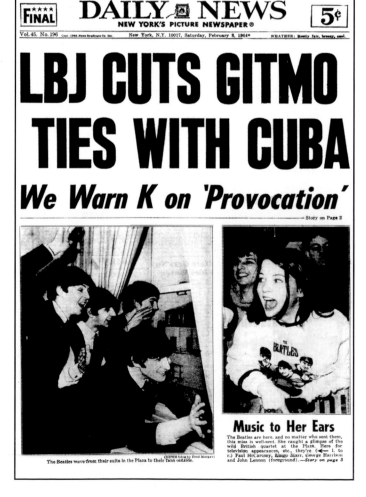

FINAL · DAILY ✪ NEWS · 5¢
NEW YORK'S PICTURE NEWSPAPER ®
Vol. 45. No. 196   New York, N.Y. 10017, Saturday, February 8, 1964   WEATHER: Mostly fair, breezy, cool.

LBJ CUTS GITMO TIES WITH CUBA

We Warn K on 'Provocation'

— Story on Page 2

Music to Her Ears

The Beatles are here, and no matter who sent them, this miss is well-sent. She caught a glimpse of the wild British quartet at the Plaza. Here for television appearances, etc., they're (← l. to r.) Paul McCartney, Ringo Starr, George Harrison and John Lennon (foreground).—*Story on page 3*

The Beatles wave from their suite in the Plaza to their fans outside.

Ringo, Paul and John relax on the drum riser on the *Sullivan* set during rehearsal (left). *Sullivan* Production Secretary Kathie Kuehl writes down the words to *She Loves You* as sung to her by Paul (center). The lyrics were used by the production crew to block out shots of the band's performance. George, accompanied by his sister Louise (right), arrived later in the afternoon, but did not sing or play guitar.

The three healthy Beatles arrived at Studio 50 at 1:30 p.m. Although Ed Sullivan normally did not attend Saturday rehearsals, the host wanted to spend some time with the group and show his presence on the set to the mass of reporters who gained admittance to the rehearsal. John, Paul and Ringo met briefly with Sullivan and his staff and then completed the required forms to join the American Federation of Television and Radio Artists. (George did his paperwork later that day.) When the three Beatles entered the stage, they were greeted by a throng of persistent newsmen and photographers. Once things settled down, they rehearsed their program with road manager Neil Aspinall standing in for Harrison. When Aspinall was called away for other duties, *Sullivan Show* production assistant Vince Calandra put on a Beatle wig and pretended to be George.

By mid-afternoon, Harrison was feeling better and was given permission by Dr. Gordon to join the others at Studio 50. The doctor told the press that George would not use his vocal chords, but was going there to familiarize himself with the stage routine for the show. Harrison was enthusiastically greeted by Sullivan and his staff, a horde of photographers and reporters and the other Beatles. After being photographed on the set, George followed his doctor's orders and returned to the Plaza for more bed rest.

Sometime after 4:00 p.m., John, Paul and Ringo, accompanied by Brian Epstein, met with Francis Hall of the Rickenbacker guitar company at the Savoy-Hilton. Hall had brought a few of his company's latest guitars to show the Beatles. John was currently playing a Rickenbacker 325 electric guitar, and the California company hoped to get the group's other guitarists to switch to Rickenbackers. One of the guitars at the room was a 360-12 12-string electric guitar. In an interview with Andy Babiuk, Hall recalled: "George

was sick so he didn't come over. John Lennon played the 12-string and he said, 'You know, I'd like for George to see this instrument. Would you mind going over with us and letting him play it?'"

Hall went with the Beatles and Brian back to the Plaza and presented Harrison with the 12-string guitar and a Rickenbacker amplifier. George took an immediate liking to the 12-string and would soon be using it on several of the songs recorded for the film *A Hard Day's Night*. This would influence other groups to incorporate the guitar's unique bell-like chiming sound into their songs. The Rickenbacker 12-string became popular with rock and pop bands, as well as folk-rock groups such as the Byrds.

That evening, John, Paul, Ringo and George Martin were treated to dinner by Capitol Records executives at the exclusive 21 restaurant. The Beatles ate chops and mashed potatoes, while the Capitol gang had pheasant. Paul had crepes suzettes for dessert. During a tour of the restaurant's wine cellar, Ringo asked if they had any "vintage Coca-Cola." After dinner, the boys were given a car tour of the city, passing by landmarks such as the U.N. Building, the Empire State Building, Broadway and Times Square.

While the others were getting a taste of New York, George was on the phone with local radio stations. When a group of disc jockeys from WMCA dropped by and asked Lou to visit their station, George expressed concern over his sister running off with them. Lou assured him it was alright because their T-shirts said they were Good Guys.

When Lou got to the station, she was persuaded to call George back at the Plaza to see how he was doing. Lou thinks George sang a little and played a few notes on his new 12-string Rickenbacker. The station recorded the exchange and played it several times over the weekend.

Thank you *for your recent request for tickets to* THE ED SULLIVAN SHOW & REH. FOR FEB. 9, 1964 *We appreciate your interest and are sorry to tell you that so many ticket requests already have been received that we are unable to send you any at this time.*

Ticket Bureau, CBS Television Network
485 Madison Avenue, New York 22, New York

February 9, 1964 **Sunday**
Evening

8:00 [7] [9] [10] **ED SULLIVAN—Variety**
England's rock 'n' rolling Beatles make their American live TV debut, and 30 policemen will be on hand in case a "Beatle-Mania" reaches the riot pitch—as it has in England. Other scheduled guests include "Oliver!" star Georgia Brown and the show's youngsters singing "Consider Yourself" and other "Oliver!" tunes, and Tessie O'Shea of Broadway's "Girl Who Came to Supper." Ray Bloch orchestra. (Live; 60 min.)

8:30 [2] [6] [12] **ARREST AND TRIAL**
"People in Glass Houses." A pair of bandits take an expectant mother hostage when they commandeer a squad car for their escape. Script by Antony Ellis. Kirby: Roger Perry. Egan: Chuck Connors. Anderson: Ben Gazzara. Miller: John Larch. Harris: Don Galloway. (90 min.)

Guest Cast
Frieda Jennison ....Katherine Crawford
Coley Mitchum ....Dennis Hopper
Frank Vose ....Henry Silva
Handley ....Ken Lynch

[4] [5] [18] [35] **GRINDL—Coca**
"Dial G for Grindl." Grindl is mistaken for a professional killer. Grindl: Imogene Coca. Foster: James Millhollin.

Guest Cast
Olive York ....Gloria Grahame
Harold York ....Tod Andrews
Riddle ....Gregory Morton
Operative G ....Douglas Henderson

9:00 [4] [5] [18] [35] **BONANZA—Western**
[COLOR] "The Cheating Game." A stranger tells Laura Dayton that she will receive a large sum from her late husband's insurance. Adam: Pernell Roberts. Ben: Lorne Greene. Sheriff: Ray Teal. Little Joe: Michael Landon. (60 min.)

Guest Cast
Laura Dayton ....Kathie Browne
Ward Bannister ....Peter Breck
Peggy Dayton ....Katie Sweet

[7] [9] [10] **JUDY GARLAND**
Tonight Judy gives a one-woman concert, singing three songs—"Liza," "Lorna's Song" and "Happiness Is Just a Thing

[TV CLOSE-UP GUIDE] 10:00 [4] [5] [18] [35] **NBC WHITE PAPER**

CUBA: THE MISSILE CRISIS

" . . . It shall be the policy of this Nation to regard any nuclear missile launched from Cuba against any nation in the Western Hemisphere as an attack by the Soviet Union on the United States, requiring a full retaliatory response upon the Soviet Union."
—President John F. Kennedy, Oct. 22, 1962

[SPECIAL] Probably we have never been closer to nuclear war than in October 1962. The point of conflict: Russian missile sites in Cuba.

In chronicling those tense days, producer Fred Freed has called on two men who were in on the Administration's planning from the start. McGeorge Bundy and Theodore Sorensen, both top Kennedy aides, recall the development of the incident from the moment U-2 photos

of the missile bases were developed. Each recounts how strategy was worked out in the series of high-level meetings at the White House.

But the final decision was President Kennedy's. On Oct. 22, he went before the Nation on TV. His plan: to stop the shipment of offensive weapons to Cuba, alert our armed forces and our allies, and call a meeting of the UN. Chet Huntley narrates. (60 min.)

A-21

FEBRUARY 9, 1964

On Sunday evening, February 9, 1964, the Beatles performed on *The Ed Sullivan Show* before a then-record American television audience of over 73 million people. CBS received over 50,000 requests for tickets to the show. Only a lucky 1,500 got to see their heroes in person. For many who watched the event, the sound and images of the group's performance was forever embedded in their minds, along with memories of where they were when President Kennedy was assassinated and when man first walked on the moon.

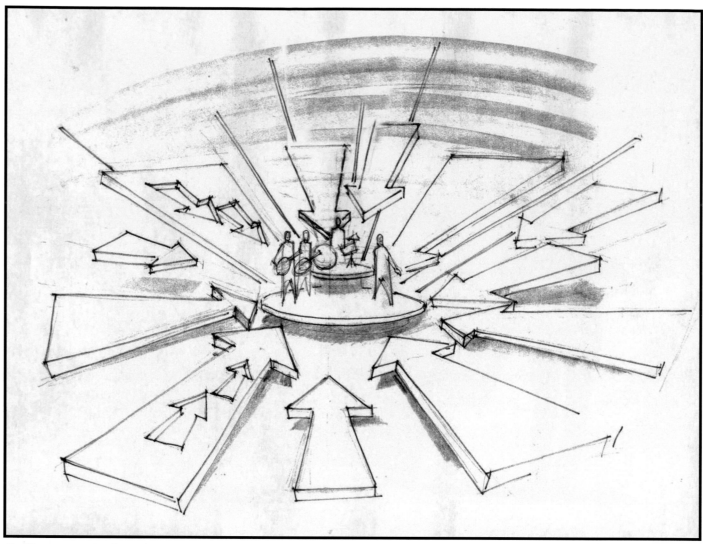

Sullivan **set designer Bill Bohnert's original sketch for the Beatles opening segment is shown above. Bohnert's design called for a series of arrows pointing to the group. The concept was to create a visual representation that "The Beatles Are Here!" on** *The Ed Sullivan Show.* **The arrows, constructed of three-inch plywood, were either hung by cables from pipes (those behind the group) or rolled out on the floor (those in front). As the set designer was not familiar with the Beatles, he drew them as a group consisting of a drummer, two guitarists and a lead singer.**

February 9, 1964. This was the day the Beatles and all of America had been waiting for. To borrow a lyric from the hit musical *Bye Bye Birdie*, the Beatles were going to be on *Ed Sullivan*, "coast to coast with America's favorite host."

Exactly one year earlier, the Beatles had performed at the Empire Theatre in Sunderland, Durham, England, as the sixth and bottom act of a tour headlined by sixteen-year-old Helen Shapiro. During the tour, the Beatles played four of the following six songs: *Chains*, *Keep Your Hands Off My Baby*, *A Taste Of Honey*, *Please Please Me*, *Love Me Do* and *Beautiful Dreamer*. One year later, the Beatles were performing on the stage of CBS Studio 50 in New York as the headline act on *The Ed Sullivan Show*. They would open the show with three songs and perform two more towards the end.

To fully understand the impact of *The Ed Sullivan Show* appearance, one must remember that in 1964, television viewers in even the largest markets were limited to a handful of choices–stations affiliated with the three networks (CBS, NBC and ABC), a Public Broadcasting System station and possibly a few independent stations. Even New York City had only eight stations. No Fox. No WB. No cable. No satellite. A big screen TV measured 20 diagonal inches. Most were 12 inches or less. Color TVs were rare luxuries and most shows, including *Ed Sullivan*, were still broadcast in black and white. American homes typically had only one television set, if they had one at all. With only one set per household, the TV variety show, which offered something for people of all ages, was ideal for family viewing. On Sunday nights, families watched television together, and that often meant they watched *Ed Sullivan*, which was broadcast by the CBS Television Network.

Sullivan lined up a wide variety of talent each week, with the goal of giving his audience a "really big show." Acts included puppeteers, magicians, gymnasts, contortionists, comedians, crooners, jazz musicians and singers, novelty performers, impressionists, daredevils, dancers and even casts of Broadway shows. One of the more memorable performers was a man who ran around the stage attempting to keep plates spinning on top of a series of poles while the orchestra played Khachaturian's frenzied classical masterpiece *Sabre Dance*. A pointless exercise, but exciting nonetheless. And then there was Topo Gigio, an Italian mouse

The Beatles are shown rehearsing their *Ed Sullivan* opener, *All My Loving*, the morning of February 9, 1964, on Bill Bohnert's arrow set. The picture was taken prior to Ringo's bass drum being fitted with a new drum head depicting the Beatles logo. The suggested caption for this UPI photo described Paul as the bouncy Beatle, George as the quiet Beatle, Ringo as the beatle Beatle and John as the sexy Beatle.

puppet who would show up from time to time to match wits with Sullivan. His tag line was, "Eddie, will you kiss-a-me goodnight?" It was very quaint.

For the youngsters, Sullivan booked rock 'n' roll singers such as Elvis Presley, Buddy Holly and Bo Diddley. But, because it was a family show, rebellious rockers were subjected to compromises. On one notorious show, Elvis was shown only from the waist up because CBS censors viewed his gyrating hip movements as being too vulgar for family entertainment. A young folk singer named Bob Dylan refused to appear on the show when told he couldn't sing his *Talkin' John Birch Paranoid Blues*. Later legendary incidents included Jim Morrison of the Doors infuriating Sullivan's people by singing "babe we couldn't get much *higher*" during *Light My Fire* after agreeing to change the lyric and Mick Jagger of the Rolling Stones being forced to change the lyrics in *Let's Spend The Night Together* to "Let's spend some time together." Although Sullivan booked rockers for the ratings and not for the love of the music, he was never condescending to his guests. While television hosts Steve Allen and Jack Paar mocked rock 'n' roll, Ed Sullivan presented it as entertainment.

Sullivan often had famous people sitting in his show's audience who he would introduce and ask to stand. At the end of the night, Sullivan reminded his studio audience to drive safely when heading home.

Sullivan's show dated back to 1948. That year, the CBS Television Network directed its manager of program development, Worthington "Tony" Miner, to come up with an hour-long variety show for Sunday evenings. The network was aware of rival NBC's plans to air *Texaco Star Theatre*, which would feature comedian Milton Berle, on Tuesday night. Rather than looking for a host who would be compared to Berle, Miner decided to go in a different direction. His idea was to have a host who would not be the talent, but rather would discover and present talent.

As fate would have it, CBS did its first remote live broadcast from Madison Square Garden on the night Ed Sullivan was there acting as emcee for the Harvest Moon Show. Miner liked what he saw and thought that Sullivan, who at the time was a Broadway columnist for New York's *Daily News*, would be the perfect host for the new variety show. Sullivan agreed to host the program and brought in Marlo Lewis to serve with him as co-producer.

While the Beatles attended the morning camera rehearsal, New York police officers mounted their horses in anticipation of the crowd of youngsters that would soon be gathering in the street outside Studio 50.

The show was titled *Toast of the Town* and made its debut on June 20, 1948, with six affiliate stations airing the program. The guests for the premiere included dancer Kathryn Lee, pianist Eugene List and the team of Dean Martin and Jerry Lewis. Although critics found Sullivan stiff and mechanical, the public loved him and the show became a fixture on Sunday evenings. By 1955, Sullivan had become the toast of the nation. CBS rewarded him with a salary increase, a long-term contract and a renaming of the program to *The Ed Sullivan Show*.

As detailed on pages 53-55, Brian Epstein reached an agreement for the Beatles to appear on *The Ed Sullivan Show* during his trip to New York in November, 1963. One month later, on December 13, CBS issued the following press release:

"The Beatles, wildly popular quartet of English record-ing stars, will make their first trip to the United States Feb. 7 for their American television debut on 'The Ed Sullivan Show,' Sunday, Feb. 9 and 16 (8:00-9:00 PM, PST) on the CBS Television Network. Their first appearance will be done at Studio 50 in New York, and their second at the Hotel Deauville in Miami, Fla. The fantastic popularity of the Beatles in England has received considerable attention not only in British newspapers but also in the American press. Their first record release is scheduled for January."

The statement that the Beatles first record would be released in January was incorrect. By mid-December, 1963, three singles had been issued in America, each of which had been a certified flop. The author of the press release was unaware of these earlier discs, but knew that Capitol was planning to release its first Beatles single in January, 1964. As detailed on pages 82-83, Capitol pushed up the release date of *I Want To Hold Your Hand* from January 13 to December 26. This turned out to be a blessing for CBS because it provided an extra few weeks for Beatlemania to take root and gain momentum prior to the *Sullivan Show* appearance.

By the time the first show aired, *I Want To Hold Your Hand* was topping the charts, with *She Loves You* and *Please Please Me* chasing after the Capitol 45. Capitol's *Meet The Beatles!* LP was about to move into the number one spot, and Vee-Jay's *Introducing The Beatles* album would soon makes its run to the second spot. With three hit singles and two albums to program from, radio stations were able to saturate the airwaves with Beatles music. And when the American press began increasing its coverage, the stage was set for a record setting television audience.

Sunday's schedule for the *Sullivan Show* began with a 9:15 a.m. - 1:00 p.m. camera rehearsal. The Beatles were required to be at CBS Studio 50 at 9:30 a.m.

Prior to the taping of the Beatles performance for later broadcast, the press was given an opportunity to photograph the group. Youngsters in the audience stood and shouted, trying to get the group's attention.

After the Beatles finished rehearsing their songs, they surprised staff members by requesting to hear a tape playback of the performances. This was a first for an act on the show. The group emphasized that they did not want their vocals to overshadow the instrumental backing. They wanted both balanced equally. In anticipation of the Beatles appearance on the show, music coordinator Robert Arthur ordered additional sound equipment. John commented that the mixing console looked like the cockpit of a German Messerschmitt fighter.

While blocking and other details were worked out, fans began to gather outside. Once again police were on foot and horseback to control the crowd as teenagers refused to stay behind the barricades.

The scene inside the building later became equally chaotic. Early that afternoon, an audience, packed with teenage girls, was let into the theater to view the show's 2:30 p.m. dress rehearsal. Every time anyone mentioned the word "Beatles" during the preliminaries, the girls began screaming. Realizing that a request for silence would be futile, Sullivan took the stage and made a deal with crowd. They could scream all they wanted during the Beatles performances if they agreed to be quiet during the other acts. The youngsters promised to comply with his request. Sullivan threatened to call a barber if the fans broke their promise.

There were all sorts of rumors spreading among the *Sullivan Show* staffers. One story had girls trying to enter the theater by climbing down through the building's air conditioning ducts. Another report stated that two girls had been ejected from the balcony for sexually stimulating themselves with Coke bottles.

Sullivan was enjoying the spectacle, but was also feeling stress. When Brian approached him and stated, "I would like to know the exact wording of your introduction," Sullivan curtly replied, "I would like for you to get lost."

The Beatles, unlike the other acts on the show, were given makeup at 2:00 p.m. because, upon completion of the dress rehearsal, they were going to tape two segments for broadcast on February 23. This would give Sullivan and America three straight weeks of the Beatles even though the group would be back in England when the third show aired.

During the dress rehearsal, the Beatles ran through the same five songs they would play that evening for the live broadcast. It was the band's first performance before an American audience. Some girls in the balcony fainted and were carried out. Staff members were concerned that the girls might fall over the railing into the lower audience level. Afterwards, those in attendance were treated to the additional performances by the band taped for later broadcast.

For the taped show, the Beatles opened with a rousing rendition of *Twist And Shout* (shown left). Exhibiting complete confidence, John belted out the rocker with nearly the same intensity as the studio recording from the previous year. The young girls in the audience bounced in their seats and screamed, particularly when the boys went "Woooo" and shook their heads. When it was over, the group bowed in unison. Paul then gave a quick count-in, and the band played their first big British hit, *Please Please Me*. Upon the song's completion, they bowed and waved to the audience. After a quick set change, the group returned to the stage for the taping of *I Want To Hold Your Hand* (shown below). At the end of the song, Sullivan came over to shake hands with each of the Beatles, who afterwards exited to the wings. Members of the audience let loose with sighs of disappointment when they realized that the Beatles had finished playing and would not be coming back on stage. The Beatles returned to the Plaza, where they were filmed by the Maysles Brothers, relaxing and being interviewed by Murray the K.

The 728-seat theater was then cleared for the evening show, which would be broadcast live before a different audience. One Sullivan staffer joked there wasn't a dry seat in the house. Because only 1,456 tickets were available for the afternoon rehearsal and the evening broadcast, CBS was only able to satisfy a fraction of the 50,000 ticket requests it had received.

During the Beatles afternoon performances, audio mixer Bob Miller achieved the proper balance between the music and vocals. He made chalk marks on the console to ensure that correct levels would be in place for the live broadcast. Legend has it that, while he was on dinner break, someone wiped the console clean of his marks, forcing Miller to recreate the balance on the fly during the live performance.

As evening approached, people across America were preparing to watch the show with family and friends. Youngsters wanted to see their heroes, while parents and other adults were curious to see what the commotion was about.

Finally, at 8:00 p.m. Eastern Standard Time, CBS began its live broadcast of *The Ed Sullivan Show*. America's favorite host started things off with a story. "You know something very nice happened, and the Beatles got a great kick out of it. We just received a wire, they did, from Elvis Presley and Colonel Tom Parker wishing them a tremendous success in our country, and I think that was very, very nice." (Sullivan actually received the telegram on Thursday evening.) After reminding the audience that his stage had been the scene of many exciting nights thanks to performers such as Topo Gigio, the Singing Nun, Milton Berle and the pairing of Sammy Davis, Jr. with Ella Fitzgerald, Sullivan got right to the point. "Now tonight the whole country is waiting to hear England's Beatles, and you're gonna hear them, and they're tremendous ambassadors of good will, after this commercial." The anticipation subsided for 60 seconds as the audience watched commercials for Aero Shave shaving cream and Griffin Liquid Wax shoe polish. After the break, Sullivan gave his famous introduction:

"Now yesterday and today our theater's been jammed with newspapermen and hundreds of photographers from all over the nation, and these veterans agreed with me that the city never has witnessed the excitement stirred by these youngsters from Liverpool, who call themselves the Beatles. Now tonight, you're gonna twice be entertained by them. Right now, and again in the second half of our show. Ladies and gentlemen, the Beatles. Let's bring them on."

Sullivan's last words were drowned out by screaming. The group opened with an energetic performance of *All My Loving*. Girls yelled and bounced in their seats the entire song. Upon its completion, the crowd screamed even louder and wildly applauded as the group bowed in unison. Paul took the spotlight again on *Till There Was You*, a lovely ballad from *The Music Man* that even adults in the audience could appreciate. Although the girls were quiet at first, the screaming resumed early on, with one shouting "Ringo" as George took his solo. During the song, the cameras focused on each member of the group, with his first name superimposed on the screen. When it came time for John, "*SORRY GIRLS, HE'S MARRIED:*" appeared below his name. The relative calm of the ballad was quickly shattered by a rocking version of *She Loves You* that provided a bold demonstration of the big beat sound. The loudest screams occurred each time John, Paul and George went "Woooo" and shook their heads. When it was over, the Beatles took their customary bow. Sullivan then restored order with "And, now, you promised," reminding the crowd of the agreement to scream only while the Beatles were on stage.

This is dedicated...

At the end of the Beatles first segment, Ed Sullivan announced, "Those first three songs were dedicated to Johnny Carson, Randy Paar and Earl Wilson." This, however, was Sullivan's dedication, not the Beatles. In all likelihood, the group did not hear Sullivan's words as they exited the stage and headed to their dressing room.

Johnny Carson was the host of *The Tonight Show*, which aired on NBC. It is not known why Sullivan honored him. This dedication would lead to an awkard encounter between Paul McCartney and Johnny Carson 20 years later on the October 23, 1984, *Tonight Show*. Carson mentioned to McCartney that the Beatles had dedicated their performance to him on the *Sullivan Show*. Paul did not know what Carson was talking about and said he didn't think it was true. This caught Carson by surprise and seemed to embarrass him.

Randy Paar is Jack Paar's daughter. Her father and Sullivan began feuding in 1961 while Paar was hosting *The Tonight Show*. Sullivan thought it unfair that Paar could book stars on his late night show for union scale wages ($320), while Sullivan paid significantly more ($1,000 to $10,000) for his guests. Sullivan threatened to pay his guests union wages if they also appeared on Paar's show. This caused some acts to cancel appearances on Paar's show. The feud went public with Paar making emotional statements on the air and CBS issuing press statements on behalf of Sullivan. After a few months, things calmed down, but Paar's showing a taped performance of the Beatles on his January 3, 1964, program rekindled the feud (see page 88).

The January 31, 1964, *Jack Paar Program* featured a segment with Paar and comedian Jonathan Winters spoofing the Beatles. Paar reminded his audience of the Beatles previous film appearance on his show and announced their upcoming live appearance on Ed Sullivan's show. After pulling two Beatle wigs out of a plastic bag, Jack mentioned that his daughter liked the Beatles. He and Winters then put the wigs on and imitated the boys.

Two nights later, on February 2, Sullivan asked his audience if anyone had extra tickets for his next show, which featured the Beatles. He stated that he needed two tickets for Randy Paar. That week, Sullivan sent tickets to Jack Paar for his daughter. Randy took Julie Nixon as her guest. Randy believes Sullivan's dedication to her was his way of apologizing for an unfortunate remark he made about her father, which he later regretted. She appreciated the gesture.

Earl Wilson was a gossip columnist for the *New York Post*. Sullivan, himself a former newspaper columnist, may have made the dedication to thank Wilson for coverage in his column or to curry Wilson's favor.

RECORD NEWS

Special Issue

bi·og′ra·phy

RINGO STARR

...sits at his drums like
...in more often than a
...ter his melancholy--

...for wearing lots
...and also the
...ny difference
...his three
...is hands--

...ad movement
...he group has made.
...everybody wants
...what makes a
...writers
...significance.

...touched

bi·og′ra·phy·phy

THE BEATLES   MCCARTNEY

Phenomenologists will have a ball in 1964 and beyond
with Beatlemania, a generally harmless form of madness which
deluged Great Britain in 1963.

As Frederick Lewis reported in the New York Times,
"Beatlemania...affects all social classes and all levels of
intelligence." Sole cause of Beatlemania is a quartet of young
Englishmen known as the Beatles, of whom Mr. Lewis said: "Their
impact on Britain has been greater than that of any other exponent
of pop music. There has been adulation before...but no one has
taken the national fancy as have the Beatles."

In less than one year, the Beatles have:

   1. Achieved a popularity and following that is unprecedented in the history of show business in England.

   2. Become the first recording artists anywhere in the
world to have a record become a million-seller before its release.
(Their disk, "I Want to Hold Your Hand," was issued in England
Nov. 29, 1963. By Nov.26, advance orders had passed the million
mark. The same record was released in the United States by Capitol
on Dec.26 and sold over 200,000 the first week.)

   3. Become the target of such adoration by their fans that
they were forced to cancel all one-night bookings because of riots.

                        (MORE)

Capitol Records

--but I wish
...ul we're
...McCartney, the
...s.

...ll of the songs
...e the group
...that some
...he rage
...some of
...fferent
...big-time
...so wrong."
...f art ("I
...e subject.
...lting
...gh"
.

He
...th

George Harrison

THE BEATLES

PRESS INFORMATION
(Inside Jacket)
This is America's Best-Selling Album!

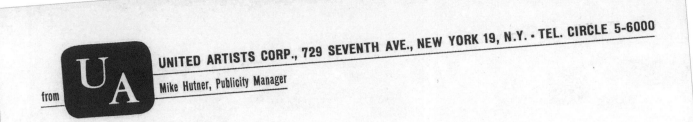

UNITED ARTISTS CORP., 729 SEVENTH AVE., NEW YORK 19, N.Y. · TEL. CIRCLE 5-6000

from **U A** Mike Hutner, Publicity Manager

Dear Friend:

You are cordially invited to attend the first American press conference with The Beatles, Britain's fabulous quartet of recording artists, who soon will be making their motion picture debut for United Artists. The conference will be held on Monday, February 10, in the Terrace Room at The Plaza Hotel, Fifth Avenue and 59th Street, at 11:00 A.M.

Sincerely,

Mike Hutner

Mike Hutner

FEBRUARY 10, 1964

The day after their triumphant *Ed Sullivan Show* appearance, the Beatles held a series of press conferences at the Plaza Hotel. Reporters received a specially-stickered copy of *Meet The Beatles!* containing glossy photos, the *National Record News* tabloid and biographies (press kit shown left). The group received gold record awards for *Meet The Beatles!* and *I Want To Hold Your Hand*.

Left: The Beatles and manager Brian Epstein (far right) pose with David Picker, United Artists Vice President for Production and Marketing, in the Terrace Room. Right: Magazine writers take notes during the afternoon press conference in the Baroque Room. Photos ©2003 www.popsiephotos.com.

The Beatles first Sunday in America had truly been a hard day's night. It began with the band heading for CBS Studio 50 at about nine in the morning and ended with their 4:00 a.m. return to the Plaza. In between, the Beatles prepared for their *Ed Sullivan Show* appearances, got their first taste of a screaming American audience during the dress rehearsal and taping of three songs for future broadcast, made their live American television debut with two sets of exciting performances and spent a night on the town with visits to the Playboy Club and the Peppermint Lounge.

On Monday morning, the group was understandably slow to venture out of their beds. The following message was delivered to the press: "We have headaches. It's not what you think. The flashbulbs did it. There were so many of them...." A rumor that the Beatles visited the Museum of Natural History proved to be a hoax. When the Beatles finally made it down to the Plaza Hotel's Terrace Room at 11 a.m., they met with reporters and columnists and were once again subjected to a large contingent of photographers armed with a seemingly endless supply of flashbulbs. At 1:00 p.m. they moved to the hotel's Baroque Room for a press conference with magazine writers. The boys later met with disc jockeys and radio and television reporters.

The Beatles gamely handled the pressures of a full day of relentless questions from the media. Highlights included the following exchanges.

Reporter: Which is the sexy one?
George: Our manager, Brian Epstein.

Reporter: Which do you consider the greatest danger to your careers, nuclear bombs or dandruff?
Ringo: Bombs. We've already got dandruff!

Reporter (referring to a review of their *Ed Sullivan Show* appearance by Theodore Strongin of *The New York Times)*: He said you had 'unresolved leading tones, a false modal frame, ending up as a plain diatonic.'
John: Well, we're gonna see a doctor about that.

Reporter: Have you got a leading lady for your movie?
George: We're trying to get the Queen. She sells.

One of the more frequently shown segments from the day is the group's response to a question about the meaning of the name Beatles. John says, "That's just a name. Y'know, like 'shoe.'" Paul adds, "We could have been called 'the Shoes' for all you know." About a dozen years later, four lads from Zion, Illinois would adopt the name "Shoes" and begin recording Beatles-influenced pop tunes.

Although United Artists sent the invitations (see previous page), press day at the Plaza was in many ways a Capitol event. The company distributed a special press kit placed inside copies of the group's recently released *Meet The Beatles!* album (see page 158). The press kit featured biographies of the band and each of its members. It may also have included a copy of the *National Record News* tabloid and two 8" x 10" promotional pictures of the group with hand stamped autographs.

The biographies were prepared in January, 1964. In an unprecedented move, Capitol produced a biography not only for the band, but also one for each of the four members of the group. The biographies were printed on gray paper. The first page of each bio has a "biography" heading and the Capitol logo in grayish-blue. The group biography is five pages and each member bio is three pages.

The biographies were probably written by Capitol press relations manager Fred Martin, who prepared the *National Record News* tabloid. The group bio contains information from the tabloid. The text of the member biographies is identical to the articles on each of the Beatles that appeared in the *National Record News*. The complete text from the Capitol biographies is printed on pages 168-173. The text from the United Artists biography is on pages 174-175.

The biographies are informative, entertaining and accurate, with the only major errors being the spring, 1963, release date for *She Loves You* and the statement that Brian discovered the Beatles at the Indra Club in Germany. He first saw the band perform at the Cavern Club in Liverpool.

Capitol distributed special copies of *Meet The Beatles!* to reporters and photographers who attended the group's February 10, 1964, press conference at the Plaza Hotel in New York. The albums have a 1½" x 6⅜" yellow-green sticker affixed to the cover, which states "PRESS INFORMATION (Inside Jacket) This is America's Best-Selling Album!" Copies of the album (shown right) can be seen in the lower left portion of the above photo. The gold record awards that were later presented to the group can be seen towards the lower right corner leaning against the end of the table. Press agent Brian Sommerville (standing at the far end of the table) directed the proceedings. Capitol Director of East Coast Operations Brown Meggs is seen at the other end of the table. Only four surviving copies of the stickered album cover have been verified.

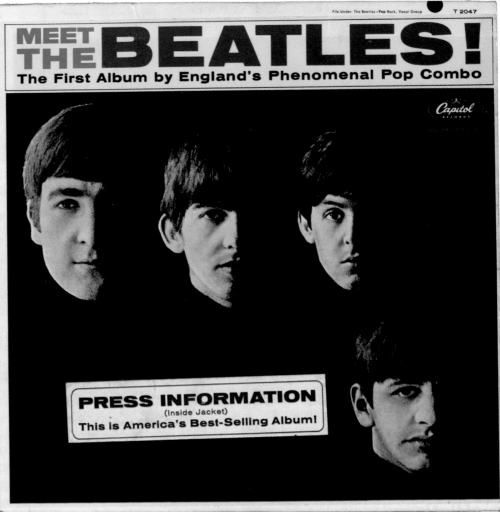

File Under: The Beatles • Pop Rock, Vocal Group   T 2047

MEET THE BEATLES!
The First Album by England's Phenomenal Pop Combo

Capitol RECORDS

PRESS INFORMATION
(Inside Jacket)
This is America's Best-Selling Album!

Dr. Brothers, I presume?

Celebrity psychologist Dr. Joyce Brothers attended the Plaza Hotel press conference hoping to gain personal insight into the group's popularity. Dr. Brothers (shown below with the boys) took notes as if she were conducting a session with her patients.

Prior to meeting the Beatles, Dr. Brothers wrote a piece about the group that ran in several newspapers. In that article, Dr. Brothers gives her theory on why the children of America love the Beatles. Before getting into specifics, she makes general remarks about youngsters.

"Teenagers, as we know, feel themselves in revolt against adult society. This is perfectly normal and natural, and is part of the process by which young people 'find' themselves.... Adolescent rebellion appears to be an unavoidable trauma in any country which allows social change, individualism, and free choice of life-style."

Dr. Brothers then talks about how difficult it is for parents when their child "coldly announces that everything they have ever done or thought is 'for the birds.'" Most parents, we are told, fight back and "advise their teenagers that his or her behavior is noisy, shiftless, vulgar, and no good, and that unless he reforms he will never amount to a hill of beans."

After setting the stage, Dr. Brothers finally discusses the group causing all the hysteria. "The Beatles are a marvelous symbol to adolescents of their rebellion against adult society. Not only do they 'get away' with being loud, vulgar, ridiculous, with gorging sweets and generally committing all the social crimes parents wring their hands at, these Beatles are actually rewarded for their behavior. They are rewarded handsomely. To the tune, it has been reported, of $100,000 a week."

While the Beatles rebellious nature was part of their appeal, Dr. Brothers' references to loud and vulgar conduct miss the mark. The Beatles rebelled against society with wit and charm. Ed Sullivan later described them as "tremendous ambassadors of good will." The Rolling Stones, who would soon follow the Beatles to America, were loud and vulgar.

Dr. Brothers next puts forth her orphan theory. "Their Oliver haircuts and too-short jackets add to their mystique in a fanciful and original way. Oliver Twist ... was an orphan. By embracing a quartet of orphans as heroes, our teenagers achieve two unconscious goals. They symbolically 'kill off' the adult generation. They show how neglected and misunderstood they believe themselves to be."

Her Oliver comparison took on an interesting twist when the cast of the Broadway show *Oliver!* was one of the other acts appearing with the Beatles on *The Ed Sullivan Show*. This gave youngsters an entire cast of orphans to go with the Liverpool orphans.

Dr. Brothers' next comments are probably intended to convey a bit of humor. "Consider the perfect significance of the very name 'Beatle,' which, while it may be spelled differently, suggests certain small crawling creatures. Beetles, like adolescents, might look unappealing and inconsequential to a majority of humans, but naturalists have long considered them 'the most successful order of animals on earth.' These insect pests show amazing tenacity, adaptability, and survival value.... Naturalists predict that beetles will survive long after man has passed away from this planet, and, similarly, our teenagers expect to have the last word (which they will get)." If Dr. Brothers was trying to say that the Beatles were going to be around for a long time, well at least she got that right.

©2003 www.popsiephotos.com

Next Dr. Brothers comments on the feminine side of the group. "The Beatles display a few mannerisms which almost seem a shade on the feminine side, such as the tossing of their long manes of hair. These are exactly the mannerisms which very young female fans (in the 10-to-14 age group) appear to go wildest over. No doubt many of their mothers have wondered why. Girls in very early adolescence still in truth find 'soft' or 'girlish' characteristics more attractive than ruggedly masculine ones. They get crushes on their female school teachers, and on slightly older girls. The male movie stars they admire most are apt to be the 'pretty boys' their big sisters would dismiss as kid stuff. I think the explanation may be that these very young 'women' are still a little frightened of the idea of sex. Therefore they feel safer worshipping idols who don't seem too masculine, or too much the he-man."

While the above observations could apply to the boy bands of the nineties, the Beatles did not appeal strictly to the 10-to-14 year old set. Older teenagers and young adult women, who were in no way frightened by the idea of sex, were also attracted to the group. While they didn't view the Beatles as he-men, these women certainly didn't find anything about the group to be feminine.

Dr. Brothers concludes with a final observation about teenagers. "Young persons wish to be unlike adults, but like other teens. The best way to succeed with them is to seem offensive to adults, and to catch the eye of the vogue-setting teen leaders. This, the Beatles have done."

Once Dr. Brothers met the Beatles, she changed her tune. After admitting she liked them, Dr. Brothers confessed, "I didn't expect to beforehand, but I just couldn't help it." She observed that, "underneath their zaniness, these boys really do have nice British manners" and that "they are disarmingly frank and unconceited." She found it important and unusual that the Beatles could "stand aside" from themselves, meaning that "while they're performing, they are also 'watching themselves from the wings'" and "enjoy their own show as much as anyone." Her one worry: "Having decided that these Beatles are really sweet kids, deserving of their success, I wonder if I should say so publicly."

> "Consider the perfect significance of the very name 'Beatle,' which, while it may be spelled differently, suggests certain small crawling creatures. Beetles, like adolescents, might look unappealing and inconsequential to a majority of humans, but naturalists have long considered them 'the most successful order of animals on earth.' These insect pests show amazing tenacity, adaptability, and survival value.... Naturalists predict that beetles will survive long after man has passed away from this planet."
>
> — Dr. Joyce Brothers

> "Psychiatrists are a menace."
>
> — George Harrison

Sociologists and anthropologists also gave their take on Beatlemania. Renee Claire Fox, assistant professor of sociology at Barnard College, observed that "There is a Chaplinesque quality to their style. They convey the image of absurd little men in an absurd, big world, bewildered but bemused by it all at the same time."

Professor Louis Orzack, chairman of the department of sociology and anthropology at Boston University, saw nothing alarming or new about the frenzy caused by the band.

"The only difference between this and other crazes is that the Beatles are more highly commercialized and that television gives them nationwide exposure. When I was in college we swallowed goldfish. Since then we have seen the swooning over Frank Sinatra and Elvis Presley. This exaggerated emotional response ... has no neurotic implication, nor does it indicate any deep-seated mass disorder in our youngsters. I believe they are highly attractive to teenagers because it's something new and different. The Beatles' youthful exuberance transmits itself to youngsters and encourages them to let themselves go, to yell and jump around and carry on. I do not see it as a revolt against parents. Rather, I believe it is their way of differentiating themselves from adults."

Professor Orzack disagrees with concerns expressed by some adults over the alleged sexual content of Beatles music. "Nor do I see any deep sex implication, aside from erotically suggestive, and I am told their songs are quite clean, not sex-stimulating."

Professor Orzack's observations are more on target than those of most psychologists and sociologists. Rather than attributing the Beatles success merely to adolescent rebellion, he focuses on positive characteristics of the group that teenagers find appealing. He recognizes that youngsters are attracted to the Beatles youthful exuberance, which encourages them to release their inhibitions. He wisely avoids silly theories and doesn't find the Beatles to be a threat or a menace to society.

While his remarks hit on some of the reasons for the Beatles popularity, he overlooks the most important factor. Nowhere does he discuss the music. The music was and always will be the reason people embrace the Beatles.

After a full afternoon of press conferences and interviews, the Beatles hosted a cocktail party for members of the press at the Plaza. While some of the attendees were satisfied with informal conversation and being photographed with the boys, others took advantage of the party as an opportunity for personal interviews with members of the band.

Having already interviewed George by telephone, newsman Ed Rudy went after Ringo, Paul and John. Ringo discussed the group's plans for the rest of the year, mentioning concerts in Israel and South Africa (which were later cancelled). Paul talked about the enthusiastic *Ed Sullivan* audience, their upcoming film and their visit to the Peppermint Lounge. He also stated that the group had achieved several of its goals, such as playing the London Palladium, coming to America and being on *Ed Sullivan*. John admitted that he didn't think the Beatles would last forever, adding "We're just gonna have a good time while it lasts." He also talked about how they worked out their arrangements in the studio.

Fred Robbins, host of the syndicated radio series *Assignment: Hollywood*, taped conversations with John and George. He later got to Paul in a more private setting while McCartney was trying to eat his dinner. A mentally exhausted Paul attempted to describe what it was like to spend a full day with reporters, photographers, disc jockeys and columnists, but could only muster, "When you've got a hectic day … it can be hectic."

The images of the cocktail party are from the contact sheets of legendary New York portrait photographer William "PoPsie" Randolph.

©2003 www.popsiephotos.com

bi·og′ra·phy

THE BEATLES

Phenomenologists will have a ball in 1964 and beyond with Beatlemania, a generally harmless form of madness which deluged Great Britain in 1963.

As Frederick Lewis reported in the New York Times, "Beatlemania ... affects all social classes and all levels of intelligence." Sole cause of Beatlemania is a quartet of young Englishmen known as the Beatles, of whom Mr. Lewis said: "Their impact on Britain has been greater than that of any other exponent of pop music. There has been adulation before ... but no one has taken the national fancy as have the Beatles."

In less than one year, the Beatles have:

1. Achieved a popularity and following that is unprecedented in the history of show business in England.

2. Become the first recording artists anywhere in the world to have a record become a million-seller before its release. (Their disk, "I Want to Hold Your Hand," was issued in England Nov. 29, 1963. By Nov. 26, advance orders had passed the million mark. The same record was released in the United States by Capitol on Dec. 26 and sold over 200,000 the first week.)

3. Become the target of such adoration by their fans that they were forced to cancel all one-night bookings because of riots. Their bookings are now for three or four days, which has succeeded in making their appearance cause for a relatively minor skirmish between Beatle fans and the constabulary.

4. Sold over 3,000,000 records in England, shattering the previous sales mark held by the now-vanquished champ, Elvis Presley.

Beatlemania has reached unbelievable proportions in England, it has become a form of reverse lend-lease and is spreading to the United States. Capitol is following up the Beatles' single record with the release of an album, "Meet the Beatles," in late January. That event will in turn be followed by the Beatles themselves, who arrive in New York Feb. 8 for three appearances with Ed Sullivan. The first show is scheduled for Sunday, Feb. 9, the second will be telecast from Miami a week later, and the third pre-taped for airing in March.

The Beatles' arrival in the United States has been presaged by a deluge of advance publicity.

Newsweek, Time, and Life have chronicled Beatlemania, UPI and the AP have done their part for the cause (including an AP wire photo of J. Paul Getty sporting a Beatle wig), and even Vogue shoved high fashion aside momentarily in its January issue and carried a full-page photo of the group.

Baltimore's respected Evening Sun took notice of the coming of the Beatles on its editorial page Dec. 30. Said the Sun:

"The Beatles are coming. Those four words are said to be enough to jelly the spine of the most courageous police captain in Britain.... Since, in this case, the Beatles are coming to America, America had better take thought as to how it will deal with the invasion.... Indeed, a restrained 'Beatles, go home,' might just be the thing."

(MORE)

BIO: THE BEATLES
PAGE 2.

Precisely how, when, and where Beatlemania got started nobody--not even the Beatles or their manager Brian Epstein--can say for sure. (It should be noted, too, that many in Britain, including psychologists and sociologists, are devoting considerable brain power to the problem of why Beatlemania got started at all.)

The Beatles' are a product of Liverpool, which has a population of some 300 rock-and-roll bands (or "beat groups," as Liverpudlians are wont to call them.) The beat groups hawk their musical wares in countless small cellar clubs, old stores and movie houses, even in a converted church, nearly all of which are in proximity to the Mersey River.

Out of all these groups came, somehow, the Beatles. And they had to go to Germany to do it. In order to better their Liverpool take-home pay of around $15 per week apiece, John Lennon, Paul McCartney, George Harrison, and Ringo (so called because of his penchant for wearing at least four rings) Starr took a tramp steamer to Hamburg and a job which moved them up a bit financially, if not in class.

There, in a raucous and rowdy strip joint, the Indra Club, the Beatles became the first entertainers ever to play louder than the audience. There, too, they were "discovered" by English promoter and talent agent Brian Epstein, who has since become deservedly known as "the fifth Beatle."

Under Epstein's shrewd guidance, the Beatles soon found themselves signing a contract with Britain's giant Electric & Musical Industries, Ltd., the largest recording organization in the world and major stockholder in Capitol Records, Inc.; headlining concerts throughout Britain; and appearing on television.

Their first recording, "Love Me Do," was issued by EMI's Parlophone label in October, 1962. It sold a respectable 100,000 copies, and it was the last time a Beatle single sold less than a half-million. Their first million-seller, "She Loves You," came out in the spring of 1963. It was followed by two albums, "Please, Please Me" and "With the Beatles." Both LP's sold over 300,000 copies. Then, finally, came the unprecedented success of the newest single record, "I Want to Hold Your Hand." In between there have been three extended-play (a 45 r.p.m. disk containing four tunes) recordings which also racked up sales of several hundred thousand apiece.

All this has resulted in what is universally known in Britain as Beatlemania and, as Newsweek said of the young Liverpudlians, "the sound of their music is one of the most persistent noises heard over England since the air-raid sirens were dismantled."

Their popularity reached a pinnacle of sorts when, in November, at the request of the Royal family, The Beatles headlined the annual command performance at the Prince of Wales Theatre. It was a glittering affair and, probably out of deference to attending royalty (including the Queen Mother--she found them "young, fresh, and vital"--and Princess Margaret), notable for the absence of even a small riot.

Despite their apparent appointment as Purveyors of Rock and Roll to the Crown, the Beatles have taken the whole thing in stride. Said Head Beatle John Lennon to the lords and ladies at the command performance:

"People in the cheaper seats clap, the rest of you just rattle your jewels."

— CAPITOL —

bi·og'ra·phy

JOHN LENNON

John Lennon is a determined 23-year-old whose somewhat stern face gives the impression of an angry young man. Without him there would be no Beatles. He was the one who organized the group and gave them their tag--one that has become, in the past year, the most important word in the English vocabulary.

Fittingly, Lennon is called the "chief Beatle." "But we don't let it count for much really," he said. "If we've got to have a leader, I'm him. How it happened is this: people kept coming up and asking who the leader was. We said nobody. They said there must be a boss. So the others said to me, 'Well, you started the whole thing off, so you're the leader.' And that's that.

"But ours is a cooperative group. We talk things over. We have our rows--nothing serious, just differences like any other human beings."

Being the leader of the most popular musical group to ever emerge in England is not John's only distinction. He's the only married member of the Beatles and he has a small son. But he sternly refuses to talk about him--"I'm dead keen to keep my private life separate from this business." The girls, however, make pilgrimages to his Liverpool home where he lives with his family. This has been a source of concern to the youthful guitarist and composer. "I want my wife to lead a normal life and not be pestered day and night just because she's married to one of the Beatles," he said.

Like his three fellow Beatles, Lennon is an individual who doesn't hesitate to speak his mind. Once, when asked about politics he replied: "Politics? They have no message for me, nor any of us. I haven't got much time for politicians. I'm 23 and I've never bothered to vote. None of them have anything for me. The Bomb? Nuclear disarmament? Well, like everyone else I don't want to end up a festering heap, but I don't stay up nights worrying. I'm preoccupied with Life, not Death."

Born in Liverpool, John attended Liverpool High School and later the Liverpool College of Art. Lennon readily admits that his school life was far from being successful ("My whole school life was a case of 'I couldn't care less.' It was just a joke as far as I was concerned. Don't think I'm proud of it all.... I wouldn't want anybody to follow my example"). The failures he had in school were more than made up for when the Beatles came into existence in a Liverpool club called the Cavern.

After some months of playing at the Cavern the boys received a booking for a tour with a Larry Parnes pop show. The job wasn't a very good one--just backing a young singer--but it was the first time they had played outside Liverpool. After that came their booking at the Indra Club in Hamburg, Germany, and a short time later their discovery by Brian Epstein.

Today, John is at the top but not overwhelmed by success. "I feel," he said, "richer and flattered by our good fortune. I am touched by the personal gifts that are showered on us now."

His philosophy sums up the feelings of the entire group. "We all go out to have fun. If others have fun, that's great. We're not rich yet, but I suppose we will be one day if our success holds. At least, I hope so because I don't wish to be singing at 80. Who wants a croaking Beatle of 80?"

bi·og′ra·phy

PAUL MCCARTNEY

"It's fabulous--the success and all that--but I wish people wouldn't think that because we're successful we're unapproachable. It's not true," emphasized Paul McCartney, the talented composer and bass guitarist of the Beatles.

McCartney, along with John Lennon, writes all of the songs for the group and has turned out over 100 tunes since the group first organized. The one thing that bothers Paul is that some people think he has changed since the Beatles became the rage of England. "I can't quite explain it, but when I meet some of my old mates, they don't seem the same. They have a different attitude towards me. Perhaps they think we've all gone big-time since getting into the charts, I don't know. But they're wrong."

Paul, however, hasn't changed. He is still fond of art ("I got my diploma in art, and I'm still very interested in the subject. I often sketch when we're on tour, that is, when I'm not writing songs or go-karting!") and he hopes some day to earn "enough" money so he can invest in his brother's hairdressing business.

Paul comes from Allerton, a typically suburban area of Liverpool, where his father still works as a cotton salesman. He was 15 when he met John Lennon who, at the time, was playing with several other musicians. Paul asked if he could sit in and that was the beginning.

"I guess it was pure chance that I met John," he said. "You see my mother was a district nurse, until she died when I was 14, and we used to move from time to time because of her work. One move brought me into contact with John."

At times, Paul wishes the Beatles could "get back to the kind of thing we were doing a year ago. Just playing the Cavern and some of the other places around Liverpool. It's only a passing mood though. Most of the time we've been living on top of the world and I'm not complaining. It's hard, but all jobs are hard if you do them well."

The sudden rise to fame by the Beatles is one of the things that Paul has thought a great deal about. "You know," he said, "we were talking about this the other day. When you're about 11, you start to think about what's going to happen to you. I've often thought about it. My plan was to go on playing the clubs until I reached 25--a ripe old age--and then go to John's Art College and hang out there for a couple of years. I never dreamt about being discovered or anything like that. I always thought discovery was something you read about."

At present, McCartney and the Beatles are being read about and studied. Paul realizes this but he can't answer why.

One critic tried to explain their success by saying "They have a sound which can only be written as 'Whoooo.' It's today's version of the eternal cry of youth." McCartney said the Beatles have no message and aren't trying to deliver one. They have nothing new to say about girls ("We like them"), war ("They should put the politicians in the ring and let 'em fight it out"), or politics ("It's like beer--we don't like the taste").

bi·og′ra·phy

GEORGE HARRISON

What makes the Beatles' Beat?

Obviously, if that question could be answered accurately, every group in England (as well as America) would be copying the formula and selling a million records.

George Harrison, who plays lead guitar, has given a good deal of thought to the question and attributes the success of the group to several factors--"We were different and, because the public was ready for a change, we've succeeded.

"Of course, apart from the music, the way we look and act has helped us. The way we have cut our hair, for example." George revealed that the haircut was arrived at completely by accident. "I went to the swimming baths in Hamburg, and by the time my hair dried out, without the benefit of brush and comb, it looked like it is now."

Despite the novel hairdo and the new approach the Beatles have to music, George feels the main reason for the phenomenal rise of the group is because "We're a different generation and so are our fans." Born in Liverpool, George left school to become an apprentice electrician ("I had to stop trying to be an electrician because I kept blowing everything up."). In 1956, he met John Lennon and Paul McCartney and in the next couple of years they played in a variety of groups--"we experimented," George recalled, "with washboard and banjo sounds."

Although Lennon and McCartney do most of the songwriting for the group, George has demonstrated his ability, too.

"I did actually write one number," he said. "The result was that we liked it and used it in the act for a short time. Now it's on one of our EPs. Though I haven't bothered about it in the same way as John (Lennon) and Paul (McCartney), I'd like to take a full stab at it sooner or later."

Songwriting isn't George's only interest. "I like parties and a bit of fun like anyone else, but there's nothing better, for me, than a bit of peace and quiet. Sitting around a big fire with your slippers on and watching the telly (television). That's the life!" George's ideal life is a far cry from his real life. Like the rest of the Beatles, his home is often surrounded by dozens of female fans. "They don't worry me," said George, "in fact, I like it. I'd be dead worried if the girls weren't around and if the screams died away. In any case, we aren't home much these days."

George did have one chance to go home this past year. It was during a two-week vacation last summer--the first the group has had since their phenomenal rise. Instead he took off for America to "see the ordinary side of America," he said, "the shops, the airports, the trains, the garages, the way people live in general."

George's thoughts are closely allied to those of his fellow Beatles. He doesn't think much about the future ("We're too busy today to talk about tomorrow") and he's disinterested in many things older people consider worthwhile. He's completely at ease and looks at the prospects of the group realistically.

"If we fizzle out--well, we fizzle out. But it will all have been a lot of fun."

bi·og′ra·phy

RINGO STARR

Ringo Starr is the quiet one. He sits at his drums like some Buddhist idol and wears a worried frown more often than a smile. Once in a while, he lets a smile shatter his melancholy--"I'm not really miserable, It's just me face."

Ringo, so called because of his passion for wearing lots of rings, is the most recent addition to the group and also the oldest member. Age or tenure doesn't seem to make any difference with Beatles fans because Ringo is just as popular as his three partners. He's been known to wear up to six rings on his hands--all gifts from admiring fans-- at the same time.

Although Ringo has been involved in the Beatle-mad movement for over a year, he is still amazed at the impact the group has made. "Suddenly," he said, "we're international figures. Everybody wants to investigate us. Get inside us. Try to understand what makes a Beatle tick. They send big writers to talk to us--writers who say they want to talk to us about our 'sociological significance.'

"In Birmingham, there were dozens of policemen controlling screaming fans at the studio doors while we rehearsed a television program. Well, if they didn't scream, I guess I wouldn't be where I am today. But don't ask me to explain it."

At home ("I daren't tell you where home is because it would be surrounded by shock troops who've gone Beatle-mad and I wouldn't like to embarrass my parents"), when he manages to find time to spend a few days there, Ringo stays indoors. "I've got records to listen to--everything from rhythm-and-blues to country and western style--and fan mail to answer."

But, all the fan mail and adulation heaped upon him hasn't changed his attitude at all. He shares the same likes and dislikes of his fellow Beatles. "I'm not interested in living it up. All money is invested, I don't even know how much it is. I don't take much out--just for clothes, a few cigarettes.

"When it ends--well, we've been skint before. But I'd like to have enough to do something--well, something with me hands. I've always loved basketwork, or pottery. Shaping something, making something. Being able to say 'I did that.'"

Right now Ringo, along with the rest of the group, is making something-- musical history. Never has England witnessed a mania as extreme as the one that has enveloped the Beatles.

"It isn't the screaming fans that affect me. That's normal. You get used to it. I love 'em and it's great to know they love you. It's a feeling that I might let them down."

Ringo tries to take his mind off the fans and the pressure with a variety of hobbies. "At the moment my great kick is science fiction. I read lots of science fiction. But I tell you this. There's been nothing so fantastic in science fiction as the monster impact the group has made.

"None of us have quite grasped what it's all about yet. It's washing over our heads like some huge tidal wave. But we're young. Youth is on our side. And it's youth that matters right now. I don't care about politics or anything-- just people."

UNITED ARTISTS CORP., 729 SEVENTH AVE., NEW YORK 19, N.Y. · TEL. CIRCLE 5-6000

from   Mike Hutner, Publicity Manager

THE BEATLES BIOGRAPHICAL FEATURE

A new show business phenomenon is sweeping the world - - Beatlemania, which is also the tentative title of a new United Artists motion picture. Beatlemania is marked by mobs of hysterical teenagers, theatres packed to the rafters with screaming, fainting youths wearing mop-like haircuts, and the most exciting new musical sound since the era of Elvis Presley.

Creators of this sound and the source of Beatlemania are four fabulously talented lads from Liverpool known collectively as The Beatles, and individually as George Harrison, John Lennon, Paul McCartney and Ringo Starr.

In assessing their fantastic popularity, Life magazine wrote: "First England fell, victim of a million girlish screams. Then Paris surrendered. Now the United States must brace itself. The Beatles are coming and already teenage Americans are keyed up as the days when Elvis first came twisting on."

On the eve of starting their first motion picture, The Beatles have emerged in a few short years from the jazz cellars and ballrooms of their native Liverpool to prominence as international recording stars and entertainment headliners.

More than 5,000,000 copies of their records have been sold in England, alone, and in three weeks their latest Capitol Records hit, "I Want To Hold Your Hand," jumped from 80th to the Number One spot on the U.S. charts.

Their American visit calls for three Ed Sullivan Shows, two Carnegie Hall concerts to be recorded for Capitol and conferences with UA executives on their film which will be produced by Walter Shenson, the same movie-maker who created "The Mouse on the Moon" and "The Mouse That Roared."

The Beatles' arrival in the United States has been presaged by a deluge of advance publicity.

Newsweek, Time, and Life have chronicled Beatlemania, UPI and the AP have done their part for the cause (including an AP wirephoto of J. Paul Getty sporting a Beatle wig), and even Vogue shoved high fashion aside momentarily in its January issue and carried a full-page photo of the group.

The Beatles are a product of Liverpool, which has a population of some 300 rock-and-roll bands (or "beat groups," as Liverpudlians are wont to call them). The beat groups hawk their musical wares in countless small cellar clubs, old stores and movie houses, even in a converted church, nearly all of which are in proximity to the Mersey River.

Out of all these groups, somehow, the Beatles.

Way back in '56 when the grind and scratch of skiffle was starting to graze the pop horizon, the three founder members of The Beatles - John, Paul and George - were busily experimenting with washboard 'n' banjo sounds at every out-of-school opportunity. After playing the Liverpool ballrooms, colorful strip clubs in the city's Chinatown and local church-hall hops, the boys outgrew their rock and skiffle phase to explode onto the highly competitive Merseyside scene in 1960 as a thoroughly groomed, supercharged quartet.

In 1960, to improve their Liverpool take-home pay of around $15 per week apiece, they boarded a tramp steamer to Hamburg and a job which moved them up a bit financially, if not in class.

There, in a raucous and rowdy strip joint, the Indra Club, the Beatles became the first entertainers to play louder than the audience. There, too, they were "discovered" by English promoter and talent agent Brian Epstein, who has since become deservedly known as "the fifth Beatle." This was the first of five successful night club sessions in Hamburg.

Under Epstein's shrewd guidance, the Beatles soon found themselves signing a contract with Britain's giant Electric & Musical Industries, Ltd., the largest recording organization in the world; headlining concerts throughout Britain, and appearing on television.

Their first recording, "Love Me Do," was issued by EMI's Parlophone label in October, 1962. It sold a respectable 100,000 copies, and it was the last time a Beatles single sold less than a half-million. Their first million-seller, "She Loves You," came out in the spring of 1963. It was followed by two albums, "Please, Please Me" and "With The Beatles." Both LPs sold over 300,000 copies. Then, finally, came the unprecedented success of the newest single record, "I Want To Hold Your Hand." In between there have been three extended-play (a 45 r.p.m. disk containing four tunes) recordings which also racked up sales of several hundred thousand apiece.

The Beatles' own built-in tunesmith team of John Lennon and Paul McCartney has already tucked away enough self-penned numbers to maintain a steady output of all original singles from now until 1975! Between them the four boys adopt a do-it-yourself approach from the very beginning. They write their own lyric, design and eventually build their own instrumental backdrops and work out their own vocal arrangements. Their music is wild, pungent, hardhitting, uninhibited ... and personal. The do-it-yourself angle ensures complete originality at all stages of the process. The Beatles can duplicate on theatre stage and ballroom bandstand every exciting sound captured within the grooves of their records.

All this has resulted in what is universally known in Britain as Beatlemania and, as Newsweek said of the young Liverpudlians, "the sound of their music is one of the most persistent noises heard over England since the air-raid sirens were dismantled."

Their popularity reached a pinnacle of sorts when, in November, at the request of the Royal family, The Beatles headlined the annual command performance at the Prince of Wales Theatre. It was a glittering affair and, probably out of deference to attending royalty (including the Queen Mother--she found them "young, fresh, and vital"--and Princess Margaret), notable for the absence of even a small riot.

Despite their apparent appointment as Purveyors of Rock and Roll to the Crown, the Beatles have taken the whole thing in stride. Said Head Beatle John Lennon to the lords and ladies at the command performance:

"People in the cheaper seats clap, the rest of you just rattle your jewels."

THUMBNAIL SKETCHES OF THE BEATLES

GEORGE HARRISON was born in Liverpool on February 25, 1943. SINGS and plays LEAD GUITAR. Met John Lennon and Paul McCartney in 1956 and the trio stayed together playing in a variety of skiffle and R. & B. groups before the formation of THE BEATLES in December 1960. He is a former apprentice electrician. Likes smallish blondes, driving, sleeping, television, Segovia and Chet Atkins guitar recordings, egg and chips, Eartha Kitt and films produced by Alfred Hitchcock. Dislikes having his dark-brown hair cut.

- - - - - - -

JOHN LENNON was born in Liverpool on October 9, 1940. SINGS and plays RHYTHM GUITAR plus HARMONICA. Has provided the remarkable FALSETTO VOICE effects on the group's best-selling records. Attended Liverpool College of Art and bought his first electrified guitar from the proceeds of a vacation building-site job. Likes steak, chips, jelly, curries, painting, modern jazz, cats, suede and leather clothing, Juliette Greco, The Shirelles and blondes who are intelligent. Dislikes traditional jazz and thick heads.

- - - - - - -

PAUL McCARTNEY was born in Liverpool on June 18, 1942. SINGS and plays BASS GUITAR. Having collected five passes in G.C.E., went on to pass English literature at Advance Level. Speaks Spanish and German. Likes Kraft Cheese Slices, steak, chips, all types of well-performed music, television, cars, Little Richard, Dinah Washington, Natalie Wood, Sophia Loren, and all girls who can makes intelligent conversation. Dislikes shaving and all types of dishonesty.

- - - - - - -

RINGO STARR was born in Liverpool on July 7, 1940. Plays DRUMS and (occasionally) SINGS. Joined THE BEATLES in 1962. Has a streak of naturally grey hair. Likes steak and chips, fast cars, "anyone who likes me," Ray Charles, sleek suits, Dinah Washington, Brigitte Bardot, small and well-built blondes. Dislikes onions, Chinese food, motor bikes and Donald Duck.

##############

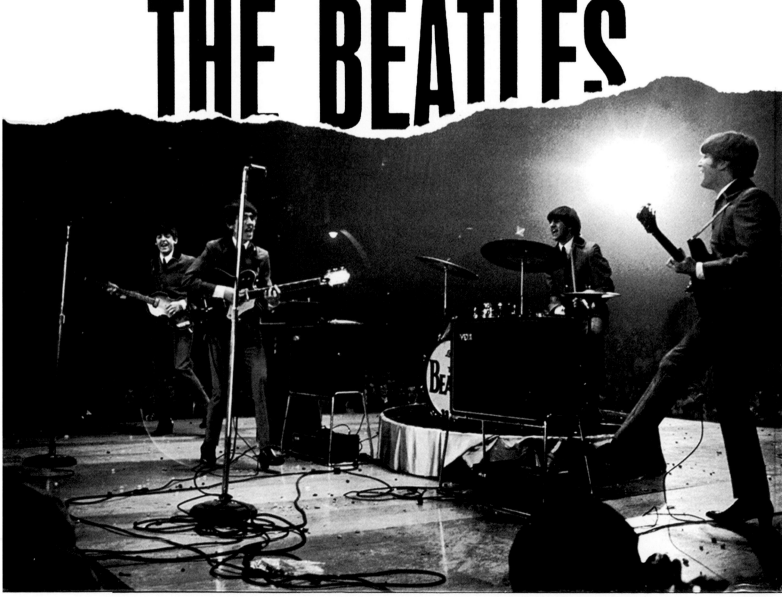

FEBRUARY 11, 1964

The Beatles first concert in America took place on February 11, 1964, at the Washington Coliseum. The show was attended by 8,092 screaming fans who paid either $2.00, $3.00 or $4.00 to see their heroes. John Lennon penned the set list for the concert on stationery from the Shoreham Hotel.

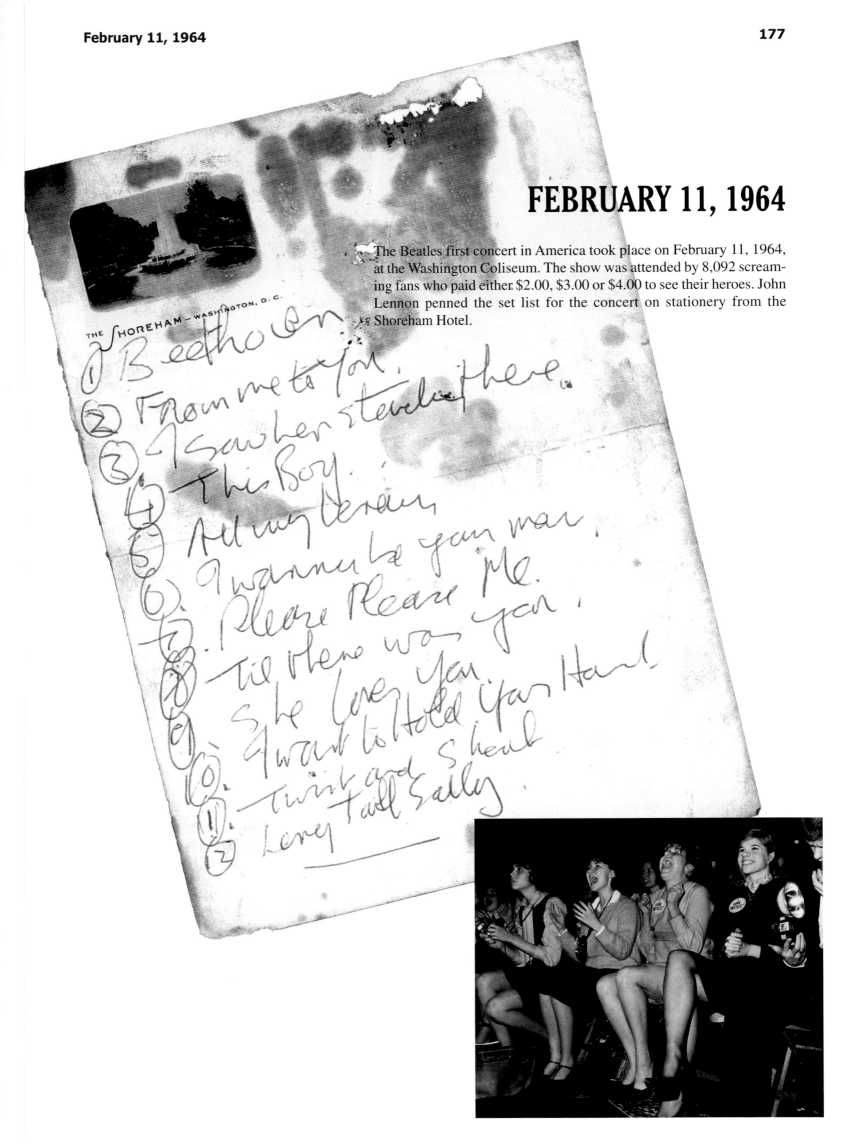

Although the Beatles were 24 hours away from playing inside the opulent setting of Carnegie Hall, their first American concert took place on a square stage centered inside a boxing arena. The group is shown performing *All My Loving* during the concert's second three-song segment. The Beatles amplifiers can be seen at the back of the stage facing the opposite direction as the band.

Because the Washington Coliseum normally hosted boxing and wrestling events, it had a square stage located in the center of the floor. In order to give everyone in attendance a frontal view of the Beatles, the group was directed to face a different part of the audience every three songs. To facilitate the moving of Ringo's drums, his kit and stool were set up on a round rotating platform. When the Beatles climbed onto the stage just after 8:30 p.m., they realized that Ringo's drums were facing the opposite direction from the microphones and amplifiers. After Ringo unsuccessfully tried to rotate the platform to the right direction, John signaled they needed help turning Ringo's round drum riser. Roadie Mal Evans and press agent Brian Sommerville came to the rescue and turned the drummer's platform to its proper position.

Even before the Beatles played a note, fans began screaming and photographers (both professional and amateur) started taking tons of pictures. The popping flashbulbs cut through the darkness with the intensity of a pyrotechnic show. The first American crowd also followed the British tradition of throwing jelly beans onto the stage. The ritual started after the group had been quoted in magazines and newspapers saying they liked "jelly babies." Unlike the soft English version of the candy, American jelly beans were hard and left a stinging sensation, causing Ringo to later observe, "My god, they hurt." The screaming was so loud and persistent that at least one of the 362 policemen present to preserve order resorted to using bullets as makeshift ear plugs.

While the Beatles had politely opened their *Ed Sullivan Show* appearance with *All My Loving* and the ballad *Till There Was You*, they began their first American concert with a raucous high energy performance of *Roll Over Beethoven*. The adrenaline rush brought on by the screaming crowd caused Ringo to lay down a faster-than-normal beat. Although George spent most of the song in search of a working microphone, it really didn't matter. The sound coming from the stage was no match for the sound coming from the audience. It is unlikely anyone present could have heard George's voice over the screaming. The opening Chuck Berry rocker was quickly followed by *From Me To You*, once again played faster and harder than the record. Paul gave an expanded introduction to the next song.

"This one which we recorded on a, a LP that we made, that's English for album, an album that we made. We'd like you, we'd like you if you would, to sorta join in, and clap your hands, you know, and stamp your feet. [John then gives his mock spastic attempt to clap his hands and stomp his feet.] Everybody just join in all together, OK? All right? The song, the song is called *I Saw Her Standing There*."

After a quick count-in by Paul, the group aggressively attacked the song. While Paul and John used separate mikes on the *Ed Sullivan Show*, they shared one microphone for this performance. Just before the instrumental break, both screamed wildly and shook their heads, causing the crowd to erupt in a frenzy. George's solo had more of an edge than the studio version, and midway through, Ringo kicked it into high gear, rapidly pounding his cymbals.

©2003 rowland.scherman@verizon.net

The Beatles performed 12 songs during their Washington Coliseum concert. The opening and closing songs were cover versions of classic American rockers that had yet to be released by the Beatles in the United States. All but two of the songs were all-out rockers. Paul is shown above singing solo on one of the evening's slow tunes, *Till There Was You*.

After the Beatles completed their third song, Mal Evans rushed on stage to rotate Ringo's drum platform to face the opposite direction. The microphone stands were brought to the other side of the stage by the Beatles assisted by stage hands wearing Beatle wigs. Once everything was in place, Paul and George surrounded John. The three singers shared a single mike for an intimate, inspired performance of *This Boy,* which was followed by a rocking version of *All My Loving*. Afterwards, Paul resumed his duties as master of ceremonies.

"Thank you very much, ladies and gentlemen, thank you. Well, uh, for this spot, we'd like to feature somebody who doesn't often get much of a chance to sing. [Paul moves one of the microphone stands to Ringo's platform, adjusts its height and hands it to Ringo.] So now, singing a song which is also on the album we made, singing a song called *I Wanna Be Your Man*, our drummer. A big round of applause for our drummer, Ringo!"

Once again, the band rocked through the song at a faster pace than the album version. Although Ringo's voice could barely be heard, the energy level made up for the technical limitations. The crowd screamed nonstop for the drummer, who at that time was the most popular Beatle in the United States. The crowd's enthusiastic reception for Ringo both touched and inspired the drummer, who spent the song smiling, shaking his head, singing with reckless abandon and pounding away on the drums.

For the next three-song segment, the microphones were set up to the left, and Ringo's drum platform was rotated a matching quarter turn. Paul's introduction to *Please Please Me*, quoted in full on page 90, demonstrates how much the group's popularity had grown in just a year. When released a year earlier on February 7, 1963, as the Beatles first U.S. single, *Please Please Me* "didn't do anything." Now, after being re-released, it was "doing something" (racing up the charts towards the number three spot behind other Beatles songs). The band ripped through *Please Please Me* before slowing the pace for the second and final time with *Till There Was You*. This was followed by *She Loves You*, which was greeted with enthusiastic screams of recognition. The volume level in the Coliseum peaked each time the boys shook their heads and went "wooooo."

The final segment of the show was played facing the audience to the right. As George tilted his amplifier on an angle and microphones were brought over to the other side of the stage, Paul explained, "The man told us to keep movin' around, you see, so we'll keep it moving." He then gave an introduction for the group's first U.S. hit to the first American city that heard the song on the radio.

"This next number we'd like to sing, we'd, before we do it, we'd like to thank everybody here in America, Washington, America.... We'd like to thank everybody for, uh, buying this particular record and starting this thing off in America. And giving us a chance to come here and see you in Washington. Thank you!"

I Want To Hold Your Hand was the song the audience was most familiar with. The fans were divided between those who screamed and those who sang along.

The Beatles opened the concert with George rocking out on *Roll Over Beethoven.*

True or False?

During their first American visit, the Beatles shared the bill with their American rivals, the Beach Boys.

False

The Washington Coliseum show was recorded in black and white video by CBS television and shown as a closed-circuit broadcast in American theaters on March 14 and 15, 1964. The Beatles performance was packaged with unrelated concert footage of the Beach Boys and Lesley Gore, leading some to believe that the three acts had given a concert together.

The concert ended with two back-to-back rockers, each worthy of closing a show. Although *Twist And Shout* had yet to be released on a single, many were familiar with the song from its inclusion on *Introducing The Beatles*. John gave his usual throat-shredding performance, and the crowd screamed wildly throughout, particularly when Paul and George shook their heads and sang "wooooo." Ringo pounded away relentlessly during the song's buildup ending. Before anyone could catch their breath, the band closed with Paul belting out Little Richard's *Long Tall Sally*. As the Beatles had not yet recorded the song at an EMI session, the crowd was not familiar with the rocker. It didn't matter. The driving beat, George's scorching guitar solos and Paul singing "We're gonna have some fun tonight" was more than enough for the fans to savor. And then, about 35 minutes after the Beatles climbed onto the stage, it was over. The Beatles, the crowd and the police were exhausted.

George Martin attended the concert with his future wife Judy Lockhart-Smith. They sat next to a young girl who kept bouncing up and down saying, "Aren't they just great? Aren't they fabulous?" When she asked if he liked them, Martin replied, "Yes, I do rather." The dignified Martin and Judy soon found themselves standing and screaming with the rest of the crowd. The girl had no idea she was next to the man who produced the Beatles records. Although some reports state that John's wife stayed at the hotel and missed the show, Lou Harrison recalls sitting next to Cynthia.

The video of the Washington Coliseum show captures the excitement of the event and reveals how different concerts of the mid-sixties were from those of today. Although the Beatles had what was then top-of-the-line equipment for their U.S. concerts, it was less than what bar bands have been using since the early seventies. While big name acts now go on the road with their own elaborate sound systems, the Beatles relied on the concert venue to provide a PA system, which did nothing more than handle the vocal microphones. For decades bands have had all their amplifiers miked separately and fed though a multichannel PA system. Several mikes are often used just for the drums. By contrast, none of the Beatles amplifiers were miked. Nor were Ringo's drums. The Beatles were relying strictly on their Vox amplifiers and the ambient sound of their amplifiers and drums picked up by the vocal mikes to fill the venue with sound. John and George each had a Vox AC-50 amp head with a matching Vox AC-50 speaker cabinet with two 12-inch speakers and a horn. Paul used a Vox AC-100 bass amp head with an AC-100 speaker cabinet with two 15-inch speakers. The Beatles relied on a mere 200 watts of power to compete with thousands of screaming lungs.

While bands now have several stage monitors to enable them to hear themselves, the Beatles had no such equipment. Considering the group could barely hear the music and vocals over the screaming crowd, it's amazing that they were able to keep it together or stay in tune.

It was also a more innocent time with limited technology. Performers now usually prohibit audio and video recording. Some even ban cameras of any type at their concerts. There were no such prohibitions at the Coliseum show. The video shows a fan in the front row aiming a home movie camera at the Beatles. The girl next to her has a small reel-to-reel tape recorder on her lap.

And then there were the jelly beans. The video shows fans gleefully throwing jelly beans onto the stage and the Beatles ducking. Photos reveal candies lying on the floor.

When the concert was over, a few dozen fans went up to the stage. They were each hoping to collect a couple of the jelly beans that had been tossed on the stage during the show. After all, some of those jelly beans had touched a Beatle! As stage hands and policemen pushed the candies towards the edges of the stage, hysterical fans grabbed at the treasures. A young girl named Jamie made eye contact with a policeman, who walked towards her. She wasn't sure what she had done and wondered if she was in trouble. But when the policeman reached her, he smiled and gave her a folded piece of paper. As she open the paper, Jamie realized she was staring at the set list from the show. The very same paper Paul had carried with him and placed on top of his amplifier! She grabbed her friend and headed to the ladies room, where she showed the item to her friend. She then placed it in her purse, praying that no one would take it away from her. Later that night she placed her jelly beans and the set list in a plastic bag, where it remained for over 30 years until purchased from her by Beatles collector Mark Naboshek. This is the set list shown on page 177.

Cooling down in their dressing room after the concert, the Beatles were exhausted and excited. The group was quite pleased with the audience response at their first American concert. Paul considered the show to be the "most exciting yet." Ringo raved about the crowd. "Some of them even threw jelly babies in bags and they hurt like hailstones, but they could have ripped me apart and I couldn't have cared less. What an audience! I could have played all night!" The Beatles reportedly received $12,184.76 for their efforts.

After recovering from the concert, the Beatles headed to the British Embassy to attend a charity ball hosted by the British ambassador to the U.S., Sir David Ormsby-Gore and his wife. The Beatles met privately with the hosts in the upstairs living quarters. They then walked down a stairway to the first floor to mingle with members of the press and inebriated guests. When a reporter asked John who he was, Lennon replied "Eric." After the reporter told the audience he was with Eric, John had to correct him by saying, "I'm John. It was only a joke."

Ed Rudy had brief interviews with John and Ringo. After Rudy told the drummer he was a sex symbol, Ringo replied, "You're joking! You can see my face." Ringo chatted with British military attaché Roger St. John, who was earlier wearing a Beatle wig. Ringo told him to buy the wig because the band needed the 10% merchandising royalty.

The Beatles, particularly John, were uncomfortable hobnobbing with high society. When Embassy officials asked them to announce the winners of the charity auction, John had had enough and was ready to leave. Ringo persuaded him to stay. Later a young lady cut off a bit of Ringo's hair with a pair of scissors. The Beatles lasted till about 1:00 a.m., when they escaped, saying that tomorrow was a busy day. Lady Ormsby-Gore apologized for the behavior of some of her guests. The Beatles later made it clear to Brian that they would never attend that kind of event again.

The New York press had fun with the Beatles trip to the nation's capital. The *Daily News* contacted several federal officials in Washington. When asked if the government had plans to defend the capital against the hysteria generated by the Beatles, a Pentagon spokesman admitted, "We ought to, but we don't." The State Department did not anticipate damage to relations between Britain and the U.S. The Treasury was worried about the "gold drain" that would be caused by the Beatles leaving with two million dollars.

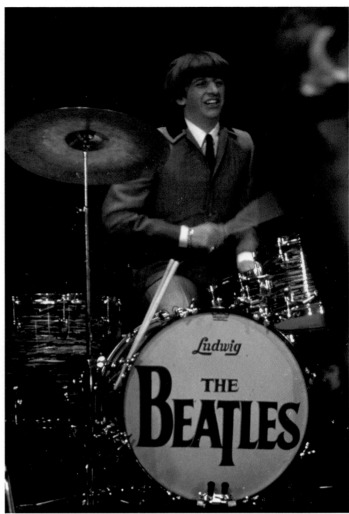

Ringo had the time of his life. "What an audience! I could have played all night!"

Although the Beatles charmed the New York media, *The Washington Post* did not fall under their spell. Leroy Aarons reviewed the audience rather than the band. "An 8,000-voice choir performed last night at the Washington Coliseum ... accompanied by ... the Beatles. [It was] like being downwind from a jet during takeoff." Columnist George Dixon described the Beatles as "a commonplace, rather dull act, that hardly seems to merit mentioning, yet people hereabouts have mentioned scarcely anything else for a couple of days. The Beatles took conversational precedence over Panama, Viet-Nam, Cyprus and the Senate investigation into the activities of Bobby Beatle – I mean Baker."

Lawrence Laurent wrote an unflattering piece about the group's *Ed Sullivan Show* appearance. He called the band "four quite ordinary musicians who happen to have unusually good diction for their own field." He also described the group as "imported hillbillies who look like sheep dogs and sound like alley cats in agony." In a later column, Laurent printed replies from Beatle fans. A woman in her thirties wrote, "I like the Beatles. I think you are a square." Two youngsters observed that "If the teenagers of today would follow the good examples set by the Beatles ... tomorrow's generation would be greatly improved." But the most astute comment came from Janice Harris of Hollywood, Maryland, who disagreed with Laurent's opinion that the Beatles were in for a brief success. She boldly predicted, "They'll never fade away, I promise you."

Before departing Washington, the Beatles wandered briefly around the Mall and were photographed with the Capitol Building in the background. By this time, millions of youngsters across America owned copies of *Meet The Beatles!* and *I Want To Hold Your Hand*, all bearing the Capitol Records logo (shown inset), which features the Capitol Building's dome and four stars.

Wednesday, February 12, 1964, was a holiday. It was 155th anniversary of the birthday of Abraham Lincoln. It was also Ash Wednesday, the beginning of Lent, the start of a 40-day season of penance. Holidays are notorious for being dull news days, but the Beatles gave the press plenty to cover.

Having played their first American concert the night before in front of over 8,000 screaming fans, the Beatles awoke in an excited mood. After checking out of the Shoreham Hotel, the group took a quick mini-tour of the nation's capital. Because it was a national holiday, there were only a handful of people present on the Mall when the Beatles exited their car for a brief photo session.

The group then headed for Union Station to board the train back to New York. Once again, the Beatles were joined by members of the press. Photographers snapped away and the Maysles Brothers rolled their cameras. Portions of the film shot on the train appear in *The First U.S. Visit* (though some footage from this day is edited out-of-sequence to give the impression it was shot the day before on the train ride *to* Washington). The boys are shown signing autographs

and being photographed with Murray the K. Playfully, George borrows one of the photographer's cameras and snaps away. Not to be outdone, Ringo puts on several camera bags and walks around the train car shooting pictures of the press. George later enters the car dressed as a porter carrying three cans of 7-Up on a tray. He then pulls back his hat and, pretending that no one recognized him, says, "It's me." Coincidentally, the group's shenanigans were similar to the fictional train ride scene filmed three weeks later for the Beatles first movie, *A Hard Day's Night*.

In the *Anthology* video, Ringo acknowledges that the group got to know quite a few members of the press during the train rides. The Beatles zaniness and fresh attitude converted even the hard-core reporters. "They started to get friendly and let us know that they were out there actually to kill us, and when we shouted at them, they loved us." One seasoned veteran observed, "Never mind their music, these boys are as good as the Marx Brothers." This proved to be a perceptive remark. When *A Hard Day's Night* opened to rave reviews in London on July 6, 1964, a British film critic called the group "a young version of the Marx Brothers."

As the train headed north, hundreds of school kids converged on the Plaza Hotel. New York television station WNBC reported that police cordons were broken down by near hysterical teenagers. One girl was trampled and taken to Roosevelt Hospital. She was not seriously hurt. Another girl fainted in the mob scene and was revived by her friends. She refused medical attention and returned to the fray. Finally, police using loudspeakers told the teenagers that the Beatles would go straight from Penn Station to Carnegie Hall, where the group would give a concert. Disappointed, some of the fans headed for Carnegie Hall, but most made a beeline for Penn Station (shown below).

WNBC reported that 1,500 screaming fans were at the station waiting for their heroes to arrive. A police officer called the mob "festive, but potentially dangerous." Tension was mounting as railroad police detoured the train to another track. The police used the strategy of sneaking the Beatles up the freight elevator to get the group past the mob without either the Beatles or the kids getting hurt. And it worked. The kids never knew that their beloved Beatles had been smuggled out of Penn Station through the subterranean passageway onto 8th Avenue and back Uptown.

But at the Plaza, there was no escaping the gathering crowd. When the Beatles car neared, youngsters surged towards the vehicle, causing the driver to panic and stop. Police had to pull young girls off the limo before mounted patrolmen could flank the car with their horses to clear the way for the final hundred yards to the hotel's drive-in entrance. Upon exiting the limo, the Beatles were guided inside a wedge of moving police through the lobby to an elevator. A couple of girls managed to squeeze into the elevator before its doors shut, but were not allowed to exit on the Beatles floor. Upon reaching their suite, the group was met by the chief of police, who warned the boys that they needed to be more careful. He looked pale and under stress, causing George to remark, "He's cracking up."

Outside the Plaza: fountain of youth; girls racing against traffic; police aiding fainted 17-year-old Eileen Harnett; cops holding back the crowd; and fans spelling out "RINGO" in sign language.

The Beatles attracted large enthusiastic crowds both inside and outside Carnegie Hall for their evening shows at the prestigious concert venue.

While the Beatles were relaxing in their suite and getting ready for their evening concerts, the action shifted to Carnegie Hall. In addition to the lucky ticket holders who attended the concerts, many fans assembled along the sidewalks to be part of the excitement. All were hoping to get a glimpse of the Beatles. Some, accompanied by their parents, were there to buy their way into the sold-out shows. Scalpers were getting up to $150 for tickets, which originally sold for $3.00 to $5.50. Police estimated that over 5,000 people gathered outside, leading Robert Alden of *The New York Times* to observe that "There were capacity audiences inside and outside."

Not all of the people in the street were there to cheer the group. A small contingent of Beatles haters made their feelings known by hoisting signs that said "Go back to English slums where you belong," "D.D.T. kills Beatles," "Flush the Pudding Basins" and "Beatles undermine artistic integrity." Another sign read "Down with the Good Guys," apparently aimed at the WMCA Good Guys who heavily promoted the Beatles on the air. These protesters, who were predominately male and college age (some were students from Fordham University), seemed to be enjoying

themselves and did not appear to be either threatening or malicious. They reportedly were swarmed by a group of girls who destroyed their signs. Realizing they were seriously outnumbered, they departed to the delight of the true believers before the Beatles arrived.

Had the Beatles seen the signs, they certainly would have taken it in stride. At their Kennedy Airport press conference, a reporter informed the group that college students in Detroit, Michigan, were handing out car bumper stickers saying "Stamp out the Beatles." Paul replied, "Yeah, well ... we're bringing out a 'Stamp Out Detroit' campaign."

Carnegie Hall employees had no idea who the Beatles were at the time the concerts were arranged. Sid Bernstein recalls telling them that the Beatles were "four young men who are a phenomenon in Great Britain." This led Iona Satescu to assume they were a string quartet. Gilda Weissberger remembers Sid telling her the Beatles were "a folk group."

On January 22, 1964, Walter Hyman, acting on behalf of Sid Bernstein, signed a license agreement for two concerts at Carnegie Hall to be held on the evening of February 12, 1964. He gave the venue a check for $1,750.

The booking ledger for Carnegie Hall shows that Wednesday, February 12, 1964, was a busy day. That afternoon, the venue was the site for the 25th annual American Music Festival, which had signed a license agreement on August 30, 1963, for $1,000. The evening was reserved for 7:00 and 9:30 concerts featuring "The Beetles presented by Walter Hyman." The license agreement was signed on January 22, 1964, at which time the rental fee of $1,750 was paid. Additional money for stage labor, ushers and security was paid at a later time.

Multiple Choice

The contract for the Beatles at Carnegie Hall was signed by Sid Bernstein and Brian Epstein in:

    A. March, 1963

    B. May, 1963

    C. October, 1963

    D. November, 1963

    E. January, 1964

Answer

This is a trick question. No contract was ever signed by Sid Bernstein and Brian Epstein for the Carnegie Hall concerts. Nor were any letters of intent ever written. The two reached a gentleman's agreement regarding the terms and conditions of the program. Thus, there is no documentation to show when negotiations began or when they were finalized.

Some accounts have Sid reading about the Beatles in mainstream British newspapers as early as late 1962 and seeing saturation coverage of the band and the hysteria they caused in early 1963. This is not possible. With the exception of music weeklies such as *Mersey Beat* and *New Musical Express,* the Beatles did not begin receiving coverage in the mainstream British press until mid-spring, 1963. Reports of frantic fans did not begin until several months later.

The breakthrough came after the Beatles October 13 appearance on *Val Parnell's Sunday Night At The London Palladium* when the Beatles attracted screaming fans both inside and outside the theater. According to Beatles press agent Tony Barrow, the *London Palladium* appearance changed everything. The *Daily Herald* described the hysteria caused by the group as "Beatle Fever!" The *Daily Mirror* called it "Beatlemania!" The latter term stuck. The British press latched onto the story of the Beatles phenomenal success and kept giving the group coverage. (See page 53.) It is these stories that first appeared in mid-October, 1963, that most likely caught the eye of Sid Bernstein.

Although Sid had not heard a single note of Beatles music, the hysteria generated by the group in England made him want to promote the Beatles in the United States. He recalls obtaining Brian Epstein's phone number from Bud Helliwell, an independent record promotion man who tried unsuccessfully to get airplay for Swan's issue of *She Loves You* (see page 139) and who was later hired by Brian during his November, 1963, visit to New York.

Sid telephoned Brian in England and offered to book the Beatles for two shows at Carnegie Hall. While Brian fancied the idea of having his boys play at the prestigious venue, he was reluctant to commit to the shows until the Beatles had significant airplay in America. He did not want the Beatles playing to half-empty houses. Apparently, Brian agreed to the Carnegie Hall shows provided that American radio began playing the Beatles. Based on the facts that Brian did not meet with Sid during his November, 1963, visit to New York and that Sid received Brian's phone number from Bud Helliwell, who was hired by Brian during that visit, Sid's first conversation with Brian probably did not take place until after Brian's return to England in mid-November, 1963. If this is the case, then Sid and Brian did not agree on the February 12, 1964, date for the shows until after Brian had already arranged for the Beatles to appear on *The Ed Sullivan Show* on February 9 and 16.

There are no documents in the archives of Carnegie Hall to indicate when Sid asked the venue to hold the February 12, 1964, date for the Beatles concerts. Gilda Weissberger, who worked in the booking department for Carnegie Hall at the time, explained that the normal procedure was for a promoter to call to see if a date was available. If so, the venue would put a verbal hold on the date. No deposit was paid at that time, but the full rental fee was due when the licensing agreement was signed. Other charges, such as stage labor, ushers and security, were paid later. Dates were normally held for a few weeks, but could be held longer if no one else requested the date. It is likely that Sid requested that Carnegie Hall hold the date for the Beatles concerts sometime in late November or December of 1963.

The Carnegie Hall shows were not finalized until mid-January, 1964, at which time the Beatles had the airplay in America that Brian was waiting for (see page 114). The Carnegie Hall booking ledger indicates that the license agreement was signed on January 22, 1964. During an interview with Harold Kelley of the American Forces Network taped on January 24, 1964, Paul mentioned that the Beatles were set to visit the United States in February for three *Ed Sullivan Show* appearances and to play Carnegie Hall. This is the first known public statement about the Carnegie Hall concerts. The first and only ad for the shows ran in *The New York Times* on January 26, 1964.

Although the above analysis indicates that Sid Bernstein did not book the Beatles in Carnegie Hall at the earlier dates reported in some accounts, this does not diminish the significance of what Sid did for the Beatles. He had the foresight to schedule two Beatles concerts in the U.S. at a time when the Beatles were virtually unknown in America. His selection of Carnegie Hall as the venue gave the concerts, and therefore the Beatles, a touch of credibility and class. He would later book the Beatles for concerts in Shea Stadium, proving that popular rock acts could sell out large outdoor venues. Dick Clark called Sid "one of the good guys" and Sir Paul McCartney said, "Sid Bernstein is a wonderful person who was instrumental in introducing the Beatles to America."

What's wrong with this picture?

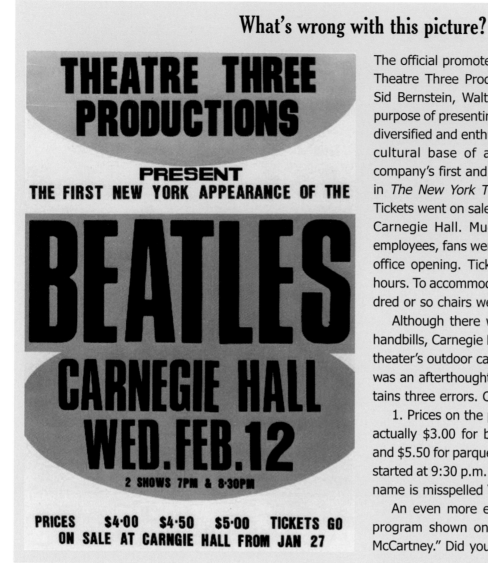

The official promoter for the Carnegie Hall concerts was Theatre Three Productions, an organization formed by Sid Bernstein, Walter Hyman and Hank Barron for the purpose of presenting "those artists who attract the most diversified and enthusiastic following through their broad cultural base of appeal to all ethnic groups." The company's first and only ad for the Beatles concerts ran in *The New York Times* on Sunday, January 26, 1964. Tickets went on sale the following morning exclusively at Carnegie Hall. Much to the surprise of the venue's employees, fans were lined up well in advance of the box office opening. Tickets for both shows sold out within hours. To accommodate additional ticket requests, a hundred or so chairs were placed on the stage.

Although there was no need to print advertisement handbills, Carnegie Hall requested posters to place in the theater's outdoor cases. Because the poster (shown left) was an afterthought, it was done without care and contains three errors. Can you spot them?

1. Prices on the poster are wrong. Ticket prices were actually $3.00 for balcony seats, $4.50 for dress circle and $5.50 for parquet and box seats. 2. The second show started at 9:30 p.m. rather than 8:30 p.m. 3. The venue's name is misspelled "CARNGIE" on the last line.

An even more embarrassing error is in the concert program shown on page 184. Paul is listed as "John McCartney." Did you notice that?

Meanwhile, back at the Plaza, Capitol of Canada's Paul White met with the group. He presented them with surveys from several Canadian radio stations demonstrating the Beatles chart dominance in his country.

Shortly before 6:00 p.m., the Beatles left their suite to head for Carnegie Hall. Rather than face the mass of teenagers still assembled near the entrance to the Plaza, the Beatles took a back elevator and exited the hotel through the kitchen. In a bit of subterfuge, the Beatles were taken to the stage entrance of Carnegie Hall in a taxi cab rather than the expected black Cadillac limo. Their cover was blown when a policeman saw the approaching cab and shouted, "There they are." This caused several fans to rush the stage door entrance. The Beatles barely beat the surging crowd and made it safely inside.

The audience for the concerts was an interesting mix of screaming youngsters and the elite of New York society, which included actress Lauren Bacall and Happy Rockefeller, wife of New York Governor Nelson Rockefeller. Each performance was attended by close to 3,000 people.

Prior to the Beatles taking the stage, the WMCA Good Guys and Murray the K of WINS took part in what the Carnegie Hall program described as a "New York disc jockeys' salute to The Beatles." Murray used the opportunity to further promote himself as the fifth Beatle and let everyone know he was "what's happening."

Also on the bill...

The opening act was the **Briarwood Singers**, a folk group from Miami signed to United Artists Records consisting of Dorinda Duncan, Stan Beach, Bob Hoffman, Harry Scholes and Barry Bobst. The closest the group came to having a hit was their recording of *He Was A Friend Of Mine*, which appeared at number 126 on the *Billboard Bubbling Under The Hot 100* listing for December 28, 1963. The tune was a traditional folk song performed by several singers, including Bob Dylan. The Byrds later recorded a version of the song with additional lyrics written by Jim McGuinn on the evening President Kennedy was assassinated. McGuinn, who later changed his first name to Roger, formed the folk-rock group the Byrds and used a Rickenbacker 12-string guitar after seeing Harrison play the instrument in the United Artists Beatles film *A Hard Day's Night*. The Byrds' version of *He Was A Friend Of Mine* appears on the group's 1965 *Turn! Turn! Turn!* album. Although the Briarwood Singers never had a hit single or album, they could, thanks to Sid Bernstein and Theatre Three Productions, brag that they played Carnegie Hall and shared the bill with the Beatles.

Prior to the start of their concert, the Beatles received an in-house gold record award for sales of over one million units of *She Loves You*. Swan owners Bernie Binnick and Tony Mammarella are shown handing the award to Paul (left). Two days earlier the Beatles were given a RIAA-sanctioned gold record award for *I Want To Hold Your Hand* (see pages 162-163). The group also received a special International Award from *Cash Box* (shown right in the hands of producer George Martin). ©2003 www.popsiephotos.com

The first show, set for 7:00 p.m., began only a few minutes late, with the Beatles reportedly taking the stage at 7:45 p.m. The band's performance lasted approximately 34 minutes. The second show, scheduled for 9:30 p.m., got off to a late start due to the logistics of clearing the hall of fans, cleaning up the trash left by the first audience and bringing in the second crowd. The Beatles didn't start playing until about 11:15 p.m.

Gilda Weissberger, the Carnegie Hall employee who had been told by Sid Bernstein that the Beatles were a folk group, wanted to see what all the excitement was about. The opening act, the Briarwood Singers, was indeed a folk group; however, the Beatles were another animal altogether. Gilda stood at the back of the theater for about five minutes, but left because she couldn't hear the music due to all the screaming.

True or False?

Capitol Records recorded the Beatles performances at Carnegie Hall.

False

Capitol announced its plans to record the concerts in a press release dated January 29, 1964 (see page 133). Capitol's Voyle Gilmore, Artists & Repertoire Vice President, was going to fly from the West Coast to personally handle the recording of an album to be titled *The Beatles At Carnegie Hall*. The company planned on releasing the live album the following April.

In a February 3, 1964, letter to Iona Satescu of Carnegie Hall, Brown Meggs confirmed that Capitol had obtained the permission of promoter Sid Bernstein and manager Brian Epstein to record the shows. The company agreed to pay $300 to record the concerts plus an additional $500 to use "recorded at Carnegie Hall" on the album cover.

Neither the archives of Capitol Records nor Carnegie Hall contain any evidence indicating that the concert was recorded. This has been attributed to the American Federation of Musicians (AFM) objecting to the recording of the performances. The reasons for the union's objection remains a mystery as it was not unusual for foreign and/or non-union musicians to perform at Carnegie Hall. Because Carnegie Hall could not risk angering the AFM, Capitol was not allowed to record the historic concerts. CBS did not encounter union objections when it filmed the group's Washington Coliseum performance.

Some accounts state that although no album was released, the concerts were recorded. This misinformation may very well have stemmed from a paragraph appearing in *The Original Beatles Book* (see page 218). The magazine, which was rushed out during the Beatles first U.S. visit, claimed that it followed the Beatles "from the cradle to Carnegie Hall." The book's author, Earl Leaf, ended his description of the Carnegie Hall concerts with:

"One man was tearing out the remains of his thinning hair. Voyle Gilmore, Vice President of Capitol Records, personally took charge of the equipment to record a new album, *Beatles Alive At Carnegie Hall*, but he could hardly hear any music over the screams and howls."

In all likelihood, Leaf assumed from the press release that the concert was recorded and fabricated his story of Gilmore tearing out his hair during the recording.

Because the concerts were not recorded, there is no way to prove what songs were played by the Beatles that evening. Both shows probably contained the same lineup as that of the Washington Coliseum show from the night before.

Under the terms of the agreement worked out between Sid and Brian, the Beatles received $6,500 plus a percentage of the gross for the two performances. Their total take for the evening was reported to be $9,335.78.

Between shows, the Beatles met with singer Shirley Bassey, who had been booked by Sid to play Carnegie Hall on February 15. Bassey, who was born in Cardiff, Wales, had nine top ten U.K. hits between 1957 and 1963. Although she began playing the American club circuit in 1961, she was not well known in the States. Bassey would gain worldwide recognition later in the year when she belted out the title song for the James Bond film *Goldfinger*. The record, produced by George Martin, became an American top ten hit in early 1965. Her recording of George Harrison's *Something* reached number four in England in 1970.

After the concerts, the Beatles went back to the Plaza to freshen up. Murray the K then took them to the Headliner Club, where Ringo once again twisted the night away. Their next stop was the Improvisation coffee house. During the evening the Beatles met starlets Stella Stevens and Tuesday Weld. They returned to the Plaza after 4:00 a.m.

The reviews of the Beatles performances at Carnegie Hall focused more on the audience than the music. John Wilson's concert review for *The New York Times* began: "Twenty-nine hundred ecstatic Beatlemaniacs gave a concert, early last evening at Carnegie Hall, accompanied by the thumping twanging rhythms of the Beatles, an English rock 'n' roll quartet. The Beatles enthusiasts, who paid from $3 to $5.50 for the privilege of outshrieking their idols, must have been 99 percent female if one judged by the level of voices that they raised. Physical evidence, however, showed that there were a considerable number of males

True or False?
The Beatles were the first rock 'n' roll group to play Carnegie Hall.

False
Bill Haley and His Comets took the stage at Carnegie Hall on the evening of Friday, May 6, 1955. The band, listed in the program as a "Rock Group," was one of several acts performing at a Jazz & Variety Concert held for the benefit of the Lighthouse. Other musicians on the bill included trumpeter Clifford Brown, drummer Max Roach, Count Basie and His Orchestra, the McGuire Sisters, Les Paul and Mary Ford, drummer Buddy Rich and singer Billie Holiday. At the time of the concert, Haley was best known for his cover version of Joe Turner's R&B classic *Shake, Rattle And Roll*, a top ten hit for Haley in the summer of 1954. His *(We're Gonna) Rock Around The Clock* would soon launch the rock era by topping the *Billboard Best Sellers in Stores* chart for eight straight weeks in July and August of 1955.

Carnegie Hall's first full-length concert featuring rock 'n' roll and R&B acts was held a half-year later on October 29, 1955. Harold Jackson presented a Top Ten Revue that included Joe Turner, Bo Diddley, the Clovers, the Charms, the Five Keys, Bill Doggett and Etta James.

present, many of whom bounced in their seats but were less vocal." The Associate Press reported that the Beatles "tore the roof off Carnegie Hall" and "set off a crescendo of teen-age squeals that could almost be heard across the river to New Jersey."

Ringo hit the dance floor at every opportunity, this time with singer Jenie Dell at the Headliner Club. Upon exiting the building, Ringo was ambushed by a female fan who broke through a police escort to plant a kiss on his face.

February 16, 1964 **Sunday**

Evening

ris. Eddie: Gary Crosby.
Before he became TV's famous bellhop, Bill Dana was a page boy. See the article on pages 8-9.

⑥ ⑪ ⑬ LASSIE—Drama
In Part 3 of a five-part story, Lassie and Ranger Stuart trail the hunter responsible for a forest fire. Tim: Jon Provost. Paul: Hugh Reilly. Ruth: June Lockhart.

Guest Cast

Corey Stuart .... Robert Bray
David Frazer .... Tim McIntire

⑨ OZZIE AND HARRIET—Comedy
Rick and Wally try to capitalize on "The Dean's Birthday" when they learn that their frat won't be permitted to hold another dance. The Nelsons portray themselves. Wally: Skip Young. Dean s: David Lewis. Fred: James Stacy.

⑧ WALT DISNEY'S WORLD
[COLOR] "The Scarecrow of Romney rsh," second of three parts. A farmer pected of smuggling is told that he ust reveal the identity of the Scarecrow—or go to jail. (60 min.)

Cast

r. Syn .... Patrick McGoohan
Mipps .... George Cole
John Banks .... Sean Scully
General Pugh .... Geoffrey Keen
Joe Ransley .... Patrick Wymark

⑥ ⑪ ⑬ MY FAVORITE MARTIAN—Comedy
Uncle Martin aids an elderly museum curator, who may lose his job because he bought a controversial piece of Egyptian art. Uncle Martin: Ray Walston. Tim: Bill Bixby.

Guest Cast

Canfield .... Cecil Kellaway
Guard .... John Qualen
Donati .... Maurice Marsac

⑨ ㊳ JAIMIE McPHEETERS
On "The Day of the Picnic," Jaimie tells a young companion about an early incident on the trip—when Billy Slocum was to be hanged for horse stealing. Jaimie: Kurt Russell. Doc: Dan O'Herlihy. Jenny: Donna Anderson. Mrs. Kissel: Meg Wyllie. Kissel: Mark Allen. Murrel: James Westerfield. Shep: Sandy Kenyon. (60 min.)

Guest Cast

Billy Slocum .... Robert Miller Driscoll

Sheriff .... Paul Fix
Little Girl .... Gina Gillespie

8:00 ⑥ ⑪ ⑬ ED SULLIVAN
The Beatles are back and so is Mitzi Gaynor; each gets an extended portion of the show. Also performing are comics Allen and Rossi; comedian Myron Cohen; the Volantes, unicyclists; and the Nerveless Nocks, sway-pole acrobats. Ray Bloch orchestra. (Live; 60 min.)

8:30 ② ⑧ GRINDL—Imogene Coca
"The Taming of a Tyrant." In a socialite's household, Grindl spearheads a strike against a tyrannical butler. Grindl: Imogene Coca. Foster: James Millhollin.

Guest Cast

Rayburn .... Harry Kroeger
Mary .... Florence Sundstrom
Lizzie .... Rowena Burack

⑨ ㊳ ARREST AND TRIAL
Arthur O'Connell in "The Best There Is." Egan's refusal to defend a suspected murderer angers his old law teacher, a once-famous lawyer who ignores his failing health and comes out of retirement to take the case. Egan: Chuck Connors. Anderson: Ben Gazzara. (90 min.)

Guest Cast

Andrew Sheridan .... Arthur O'Connell
Joyce .... Merry Anders
Sergeant Kelliher .... Adam Roarke
Lieutenant Handley .... Ken Lynch
Rudy Sanchez .... Alejandro Rey

9:00 ② ⑧ BONANZA—Western
[COLOR] "Bullet for a Bride." Little Joe wants to marry Tessa Caldwell—whom he blinded in a hunting accident. Little Joe: Michael Landon. Ben: Lorne Greene. Hoss: Dan Blocker. (60 min.)

Guest Cast

Tessa Caldwell .... Marlyn Mason
Mr. Caldwell .... Denver Pyle
Lon Caldwell .... Steve Harris

⑥ JUDY GARLAND—Variety
Jane Powell and Ray Bolger guest. Judy and Ray recall their performances in "The Wizard of Oz" (Ray was the scarecrow) with "We're Off to See the Wizard" and "If I Only Had a Brain." Jerry Van Dyke, Ernie Flatt dancers, Mort Lindsey orchestra. (60 min.)

Highlights
"I Feel a Song Comin' On," "A Lot
Continued on next page

FEBRUARY 13-20, 1964

The day after their Carnegie Hall concerts, the Beatles flew to Miami for some vacation time and to appear again on *The Ed Sullivan Show*, this time broadcast live from the Deauville Hotel in Miami Beach on February 16, 1964.

Female fans, many armed with cameras and binoculars, await the arrival of the Beatles at Miami International Airport.

Exhausted from an exciting and long day that included a train ride, two concerts at Carnegie Hall and visits to New York night clubs till four in the morning, the Beatles took advantage of some down time to sleep late. They left the Plaza Hotel for the final time shortly after lunch on Thursday, February 13, to catch a 1:30 p.m. flight to Miami. Both the New York police force and the staff at the Plaza breathed a heavy sigh of relief.

Upon arriving at the airport, the group was surprised to learn that they would be flying in the back of the plane. Apparently a prankster had called National Airlines the night before requesting that the Beatles tickets be switched from first class to tourist. Meanwhile, city and police officials in Miami were bracing for the Beatles invasion.

WFUN was the first Miami radio station to jump on the Beatles bandwagon when it played *I Want To Hold Your Hand* shortly after the record was released. According to disc jockey Dick Starr, "The reaction was fantastic. Our switchboard was jammed with requests for more, from both teenagers and adults." Within three weeks, the station's top three songs were *I Want To Hold Your Hand, She Loves You* and *Please Please Me*. In late January, the station announced plans to throw a gigantic greeting party for the group when they arrived at the Miami airport.

Within days of the Beatles invasion, WFUN and WQAM began informing listeners that the band would be arriving on National Airlines Flight 11 shortly before 4:00 p.m. In a repeat of the previous week's spectacle in New York, Florida youngsters headed to Miami International Airport to greet their heroes. Crowd estimates ranged from a low of 4,500 to a high of 7,000. This was significantly less than the 20,000 to 40,000 predicted earlier in the week by Miami newspapers, but greater than the crowd of 3,000 at Kennedy Airport one week earlier.

The group's arrival was broadcast live on Miami radio station WQAM. The tape reveals the crowd chanting "We want the Beatles, we want the Beatles" over and over again in anticipation. Disc jockey Charlie Murdock described the scene as "almost frightening." Fellow DJ Jack Sorbi was both excited and apprehensive. "This is getting to be a little bit too much, the people are still trying to force [airport terminal] windows open so they can get a better view."

After the plane arrived, Miami police were unable to contain the crowd behind fences and barricades. A second line of defense was formed on the outdoor tarmac. The Beatles remained on the jet until the other passengers were allowed to escape. The excitement reached a fever pitch when the group finally emerged from the plane and headed down the portable staircase. WQAM disc jockey Charlie Murdock shouted the following description:

"Here come the Beatles! Here they come, here they come, there's Ringo! Who else do we have there? There's George! Here they come, the four Beatles. They've stopped about half-way down, the crowd moves on, the police are trying to hold them back. This is the crowd that's on the apron, we're moving with them. They're trying to hold them back the best way they can. There go the WQAM Sweethearts up there near the ramp. They're going to try to give them the kisses. The Beatles have stepped down to the bottom of the ramp. And there they go, they're getting ready to try to come through this enormous crowd here at Miami International Airport. This will be a time that no one will ever forget, I don't believe, who was at the airport at this particular moment."

As the Beatles made their way to the waiting limousines, a young girl told the disc jockeys and WQAM listeners that she touched Ringo and Paul and that she was never going to wash her hand again. Another said they were even more wonderful than she'd imagined.

The Saturday Evening Post later wrote that the Beatles "were greeted at the airport by a chimpanzee, four bathing beauties, a four-mile-long traffic jam and 7,000 teenagers." UPI reported that the Beatles were "greeted by an exterminating truck and 4500 squealing teenagers who kicked out airport windows" and that "despite the crush of the thousands of screaming and singing fans, the young singers with the seaweed hairdos made it through the Miami airport unmolested and were rushed off to Miami Beach in a shiny limousine, flanked by police escorts." The truck sported a sign that read "We welcome the Beatles but we hate bugs." One of the policemen struggling to hold a door closed against the surging crowd felt differently. He muttered, "If I ever caught my kid out here, I'd beat the hell out of her. This is disgusting."

A local Miami newspaper reported that the group received a "smashing welcome at the airport–smashed doors, smashed windows, smashed furniture, a smashed auto roof" and that the Beatles "were nearly squashed when their big National Airlines DC-8 touched down, and scores of screaming teens broke through police lines and hurled themselves at limousines waiting to whisk the Beatles away." Airport Director Alan Stewart blamed the radio stations and news media for stirring the kids up to come to the airport and estimated over $2,000 worth of damage. A thick plate glass door leading to Concourse 3 was smashed to bits and several jalousie windows near Gates 25 and 27 were smashed out by chair-wielding teens wanting a better view of the band.

The ride to the hotel was as wild and memorable as the airport reception. The Beatles limousines were given a motorcycle escort by police that ran red lights and often traveled on the wrong side of the road against traffic to save time. Another large crowd greeted the Beatles upon their arrival at the Deauville Hotel. John and Cynthia had a private room, Paul and Ringo were roommates and Murray the K talked his way into sharing a room with George, who never understood how the disc jockey pulled that one off.

After dinner and a meeting with *Sullivan* staff, the Beatles, Brian Sommerville and Cynthia ventured out to sample the Miami nightlife. Murray the K served as tour director and Miami Beach Police Sgt. Buddy Dresner (shown top right) provided security. Their first stop was the Miami branch of the Peppermint Lounge, where they caught R&B singer Hank Ballard's show. The Beatles sat at a table in the dark, but were quickly spotted and approached by autograph seekers. They stayed until about 1:00 a.m. before heading to the Wreck Bar at the Castaways Hotel. After a round of drinks, they returned to the Deauville.

The next morning, Friday, February 14, the Beatles were scheduled for a photo session at the Deauville for an upcoming *Life* magazine story. When *Life* reporters lamented about the mobs of fans at the hotel, comedian Myron Cohen suggested that the session be moved to the backyard of a friend of his, retired jazz singer Jerri Kruger Pollak, whose husband Paul owned the Driftwood and Thunderbird Motels. The group arrived at the Pollak residence on North Bay Road and was photographed in and around the swimming pool. Jerri prepared a luncheon buffet for the boys and told them they could drop by any time. Photos from the session appeared in *Life* and other publications. The German magazine *Stern* featured a cover story titled "Up to their necks in world success" (shown middle right).

Early that afternoon the group boarded the motor yacht *Southern Trail* (bottom right), which was turned over to them, crew and all, by local businessman Bernard Castro. Paul, George and Ringo wore white terry cloth shirts sporting the Deauville Hotel crest. After the press was given the opportunity to snap their pictures, the vessel pulled out to sea. When a local photographer and reporter showed up as stowaways, Brian Sommerville had the yacht brought back to the dock to discharge the pair. The boat then left the harbor for a brief cruise during which time the group soaked up the sun. While the yacht was anchored, John, Paul and George went swimming, with Ringo opting to stay on board.

© CBS Photo Archive 2003

Paul later sat behind the yacht's piano and played a bit of *Can't Buy Me Love* for the ever-present Murray the K. Several boats passed by with their passengers waving, shouting and setting off sirens. Upon returning to shore, the Beatles went back to the Deauville.

Although original plans called for the group to begin their journey home the day after their second *Sullivan Show* appearance, the boys were having such a good time that they began to inquire about extending their stay in sunny Florida. Brian Epstein later worked out the details allowing the group to remain in Miami an extra four days.

At 6:00 p.m., the group held a rehearsal in one of the hotel's lower level rooms. Rather than changing into their jackets and ties, the boys went casual, with Paul, George and Ringo remaining in their Deauville terrycloth shirts. Ringo and George didn't bother changing out of their swimsuits. For part of the rehearsal (shown above), Harrison tried out his new Rickenbacker 12-string guitar while John, dressed in black and wearing sunglasses, strummed away on George's Gretsch Country Gentleman.

That evening the group went to Sgt. Dresner's home for a family-style American dinner. They met Buddy's wife, Dotty, and the couple's three young children, Barry, Andi and Jeri. The group wore ties as did Dresner's son, Barry. His two daughters wore fancy dresses. The meal consisted of a salad, roast beef, baked potatoes, green beans, peas and a strawberry iced cake for dessert. The Beatles appreciatively signed autographs and pictures for the family.

After returning to the Deauville at approximately 11:00 p.m., the group headed to one of the hotel's night clubs to see comedian Don Rickles, whose routine consisted of launching insults at members of the audience. Everyone was fair game, including little old ladies and, of course, the

Beatles and Sgt. Dresner. "Look at this. A police sergeant guarding four Zulus when all over the city there's fighting and burglary going on." Although the Beatles laughed along with the audience each time Rickles took aim at them, they were not amused. The group was trying to keep a low profile and resented being publicly embarrassed by the comedian. George thought it unfair that only Rickles had a microphone. "If we'd had him on our own terms we could have made mincemeat out of him."

After the show, John went off to bed, while the others headed to the Deauville's other night club to see singer/dancer Carol Lawrence and comedian Myron Cohen, who would be one of the acts on the upcoming *Ed Sullivan Show*. Afterwards they made the short walk back to their rooms.

Saturday, February 15, was a day mixing work and play. The Beatles spent the morning soaking up the sun and fishing. They were taught the basics by Sgt. Dresner, who recalled, "They wouldn't put the bait on and wouldn't take the fish off the hook, but they liked fishing." George caught a red snapper. Much to the surprise and delight of 16-year-old Linda Pollak, the Beatles acted upon her mother Jerri's offer by returning to Pollak home. The group spent a few hours relaxing around the pool with Linda and her friends.

Later that afternoon the Beatles attended a camera rehearsal (shown on the following page). In contrast to New York, dress was casual, with Ringo, George and John showing up in their Deauville shirts. John band Ringo wore sunglasses. While in Miami, the Beatles went to see the Coasters, who were performing at a local club. In their early days, the Beatles included several Coasters songs in their stage show. At their January 1, 1962, Decca audition, they performed three songs by the American R&B group: *Three Cool Cats*, *Searchin'* and *Besame Mucho*.

Sunday, February 16, started with a morning camera rehearsal. Once again the Beatles dressed casually.

Shortly after 1:30 p.m., approximately 3,500 lucky ticket holders filed into the hotel's Napoleon Room for the show's dress rehearsal, which was taped but not broadcast by CBS. The tape survives, but has yet to be released.

The Beatles opened the rehearsal with *She Loves You*, which was plagued by technical problems. John's microphone was aimed too low and failed to properly pick up his voice. When John tried to adjust it during the song, he became distracted and muffed the lyrics to the last verse. Things settled down for the first segment's remaining songs. John, Paul and George shared a single microphone for *This Boy*, which was performed to near perfection. At the end of the song, Paul told the audience "Good afternoon" and explained that the previous song, as well as the next one, *All My Loving*, was from the group's Capitol album.

Prior to the Beatles second segment, Sullivan quoted American composer Richard Rodgers as saying that the youngsters' response to the Beatles was "healthy" and that it was a "wonderful thing if they continue all through their lives to get that enthusiastic about anything." The gremlins struck again for the segment's opening number, *I Saw Her Standing There*. Paul's mike was not on for the first verse and had trouble picking up his voice until after the guitar solo. Fortunately both vocal microphones were set at the proper volume for the next tune, *From Me To You*, but as was the case with the previous song, the music was not loud enough. During Paul's introduction to the final song, the crowd kept screaming, causing John to say, "Shut up while he's talking!" Paul asked the crowd to "join in...clap your hands...stomp your feet" while John went through his spastic routine. They closed with *I Want To Hold Your Hand*.

After the song ended, Sullivan called the group over. At first he instructed the crowd to yell, but then said "Please, please be quiet because I know you want to hear what I'm going to say here. These are four of the nicest youngsters...we've ever had on our stage...And I want to tell them...how much we've enjoyed having them."

The Beatles then headed back to their rooms to relax and prepare for the evening's live broadcast. Unbeknownst to the band, total chaos would precede the show.

Early in the week, Sullivan's staff had warned the Miami Beach police and the Deauville of the ingenuity and tenacity of Beatles fans and the trouble the New York police had controlling the crowd outside the Plaza. Both assured Sullivan's people that, in Miami Beach, they were perfectly capable of handling crowds and that the hotel would be properly secured. Things did not turn out that way as youngsters swarmed the hotel's lobby and hallways.

In what Miami Beach promoter Hank Meyer later described as a "public relations disaster," several ticket holders were unable to get inside the Napoleon Room to see the show. The problem was caused by issuing more tickets than available seats, compounded by the dress rehearsal ending late, which made it difficult to get the first audience out and the second crowd seated in time for the live broadcast. Over 200 seats remained empty while several hundred ticket holders were denied entry. In addition, a few thousand fans without tickets gathered outside the hotel and in its lobby hoping to gain admittance.

The hotel's jammed lobby caused problems when it came time for the Beatles to journey from their rooms to the stage. The schedule called for the Beatles to open the show, but when *The Ed Sullivan Show* went on the air, the group had not even reached the Napoleon Room.

EXECUTIVE OFFICE

Deauville HOTEL

ON THE OCEAN AT 67th STREET • MIAMI BEACH, FLORIDA

February 14, 1964

Dear Deauville Guest:

Thank you very much for being with us at the Deauville.
To add to the enjoyment of your visit, I am enclosing
two tickets for the Ed Sullivan TV Show. The Show will
be at 8:00 p.m. Sunday, February 16 in the Napoleon
Room, Deauville Hotel, 6701 Collins Avenue, Miami Beach.

Appearing will be MITZI GAYNOR, THE BEATLES, MYRON COHEN,
THE NERVELESS KNOX'S, DANNY LEWIS, and ALLEN AND ROSSI.
Plus, of course, the RAY BLOCH orchestra, and Mr. ED
SULLIVAN.

The Napoleon Room will open at 7:00 p.m. and the doors
will <u>close</u> <u>promptly</u> at <u>7:40</u> <u>p.m.</u> No one will be admitted
to the Show after 7:40 p.m.

Admission will be by TICKET ONLY, so be sure, please,
to take your tickets with you. Seating is on a first-
come, first-served basis. Please be early and <u>please</u>
<u>be seated in the Napoleon Room by 7:40 p.m.</u> The Show
will last for approximately one hour.

I sincerely hope you enjoy this entertainment extra
we have planned for you.

Cordially,

Morris Lansburgh

Morris Lansburgh
President

P.S. Please do not leave the Napoleon Room before the
show is over, and please remain in your seats during
the show.

© CBS Photo Archive 2003

Sullivan was told to extend his introduction. "And now this has happened again. Last Sunday on our show in New York, the Beatles played to the greatest TV audience that's ever been assembled in the history of American TV. Now tonight, here in Miami Beach...again the Beatles face a record-busting audience." With the group still nowhere in sight, Sullivan talked about the weather and was forced to go to commercial. He brought out George Fenneman to introduce a Lipton Tea commercial taped earlier in the week by the Deauville Hotel swimming pool.

During the commercial break, the Beatles, flanked by Sgt. Dresner and a flying V wedge of officers and security guards, entered the room and ran through the audience to the stage. The band plugged in their guitars seconds before Sullivan gave his introduction. "Ladies and gentlemen, here are four of the nicest youngsters we've ever had on our stage, the Beatles. Bring them on now." As the curtain opened, Paul, George and John stepped up to the mikes and went straight into *She Loves You* and *This Boy*. This time there were no sound problems.

Prior to the next song, *All My Loving*, Paul greeted the audience. "Thank you, thank you very much everybody, and good evening. How are ya?" He and John then engaged in entertaining stage banter in which Paul showed his appreciation for Capitol's contribution to the band's breakthrough in America. "This song that we've just done was called *This Boy* and it is off the album we made for Capitol, LP, that's LP in English." After some members in the audience complained that they couldn't hear Paul, he repeated his message "It was off the LP we made for Capitol Records." This prompted John to shout "Oooo" and mouth off-mike "You can't say that," to which Paul replied "Of course you can!"

Paul was not about to pass up an opportunity to plug the Capitol album. Interestingly enough, neither Paul nor John ever introduced *Twist And Shout* or *Boys* as being off the Vee-Jay LP. Perhaps they were asked not to say the "V word" on stage. Vee-Jay may have been the first label in America to release Beatles records, but the band's initial success and future in America was with Capitol.

Viewers in the television audience had no idea of the chaos at the Deauville. Even those in the Napoleon Room were unaware of a close call that took place in the hotel's parking lot as the show came on the air. The TV cameras were connected by cables running outside to a truck containing the *Sullivan* production crew, monitors, consoles and communications, audio and switching equipment. Because of the heat generated by the equipment, the back doors to the vehicle were left open. Some of the fans who had been denied entry to the show noticed the truck and realized it contained TV monitors. Deciding that this would be a good place to watch the program, a horde of youngsters started running towards the open vehicle. Bill Bohnert noticed the advancing wave of frenzied fans and shut the doors seconds before their arrival. It caused some anxious moments. "They were pushing against the truck and it started to rock. I was worried that the wires would break and electrocute somebody and knock us off the air." Fortunately, once the crowd realized they needed to find another place to watch the remainder of the show, they went away.

The audience in the Napoleon Room was much more sedate than the mass of fans gathered outside. Although some local youngsters had managed to get tickets for the show, most of the audience members were guests of the Deauville and other Miami Beach hotels owned by Morris Lansburgh (see letters on previous page). The men were in suits and tuxedos and the women wore cocktail dresses. Although obviously not fans of the group, they politely applauded at the end of the group's performance.

After the Beatles left the stage, Ed Sullivan introduced then heavyweight boxing champion Sonny Liston and former champion Joe Louis, who were sitting together in the audience. Liston was in training for his February 25th fight with Cassius Clay. After another Lipton Tea commercial, the boxing theme continued in a comedy sketch by Marty Allen and Steve Rossi. Straight-man Rossi interviewed "Rocky Allen," who supposedly was going to fight the winner of the Clay/Liston fight. When asked if he was a fighter, Allen replied, "No, I'm the mother of the Beatles." This caused both laughter and screams from the audience. At the end of the interview, Allen put on a Beatle wig and went into a wild dance routine.

Next up was show headliner Mitzi Gaynor, who danced and sang *Too Darn Hot* followed by a group of standards. When her performance was over, Sullivan told the audience that the Beatles were thrilled to meet her. The next feature was a taped performance of a sway pole routine by the Nerveless Knocks filmed earlier at Florida's Hialeah Race Track. This was followed by comedian Myron Cohen.

Prior to the Beatles second segment, Sullivan attempted his own humor. "You know, Sonny Liston, actually some of these songs could fit you and your fight. One of them is *From Me To You*, that's one song they're gonna sing. And another one could fit Cassius, 'cause that song is *I Want To Hold Your Hand*. Ladies and gentlemen, here are the Beatles."

After the curtain went up, the Beatles walked to the microphones, which had been placed on the stage in front of the curtain. Unfortunately they were not set at the proper height (see photo on previous page). Paul's vocal was barely audible during *I Saw Her Standing There*. John unsuccessfully tried to adjust his flopping mike and had to bend his knees when singing his lines. After the first song, Paul and John fixed the problem by adjusting the mikes before launching into *From Me To You*. When it was over, Paul greeted the audience and used a joke of his that got laughs at the *Royal Variety Show*. "We'd like to finish off this bit with a song which has always been a great favorite of ours, this is one that was recorded by our favorite American group, Sophie Tucker." When Paul's line was met with total silence, John mockingly went "Ha, ha, ha, ha." The group then closed their *Sullivan Show* performances with the song that started it all in America, *I Want To Hold Your Hand*.

At the end of the song, the Beatles gave their customary bow and went over to Sullivan, who praised the group. "I just wanted to tell you fellows ... that Richard Rodgers, one of America's greatest composers, wanted me to congratulate you and tell the four of you that he is one of your most rabid fans. And that goes for me too. Let's have a fine hand for these youngsters."

After the program ended the Beatles attended a party thrown by Deauville Hotel owner Morris Lansburgh for the *Sullivan Show* staff and guest acts. While the other Beatles were in an upbeat mood, Ringo appeared sullen. When asked by *Sullivan* Associate Director John Moffitt

why he was feeling somber, Ringo replied, "It will never be any better than this. It's all straight down from here."

In a review published in the *Miami News* the following day, Agnes Ash called the Beatles act "high spirited and amusing." She added, "The music produced by the rock 'n' roll quartet did have a compelling rhythm. I'll bet even the old fogies...could not resist tapping a toe when the Beatles sang, 'From Me to You.'" She reported that after the show ended, the Deauville received hundreds of calls from fans who wanted to talk to the Beatles. The hotel operators took down the names and addresses of the callers for the Beatles, who promised to write the fans upon their return home. Miami station WTVJ, which broadcast the show, got complaints from viewers who described the Beatles performance with words such as "absurd, phony, nauseating, disgraceful, crude and disgusting."

With the second *Sullivan Show* over, the Beatles could now relax. By this time, the decision had been made to remain in Miami Beach until Friday. The group would have four full days of doing whatever they wanted.

Murray the K headed back to New York on Monday, leaving Sgt. Dresner to serve as both security officer and tour guide. He also became George's roommate for the next few evenings. While the group's later tours were described by John as a scene out of Fellini's orgy-filled *Satyricon*, Sgt. Dresner did a bed check every night in Miami Beach. According to Dresner, "There were no women in the rooms, no drugs–no way, shape or form. Only Scotch and Coke. That's a fact. These were the straightest, cleanest kids."

Dresner arranged for the use of a private home on Star Island. The Beatles were able to run on the beach and frolic in the waves. They also went water-skiing for the first time. Paul was described as a good water-ski pupil, who could stay upright longer than the others. John did well, and George, who preferred sitting in the shade and fishing, was the most upright when he gave it a try.

Back at the Deauville, the Beatles sat around and watched TV. From their rooms, they could see "love messages" written in the sandy beach below by female fans. Monday evening they watched the science fiction series *The Outer Limits*. During the episode, titled "The Children of Spider County," Sgt. Dresner marveled at an alien weapon and observed, "If I had one of those guns, I could zap all the criminals." The Beatles found the expression interesting as they were unfamiliar with the meaning of the word "zap." John later used it in his lyrics to *The Continuing Story Of Bungalow Bill*, "So Captain Marvel zapped him right between the eyes."

On Tuesday, February 18, the Beatles attended the workout of Cassius Clay. The meeting was set up by fight promoter Harold Conrad, who attended *The Ed Sullivan Show* with Sonny Liston. According to Conrad, Liston was not impressed with the band and commented, "Is these bums what this fuss is all about? My dog plays better drums than that kid with the big nose." After the show, Sullivan arranged for Conrad to meet the Beatles in their suite. When the group expressed interest in meeting Clay, Conrad invited them to attend the boxer's workout at the Fifth St. Gym.

UPI reported that the meeting between "Britain's bush-haired Beatles" and Cassius Clay "ended up in clowning, off-key pandemonium" and that "boxing and singing probably were set back 100 years." Clay, who often recited poetry to predict the outcome of his fights, boldly stated "When Liston reads about the Beatles visiting me, he'll be so mad I'll knock him out in three." For the first time, Cassius called someone other than himself "great" by admitting, "Man, you guys are the greatest. The whole world is shook up about you."

The meeting was attended by many reporters and photographers. Clay took charge and set up several posed shots of him triumphant over the group. Although the Beatles appeared to be enjoying themselves, John did not like being upstaged by the boxer. While Clay was scoring points with ringside observers, Lennon got in one devastating jab during the following exchange.

Cassius: You guys got to be making a lot of money. You ain't as dumb as you look.

John: But you are.

Clay would go on to defeat Liston and change his name to Muhammad Ali. The Beatles would go on to defeat their critics and change the face of popular music forever.

Sgt. Dresner took the group to see Elvis Presley's *Fun In Acapulco* at a drive-in theater. Five months earlier George had been the first Beatle to see a movie at a drive-in.

The Beatles also ventured out for a few shopping trips. They were fascinated with American clothing and reportedly spent over $6,000 in a Miami men's store. And, of course, they purchased several record albums.

Miami's elite were constantly offering the Beatles the use of beachfront homes and boats. Ringo was put behind the wheel of a speedboat and proceeded to run it into the dock. Nobody seemed to mind. Legendary powerboat designer Don Aronow took the group for rides in his

Formula 233 vessel *The Cigarette*. Paul recalls a car dealership lending each Beatle his own MG to drive around in.

The group also spent time hanging out at the Deauville. The cabana manager taught them how to snorkel in the hotel's swimming pool.

After an exciting but grueling week in the frigid Northeast, the Beatles enjoyed a week of relaxation in sunny Florida. It was a happy and innocent time. According to Paul, Miami was just like paradise because they had never been anywhere with palm trees.

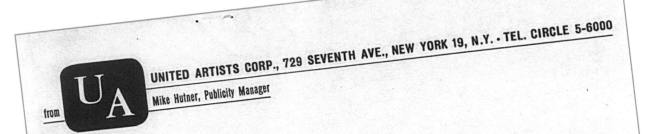

FOR IMMEDIATE RELEASE

BEATLES SING GOODBYE TO U.S.;

WILL PREPARE FOR FIRST UA FILM

- - - - - - - -

The Beatles, England's famed singing quartet who have taken the United States by storm during their two-week visit, will leave New York Friday (21) for London to prepare for their first motion picture, a United Artists release, which goes before the cameras March 2.

Six new songs have been written by The Beatles for their UA film to be produced by Walter Shenson and directed by Richard Lester from an original screen-play by Alun Owen.

Wilfrid Brambell, one of England's most popular television comedy actors, has been signed for a leading role in the motion picture.

2194

###############

FEBRUARY 21, 1964

On Friday evening, February 21, 1964, the Beatles boarded a Pan American Airways Boeing 707, appropriately renamed *Jet Clipper Beatles*, for the journey back to London. Thousands of fans braved the cold New York winter night to bid their heroes good-bye.

Thousands of fans showed up at New York's Kennedy Airport to say goodbye to the Beatles.

Two weeks after arriving in America, the Beatles began preparations for their trip back home on Friday, February 21. Because their flight from Miami to New York was not until late afternoon, the group easily had time for a farewell interview with Jack Milman of radio station WQAM. The interview took place at the Deauville Hotel and consisted of the boys thanking everybody who made their trip to Miami so successful and enjoyable.

George went first, thanking the fans for buying all the records and coming to see the group, the disc jockeys for playing the records and the police for helping the group out and organizing everything.

Paul was next, thanking Mr. Ed Sullivan for looking after the group and making them feel at home, causing John to shout "good ole Eddie!" Paul also thanked the police and singled out Sgt. Buddy Dresner, who took the group to his house and treated them to what Paul described as one of the biggest meals he'd ever eaten. He further thanked the people at the hotel, the people on the sand outside, hotel owner Morris Lansburgh and the wonderful fans.

John, referring to a presentation of a plaque by Sigma Chi fraternity members, thanked the University of Miami for giving them a plaque making them members of the fraternity. He apologized to the fans for not being able to go water skiing with them, claiming that they had to go to private homes to do it. He thanked the owners of the private homes "who shall remain omnibus" and "the press, who've been so kind," adding "most of them anyway, and the ones who weren't kind, keep trying."

Ringo thanked the disc jockeys who did such a great job plugging all their records, Capitol Records who did such great promotion and the mayor and people of Miami themselves. The group then shouted out their goodbyes to the Miami listeners.

That afternoon, Albert Maysles arrived with a camera and a friend to capture the Beatles final moments in Miami. While John and Cynthia remained in their room packing, George dropped by to visit Paul and Ringo, who were desperately trying to stuff their clothes and souvenirs into their suitcases. The three Beatles clowned around for the cameras, with Ringo playing bongos and combing his hair, Paul feeding seagulls on the balcony and George playing a blues number on an out-of-tune acoustic guitar. They also ventured out on the balcony, shouting to the fans on the sand below. These events appear on the video *The First U.S. Visit*.

In order to avoid another airport mob-scene, details of the Beatles departure were kept secret from the public. The Miami radio stations cooperated with the plan and did not broadcast flight information. The group boarded their flight from Miami to New York in relative obscurity.

Port Authority Police did their best to keep the girls from pushing through the barricades.

Multiple Choice

Which airline did the Beatles fly from Miami to New York?

A. B.O.A.C.
B. National Airlines
C. Eastern Airlines
D. Pan American Airways

Answer

Although the song *Back In The U.S.S.R.* contains the line "Flew in from Miami Beach B.O.A.C.," the Beatles did not fly British Overseas Airways Corporation during any part of their first visit to America. The group flew on National Airlines from New York to Miami, but did not purchase round trip tickets on National.

Some accounts state that the Beatles flew back to New York on Eastern Airlines; however, this is not correct. The reason this mistake was made is that there are pictures of the group descending an Eastern Airlines portable stairway in New York. While the stairway belonged to Eastern, the plane the Beatles arrived on was Pan American Airways *Jet Clipper Northern Light*.

The scene at New York's Kennedy Airport was reminiscent of the frenzied reception that greeted the band two weeks earlier. Hordes of fans braved the cold winter night to get a final glimpse of their departing heroes. Upon their arrival, the Beatles exited Pan Am *Jet Clipper Northern Light* and were escorted by members of the Port Authority Police to the plane that would take them home. Pan Am temporarily renamed the Boeing 707 *Jet Clipper Beatles* for the occasion. After climbing the stairway to the plane's entry door, the Beatles stood at the top and waved goodbye to their American fans.

Minutes later *Jet Clipper Beatles* rolled down the runway at Kennedy Airport bringing to an end the Beatles triumphant first U.S. visit. It was two weeks that neither the Beatles nor America would ever forget. The March 21, 1964, *Saturday Evening Post* observed that "When it was all over, America could relax–at least until the Beatles return this summer."

Two of the three companies that had worked so hard to make the Beatles first American visit a smashing success could also relax. Although the Beatles would appear two nights later on *The Ed Sullivan Show*, CBS merely broadcast a taped program (see page 209). In contrast to the previous weekends, the network didn't have to worry about crowd control problems or ticket requests.

Murray the K with a Port Authority Police officer.

Capitol Records could also catch its breath, though the money never stopped rolling in. *Newsweek* reported that when the Beatles left America, "they had in hand $253,000 from Capitol Records–their royalty share of the fantastic sale of 2.5 million albums and single records in just four weeks time." According to Capitol president Alan Livingston, "After that, there was no Beatles Campaign. All we had to do was release the records and meet the demand."

For United Artists, work was just beginning. Ten days later the company would commence filming the Beatles first movie, which was still untitled. That summer the film company and its United Artists Records division would run an elaborate promotional campaign for the movie *A Hard Day's Night* and its soundtrack album.

As *Jet Clipper Beatles* made its way across the Atlantic, the Beatles could also relax, but only for a few hours. They would soon face over ten thousand fans and the British press at London Airport. On Sunday, February 23, while Americans were watching a tape of the Beatles performing three songs on *The Ed Sullivan Show*, the group taped a television appearance for the variety show *Big Night Out*, which included a skit of their luggage being searched by British customs upon their return from America. Naturally their travel bags were full of cash. On Tuesday, February 25, they celebrated George's 21st birthday at Abbey Road studios where they finished their next 45, *Can't Buy Me Love* and *You Can't Do That*, and began recording songs for their upcoming movie soundtrack. On Monday, March 6, they began filming their first feature-length movie.

But on that evening of February 21, they had a few private moments to savor their triumphant conquering of America. Although they were excited by the events of the past two weeks, the Beatles were at a loss to explain why

they had been so enthusiastically embraced by America. Their reception had been beyond their wildest dreams.

The Beatles also had no idea of the effect they would have on American culture as evidenced by the following exchange between Paul and a reporter from WNBC-TV taped on February 12, 1964.

Reporter: Paul, what place do you think this story of the Beatles is going to have in the history of Western culture?
Paul: Western culture? Ah, I don't know. You must be kidding with that question. Culture, it's not culture.
Reporter: What is it?
Paul: It's a good laugh.
Reporter: You laughing at your audiences or with them?
Paul: We're laughing at ourselves, which is the main thing, isn't it?

The Beatles also had little knowledge of the convoluted chain of events that shaped the delayed birth of Beatlemania in America. They knew the names of some of the key players, such as Ed Sullivan, Murray the K, Carroll James, Sid Bernstein and Capitol Records. But they did not know about or fully understand the significance of the roles of Dave Dexter, Paul Marshall, Ewart Abner, Dick Biondi, Paul White, Bernie Binnick, Peter Prichard, Alexander Kendrick, Alan Livingston, Brown Meggs, Freddy Martin, Walter Hofer, Walter Cronkite or 15-year-old Marsha Albert.

Timing was key. What if Walter Cronkite had not aired the Alexander Kendrick story on the Beatles on December 10, 1963? Then Marsha Albert would not have written WWDC about the group, Carroll James would not have played *I Want To Hold Your Hand* on December 17, 1963, and Capitol Records would not have released its first Beatles single on December 26, 1963. Instead, the record would have been issued as planned on January 13, 1964. This would have delayed America's exposure to the group by three weeks. Had that happened, there would have been less time for the Beatles dominance of American radio to develop and therefore significantly less interest in the Beatles when they arrived in America on February 7 and played on *The Ed Sullivan Show* two days later. The enthusiastic airport reception and the record breaking television audience would not have happened without those three extra weeks of exposure and anticipation.

One must also consider the role of Dave Dexter, the man who kept turning down the Beatles as unsuitable for the American market. What if Capitol Records had released *Love Me Do* back in late 1962? The record probably would have bombed and reinforced the belief of Capitol, as well as the other major labels, that there was no interest in British music in America.

These were things the Beatles never gave any thought to. Similarly, the group didn't concern themselves with how long they would remain popular. As George stated in the first CBS story to air on the Beatles, "It's not worth missin' your sleep for, is it?" During that same interview, Paul acknowledged that their fans could lose interest tomorrow, but summed it up with, "We just hope we're gonna have quite a run." And what a run they had.

THE THIRD SULLIVAN SHOW

On Sunday, February 23, 1964, Ed Sullivan presented the Beatles for a third straight week. Although the group had departed New York two days earlier, Sullivan implied that the Beatles were appearing live on his show. Many Beatles fans watching that Sunday evening were not fooled because they knew that the group was already back home in England.

The idea for the third show came from Sullivan producer Bob Precht. After Sullivan and Brian Epstein agreed on having the Beatles appear live on two consecutive programs in February, 1964, Precht suggested the taping of an additional performance. He figured that because the *Sullivan Show* would be responsible for transportation and lodging for the group, it made economic sense to tape a third performance of the band for later broadcast.

The original plan called for holding the taped Beatles songs for a show later in the 1963-1964 television season. The December 13, 1963, press release issued by CBS referred only to the two live shows (see page 152). But by mid-January of 1964, Sullivan realized how hot the Beatles had become. He decided to run the extra performance the week after the second show. This would give Sullivan and America three consecutive weeks of the Beatles.

The third *Sullivan Show* to feature the Beatles was a bit of an anomaly for a winter broadcast. Not only was the Beatles performance on tape, but so was the rest of that show. Although *The Ed Sullivan Show* was normally broadcast live on Sunday evenings, some of the programs were shows that had been taped before a studio audience on a Monday. Most of the taped shows were shown during summer, thus enabling the Sullivan staff to vacation while viewers got fresh new shows rather than reruns. Bob Precht normally ran one taped show in February so he could vacation in the Caribbean. When the show was broadcast live, it opened with the announcement "Good evening ladies and gentlemen. Tonight, live from New York, *The Ed Sullivan Show*." When the show was on tape, the word "live" was not used.

The opening for the February 23, 1964, program does not contain the word "live." For this show, Associate Director John Moffitt edited the two Beatles segments taped on the afternoon of February 9, 1964, into the body of a show that had been previously taped on a Monday. The Beatles were used to open and close the program.

To complete the illusion that the show was a single and timely broadcast, the crew taped segments with Ed Sullivan thanking some of the acts and mentioning that the Beatles would be back later in the show. For these segments, Sullivan wore the same tie he wore on the February 9 show with the Beatles. During the Monday taping of the other show, Sullivan had worn a different tie. On the segments where Sullivan interacts with guests other than the Beatles and for most of the program's introductions, Sullivan is seen in his Monday tie. If you look closely at the video, you will notice that the stripes on the Monday tie run in a different direction than on the February 9 tie.

Sullivan opens the February 23 program in his February 9 tie and tells the television audience, "Tonight's show again stars the Beatles before their return to England. You know, we discussed it today, we're all gonna miss them. They're a bunch of nice kids." After Chef Boy-ar-dee pizza and Aero Shave shaving cream commercials, Ed introduces the band in a segment taped on February 9.

"You know all of us on the show are so darn sorry, and sincerely sorry that this is the third and thus our last current show with the Beatles because these youngsters from Liverpool, England, and their conduct over here not only as fine professional singers, but as a group of fine youngsters will leave an imprint with everyone over here who has met them. And that goes for all of us on our show. Let's bring them on. The Beatles."

Sullivan's last words are drowned out by the screaming leading into the group's performances of *Twist And Shout* and *Please Please Me* (see page 154). At the conclusion of the songs, the Beatles give their customary bow. Another taped segment is used with Sullivan telling the audience that the Beatles will be right back. This is followed by a cut to Sullivan interacting with the next guest, comic singer Gloria Bleezarde. This marks the first time the Monday tie appears. The Monday tie is also seen during Sullivan's introductions of the other acts of the show: puppets Pinky & Perky, British comedians Eric Morecambe and Ernie Wise, clarinetist Acker Bilk, Gordon & Sheila MacRae (doing a take-off on *The Garry Moore Show*), comic Dave Barry, jazz singer Cab Calloway and comic Morty Gunty. The February 9 tie is seen during most segments in which he thanks an off-camera guest. The segments appear to have been taped at another time, perhaps on February 10.

The February 23 *Sullivan Show* was not the only time the Beatles were on the same television program with Morecambe and Wise, who were the hosts of a popular program broadcast on ATV, a British television network. On December 2, 1963, the Beatles taped four songs for *The Morecambe And Wise Show* that were first broadcast on April 18, 1964. Parts of the performance appear on *Anthology 1* and on the *Anthology* video.

Sullivan's introduction for the Beatles second segment on the February 23 program was taped on February 9 before the studio audience. He is shown walking in front of the group, extending his arm and saying, "And now, ladies and gentlemen, the Beatles." The Beatles then perform *I Want To Hold Your Hand* (see page 154). After the Beatles meet with Sullivan, they leave the stage and the host announces the guests for the next week's show.

Beatles fans watching that evening were, in Sullivan's words, "so darn sorry" because they knew that they had just watched the last current show with the Beatles. Although the group would later send promotional films of their songs to the *Sullivan Show* for broadcast, the Beatles only other performance at CBS Studio 50 took place on Saturday, August 14, 1965, when the band taped six songs for the September 12, 1965, season opener of *The Ed Sullivan Show*.

YOU HAVE JUST READ HOW BEATLEMANIA EVOLVED IN THE AMERICA OF YOUR WORLD. BUT THERE ARE OTHER WORLDS IN THE MULTIVERSE...WORLDS WHERE A WHOLE NEW REALITY DEVELOPED BECAUSE A SEEMINGLY UNIMPORTANT EVENT OCCURRED JUST THE SLIGHTEST BIT DIFFERENTLY THAN ON YOUR WORLD...

...I AM **THE WATCHER!** IT IS MY DESTINY AND PRIVILEGE TO OBSERVE ALL WHICH OCCURS THROUGH-OUT THE MULTIVERSE--NOT JUST ON YOUR WORLD, BUT OTHERS AS WELL!

ON YOUR WORLD, CAPITOL RECORDS TURNED DOWN THE BEATLES 4 TIMES BEFORE AGREEING TO ISSUE "I WANT TO HOLD YOUR HAND" IN LATE 1963! BUT I HAVE VIEWED A WORLD WHERE CAPITOL REALIZED THE BEATLES POTENTIAL IN THE SUMMER OF 1963. HAVING OBSERVED THAT ALTERNATE REALITY, I CAN NOW ANSWER THE QUESTION...

WHAT IF CAPITOL RECORDS RELEASED "SHE LOVES YOU"?

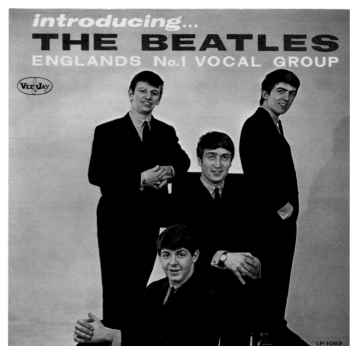

Dexter then programmed a 12-song Beatles album containing both songs from the Capitol single, the B side of the British 45 and all but two of the Lennon-McCartney originals (Vee-Jay still had the rights to *Please Please Me* and *Ask Me Why)* plus four cover tunes from the album. He decided to call the LP *Meet The Beatles!* The lineup was:

Side One
1. She Loves You
2. I Saw Her Standing There
3. I'll Get You
4. Misery
5. Boys
6. Love Me Do

Side Two
1. P.S. I Love You
2. Baby It's You
3. Do You Want To Know A Secret
4. A Taste Of Honey
5. There's A Place
6. Twist And Shout

The next week Livingston held a meeting with Dexter, Brown Meggs and Freddie Martin to put together a Beatles Campaign. And, as you'll see, the campaign was the same on this alternate world as on your world. It just started a few months earlier. Meggs came up with the slogan "The Beatles Are Coming!" and Martin pitched marketing ideas of two-page ads, counter standees, stickers, buttons and a tabloid newspaper heralding the group. Livingston requested an elaborate point-of-purchase motion display. The single was set for release on September 30, 1963, with the album to come out on October 21.

Capitol ran its first "The Beatles Are Coming!" teaser ad in the September 7, 1963, *Billboard.* Shortly thereafter, "The Beatles Are Coming!" stickers began appearing on fences, walls, school lockers and other surfaces all over

America. A special all-Beatles issue of *The National Record News,* a tabloid prepared by Capitol, was distributed in record stores, schools and colleges across the nation. The Beatles Campaign was working to perfection as all of America was asking "Just who or what are the Beatles?" *Time* magazine ran a story in its September 20 issue solving the Beatles mystery. Readers learned the Beatles were a British rock 'n' roll band with three number one hits in a row in their homeland.

Dick Biondi, who had previously played the Vee-Jay single *Please Please Me* while at WLS in Chicago, began spinning the disc at KRLA. Other stations soon followed. Vee-Jay began receiving substantial orders for its first Beatles single, which had flopped earlier in the year. With *Please Please Me* getting airplay and interest in the group growing, Capitol was forced to begin distributing its *She Loves You* single a few days earlier than planned. The disc entered the *Billboard Hot 100* on October 5 at number 78. A week later it moved up to 45. In its third week it was number three. That week the single topped the *Cash Box* chart. The next week it was also number one in *Billboard* and *Record World.* Vee-Jay's *Please Please Me* also raced up the chart and on November 2 spent its first of three straight weeks at number two behind *She Loves You.* When Vee-Jay began promoting its *From Me To You* single, that record also became a hit. On November 9, it reached the number three spot behind the other two Beatles singles.

But the Beatles success was not limited to the singles chart. Vee-Jay surprised Capitol by issuing an album titled *Introducing The Beatles* on October 4. Capitol responded with a law suit on October 7. When Vee-Jay filed an answer the next day in which it denied Capitol's allegations that Capitol had exclusive rights to the Beatles, the judge refused to grant Capitol's request for a temporary injunction and set the case for a trial on the merits to be held in early 1964. Capitol then pushed out its Beatles album on October 14. Although the two competing LPs had 10 out of 12 songs in common, both albums sold well;

however, the Capitol disc had the edge because it contained the hit single *She Loves You*. In hopes of better competing with the Capitol LP, Vee-Jay reconfigured its album by replacing *Love Me Do* and *P.S. I Love You* with *Please Please Me* and *From Me To You*. By November 9, the top two albums in the country were *Meet The Beatles!* and *Introducing The Beatles*.

Brian couldn't believe how perfect the timing was. His boys held the top three spots on the singles charts and the top two spots on the album charts. Livingston had set up a Sunday night appearance on *The Ed Sullivan Show*. Then, after a day of meetings with the press, the group would play a Tuesday night concert in the nation's capital and two shows at Carnegie Hall the following night. Brian never would have dreamed of such a perfect set up. And all because Capitol Records had released *She Loves You*.

American radio was saturated with Beatles songs. In addition to the three hit singles, stations were playing songs from the albums. *Twist And Shout* and *Do You Want To Know A Secret* were being played almost as much as the 45s. Program directors were surprised to find that *Boys*, a rocker sung by Ringo, was getting numerous requests. To further build excitement, Capitol supplied radio stations with open-end interview discs.

That November, the Beatles were the talk of the nation. American youngsters were anxiously awaiting the day the group would arrive in New York. Capitol gave the press full details of the Beatles travel plans and encouraged disc jockeys to tell listeners to meet the Beatles at the airport.

When the Beatles plane landed in New York at 12:20 p.m. on an overcast Friday afternoon, the group was greeted by over 3,000 screaming fans. After clearing customs, the Beatles gave their first American press conference. The scene inside the press room was total chaos. Photographers were fighting to get the best shots of the "long-haired kids." Reporters were shouting out questions. Press agent Brian Sommerville lost his cool and yelled for everyone to "please shut up!" Once order was restored, the Beatles began charming the press with their clever answers.

Suddenly, a few reporters in the back of the room began talking loudly. As John looked out, he could see several members of the press were agitated and were heading towards the exit. He called out, "Hey, is it something we said? We were only kidding about the campaign to stamp out Detroit. We love the city because it's the home of Motown and Tamla Records." As John was speaking, a reporter came up to Brian Sommerville and told him what was going on. Sommerville's face turned pale. He motioned for John to be quiet and grabbed a microphone. "I don't know if all of you have heard the news, but President Kennedy has been shot. Obviously, you may need to call your papers and stations. Out of respect for the President, this press conference is over. Let us pray, let us pray."

The Beatles stood behind the rows of microphones in total shock. A few photographers managed to put their emotions aside and shoot pictures of the Beatles and the members of the press leaving the room. The group was quickly escorted to their limousines and driven to the Plaza Hotel. They listened to the radio and heard the details of three

shots ringing out in Dallas, Texas. The announcer speculated as to whether or not the President had survived, warning listeners that United Press had reported that the shots may have been fatal. By the time the cars neared the Plaza, it was official. President Kennedy was dead.

Only a few fans remained by the hotel when the Beatles arrived. Most had gone home to be with their families. Those outside had sullen faces and waved in slow motion. The group was escorted to their rooms, where they remained for the rest of the day, watching television coverage of the assassination.

That evening, the group had dinner in their suite. Shortly after 7:00 p.m., Maureen Cleave, a reporter for the British newspaper *Evening Standard*, called the Beatles to see how the boys were doing. She had traveled to America with the group and was staying at the Plaza. Ringo invited her to their suite.

When Maureen arrived, she sat down and watched coverage of the assassination with the others in the room. Brian Epstein had cancelled both a telephone interview with Brian Matthew of the BBC and the Maysles Brothers' filming of the group's visit. Maureen had gained access to the Beatles suite as a friend, not as a reporter. Unbeknownst to the boys, she planned on obtaining a few quotes for an article on how the Beatles trip had been altered by the day's tragic events.

Later that evening, she telephoned the *Evening Standard* with the story, which contained several quotes from John. "It's been a horrible day, you know. We didn't know much about President Kennedy, but from what we've seen on the telly, he was a great man loved by his country. We've been sitting around in shock."

When asked whether the group was going to play *The Ed Sullivan Show* on Sunday, John replied, "They haven't called us, so we don't know if the show's been cancelled or not. I mean, I don't think we should play. It doesn't seem right, you know? But if they want us to do the show, we will. You know, the show must go on and all that. Maybe Americans need a diversion. If so, we'll make them forget about Kennedy for a while."

On Saturday morning, Ed Sullivan telephoned Brian Epstein to inform him that there would be no show on Sunday because CBS had cancelled all regular programming. George, who had a nasty sore throat, remained in bed, while the others ventured out for a walk through Central Park. Only a handful of people were in the park, so the boys were able to move about freely. That evening, Capitol Records took John, Paul and Ringo to dinner.

Meanwhile, a reporter for *The New York Times* was putting together a story on foreign reaction to the President's death. He heard about Maureen Cleave's article on the Beatles American visit and thought it would be interesting to include a quote from the group. Although he wrote a full paragraph on the band's comments, his story was edited and ended with John saying, "We'll make them forget about Kennedy."

On Sunday morning Brian Epstein was having breakfast in his room when Brian Sommerville barged in. He explained to Epstein that they had a problem. John had been quoted in *The New York Times* about the Kennedy assassination. His exact words, "We'll make them forget about Kennedy." Sommerville explained that radio stations WMCA and WABC were airing phone calls from angry listeners. Most interpreted Lennon's remark to mean that John thought the Beatles were more popular than Kennedy. Listeners were outraged that a group of long-haired British musicians thought the youth of America cared more about them than the slain President. Disc jockeys were assuring listeners that their stations would never play a Beatles record again. It would only be a matter of time before the story spread across the nation. The group had to put out a statement as soon as possible to control the damage.

Epstein wanted to protect his boys, so he decided that the press would not be allowed to talk directly to the group. Instead, he issued a press release.

"The Beatles are saddened by the tragic death of President Kennedy and have cancelled all scheduled American performances out of respect for the President, his family and the people of America. Comments from John Lennon that appeared in *The New York Times* were taken out of context and do not accurately reflect the group's feelings. The Beatles send their condolences to the Kennedy family and the people of America."

Because the television and concert appearances had been cancelled, the Beatles headed back to England on Monday, November 25, the day President Kennedy was buried. In contrast to the reception that greeted the band just three days before, no one was at the airport to see them off. Out of fear for the boys' safety, their travel plans had been kept secret from the media and radio stations.

During the week the full force of the fallout from John's remark became known. Nearly all radio stations in America had pulled all Beatles records from their playlists. Editorials and columns in newspapers and magazines blasted the band. Letters to the editor were brutal, with only a handful of writers protesting that John's remark had been taken out of context. Radio stations felt betrayed because they had been the Beatles biggest supporters. Many organized bonfires to burn Beatles trash and crush their records.

On Friday, November 29, a 45 containing *I Want To Hold Your Hand* and *This Boy* was released in the U.K. as the Beatles fifth single. The record had advance sales of over one million units and jumped to the top of the charts.

In America, it was a totally different story. Capitol had planned on issuing the same single on December 6, but delayed the release until December 13 to allow things to cool off. The company knew that it would be difficult to get airplay, so it only pressed 50,000 copies. Although program directors admitted to Capitol sales reps that the song was terrific, they explained that America had not forgiven John and that there was no way they could play the record. Knowing that radio airplay would be minimal and that many parents would not allow their children to play records by "those British bums," record store orders were dismal, with some stores even refusing to stock the 45. *Billboard* charted *I Want To Hold Your Hand* at 99 for one week and then at 86 before dropping the song altogether.

In early January, 1964, Brian received a call from Bud Ornstein of United Artists informing him the company was not going to do a Beatles movie. Ornstein explained that the reason UA wanted to do a film was to obtain the rights to issue a soundtrack album in the States. Because no one was buying Beatles records in America, UA could not count on making money from record sales and was worried that the film would lose money. Ornstein told Brian that UA would send the Beatles a check for one thousand pounds as per the contract's cancellation clause.

The Beatles had a few more hit singles in England, but were soon eclipsed by other bands such as the Dave Clark Five, Gerry & the Pacemakers and the Hollies. By late November of 1964, the Beatles broke up.

Ringo decided against joining another band and opened a string of beauty salons. George Martin and Ron Richards frequently booked him as a session drummer to provide his steady beat for recordings by Cilla Black and others.

John and Paul continued their songwriting partnership and penned several hits for groups managed by Brian Epstein. They also wrote songs for musicals developed for London's West End theaters. However, out of fear that John's name would preclude a song from getting airplay in the States, all Lennon-McCartney originals were credited to "Bernard Webb."

George visited his sister Louise in Benton, Illinois, during the Christmas season of 1964. While there, George met with Gabe McCarty, who talked him into moving to America and joining his band, the Four Vests. Gabe was going to rename the group the Five Vests, but Harrison thought the vest gimmick was outdated and suggested that the band be called the Dark Horses. A few months later, the group signed a contract with A&M Records. During the next few years, the Dark Horses had several hit singles, all penned by Harrison. *I Need You*, *Taxman*, *Something*, *Here Comes The Sun*, *All Things Must Pass* and *My Sweet Lord* topped the charts on both sides of the Atlantic.

And that's the way it was on that alternate world. And all because Capitol Records released *She Loves You*. In the multiverse, things happen for a reason. I know because... I am the Watcher!

Radio, Radio

Shortly after arriving at their Plaza suite on February 7, 1964, the Beatles were met by a representative of the Pepsi Cola company, who presented each of the Beatles with a transistor radio designed to look like a Pepsi Cola vending machine (shown actual size right). It came with a black wrap-around case and an earphone.

The Beatles immediately put the radios to use, sampling the New York stations. The Pepsi radios appear in some of the pictures taken at the Plaza (see page 138). They also appear throughout the New York scenes in *The First U.S. Visit* video. Paul is shown carrying his radio as the Beatles leave the Plaza on Saturday morning. During the Central Park photo session, Paul pulls the Pepsi radio out of his pocket and says, "For the continuity of the story, I'd like to reintroduce the radio." McCartney is shown listening to WINS during the ride from Central Park to the Saturday afternoon *Ed Sullivan* rehearsal. He and George have their transistors playing on Saturday evening when the boys are on the phone with Murray the K. All four Beatles are shown listening to *I Want To Hold Your Hand* through their radio earphones as they leave their Plaza suite on Sunday evening to perform on *The Ed Sullivan Show*. The Pepsi radios also appear in segments taken at the Plaza and edited into the closing credits.

The Beatles were totally infatuated with American radio. They were also impressed with New York's flamboyant disc jockeys, who took advantage of the situation by recording bits of conversation with the boys for use in station promos. The disc jockeys would ask a Beatle to repeat a line, answer a question or say whatever he wanted. And, most important of all, mention the station's call letters. WMCA edited over a dozen Beatles promos from tape recordings made by the Good Guys.

Murray the K had the edge over the other disc jockeys due to his special relationship with the band. While the Beatles were relaxing in their suite prior to their *Ed Sullivan Show* performance, Murray kept an open phone line to his station. He got each of the boys to shout out the station's call letters. John and Ringo obliged with "WINS 1010," while Paul went with "WINS Winston Churchill."

When Brian found out about this, he was upset with the group for giving away valuable promotional spots to radio stations for free. By the time the band was in Washington, Brian's message had gotten through. At the end of an interview, Ringo says, "Everything's happening, baby! With Murray the K on, I'm not allowed to say that."

John admitted that the group was "over-awed" by American radio. "Epstein, our manager, had to stop us. We phoned every radio [station] in town, just saying, 'will you play the Ronettes?' We didn't ask for our own records, we asked for other people."

The Beatles infatuation with American radio was mutual. By the time the group arrived in America, several of their songs were being played in heavy rotation, particularly by stations in two of the cities that hosted the Beatles.

WMCA was the first station in New York to play *I Want To Hold Your Hand*, listing the single as a "Sure Shot" on its January 1, 1964, survey. The next week the song debuted at ten before reaching the top on January 15. It held down the top spot for two more weeks before being replaced by *She Loves You* on February 5. That same week *Please Please Me* was number ten. *She Loves You* topped the WMCA chart for seven weeks. WABC charted *I Want To Hold Your Hand* at 35 on its December 31, 1963, survey. The next week the song spent its first of six weeks at the top before being replaced by *She Loves You*. The February 11 chart listed *I Want To Hold Your Hand* at one, *She Loves You* at two, *Please Please Me* at nine, *My Bonnie* at 19 and *All My Loving* and *Till There Was You* (both played on the *Sullivan Show*) as album cuts. WINS charted the three major Beatles hit singles in the top three spots.

In Miami, WFUN played *I Want To Hold Your Hand* shortly after the record's release. Although WQAM was a week or two behind, the station's January 25, 1964, survey debuted the single at number one. Its February 1 chart added *She Loves You* at 25. The next week the two Beatles singles held down the top two spots with *Please Please Me* at 36. The February 22 survey had the Beatles holding down the top three spots (*She Loves You*, *I Want To Hold Your Hand* and *Please Please Me*) plus *My Bonnie* at 13. WFUN also gave the Beatles the top three spots.

MAGAZINES

Although the Beatles would soon appear on the cover of numerous magazines, only a handful of American publications featured the Beatles prior to or during their first U.S. visit. The February 24, 1964, issue of *Newsweek*, which hit newsstands a week earlier, ran the first American cover story on the group. The article showed a picture of the band performing at the Washington Coliseum superimposed in front of the unused Beatles backdrop from *The Ed Sullivan Show* (see page 147). PYX published a Beatles magazine (shown upper right) featuring a colorized version of the Dezo Hoffmann photo that appeared on the back of the *Meet The Beatles!* album. Several radio stations, including Miami's WQAM, ordered customized copies of the magazine with their call letters on the cover to distribute to their listeners. Pictures taken at Penn Station and outside the Plaza (see pages 186 and 187) show Beatles fans holding copies of the *Beatles 'Round The World* magazine. *The Original Beatles Book* was rushed out immediately after the Carnegie Hall concerts.

MERCHANDISING

Beatles fans would soon be able to purchase Beatle lunch boxes, school supplies (book covers, 3-ring binders, pencils and pens), posters, pennants, pillows, scarfs, socks, sneakers, stockings, shoulder bags, purses, wallets, jewelry, trays, glasses, dishes, lamps, plastic model kits, bobbing-head dolls, inflatable dolls, record players, record carrying cases, headphones, plastic guitars, bongos, licorice, ice cream, bubble gum trading cards, Halloween costumes, combs, shampoo, bubble bath and even hair spray. But in February, 1964, only a few Beatle merchandise items were available in America.

Department stores carried official Beatle sweatshirts, with prices ranging from $1.57 to $3.98. The February 24, 1964, *Newsweek* reported that 200,000 of the sweatshirts were shipped and that over a half million Beatle wigs were on back order. Ed Sullivan put on one of the silly-looking wigs before the February 9, 1964, dress rehearsal. Fans could also cover their heads with funny beach hats that came in red and white and blue and white versions. A couple of different buttons were available. Although the official button sold at the Beatles first U.S. concert in Washington, D.C., misspelled the group's name as "Beetles," fans still bought and wore them that evening. *Newsweek* reported that, "For those who want to hug a Beatle (or stick a pin in one), the market will soon be crawling with Beatles dolls [from Remco]."

Reliance Manufacturing Co. secured the exclusive right to manufacture clothing with images of the Beatles. In its first two weeks, the company sold Beatles merchandise valued at 1.4 million dollars wholesale (2.5 million dollars retail). Lowell Toy Company obtained the right to produce Beatle wigs. Lawyers pursued several businesses for the unauthorized production and sale of Beatles items.

© CBS Photo Archive 2003

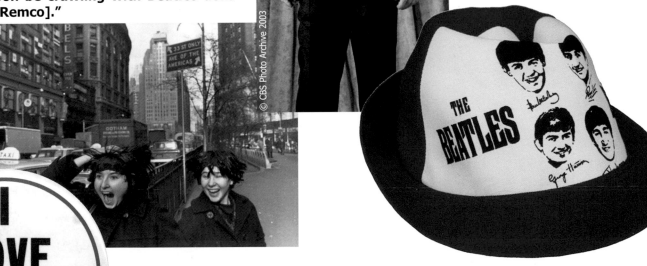

MISCELLANEOUS MYTHS

Myth

During the hour the Beatles were on *The Ed Sullivan Show*, no crimes were committed in America.

Fact

It is highly unlikely that all criminals suspended their activities to watch the Beatles on television on February 9, 1964. The myth grew from the following paragraph appearing in the February 24, 1964, *Newsweek*:

There were many post-teen-agers, however, who took an uncharitable view of the swarms of Beatle fans. Bill Gold, writing in The *Washington Post*, expressed this position rather sharply: "'Don't knock the Beatles,' counsels B.F. Henry. 'During the hour they were on Ed Sullivan's show, there wasn't a hubcap stolen in America.'"

Myth

The Beatles were taken from Miami International Airport to the Deauville Hotel in a red double-decker bus.

Fact

Although Deauville owner Morris Lansburgh sent Ed Sullivan a telegram informing him that the group would be driven to the hotel in a double-decker bus that once was part of the London transportation system, this plan was abandoned. Instead, the group traveled in limousines. The same telegram told Sullivan that Sonny Liston and Carol Lawrence would be at the airport to greet the band. Those plans also fell through.

Myth

During the reception held at the British Embassy on February 11, 1964, the wife of a British dignitary snipped off a lock of Ringo's hair.

Fact

Although a female snipped off a bit of Ringo's hair, she was not a British socialite. The "Embassy Barber" was 18-year-old Beverly Markowitz of Silver Spring, Maryland, who had crashed the party. Prior to sneaking up on Ringo with a nail scissors, she obtained the drummer's autograph.

Myth

The Beatles resented Capitol Records for initially turning them down and reconfiguring their records.

Fact

Although the Beatles later grew to resent Capitol's restructuring of their albums, the group was appreciative of Capitol's promotional efforts and voiced no objections to the *Meet The Beatles!* album. At the Washington Coliseum press conference, George was asked when the group's records first came out in America. He replied, "Actually, the first one was released about a year ago, but it wasn't until we got on to Capitol and got a bit of promotion that the records caught on." Paul plugged Capitol during the second *Ed Sullivan Show* (see page 201). Ringo also had praise for Capitol during the group's final interview of the first U.S. visit on February 21, 1964.

Myth

The Beatles only attracted young female fans.

Fact

The Beatles also appealed to older women as well as male youngsters. Film shot by CBS at Kennedy Airport (see image center) shows a reporter interviewing and being bumped by a large group of teenage boys. Some are there because they like the group. Others are there to protest or to be part of the action. One shouts out "the Beatles are great. All Manhattan says so." Another screams "the Beatles are phony." The reporter asks the boys if they like the Beatles and gets a variety of answers. "They're great. I think they're boss." "I think they're perfect. Just great." "I like the Trashmen [a group from Minneapolis who had recently scored a number four hit with the garage band classic *Surfin' Bird*]." One young man protests that "they're taking money out of America and bringing it to England when we need money here." The reporter finally gets around to asking a young woman what she thinks of the group and is told, "I think they're sharp. I like the beat."

Myth

Poor Ringo was the least popular Beatle.

Fact

The Beatles drummer was the favorite of the American crowd. His name frequently appeared on signs (see page 187) and was shouted out by fans during performances. When asked by Murray the K why he was the fan favorite, he replied, "I don't understand it. Maybe it's the name. A lot of people remember Ringo 'cause the name stands out. I just don't know." Much to the surprise of everyone, Ringo received more American fan mail than any of his fellow band members. When asked why, Ringo replied, "I dunno. I suppose it's because more people write me."

Myth

The Deauville Hotel had to sue to the Beatles to collect incidental charges made by John, Paul, George and Ringo to their rooms.

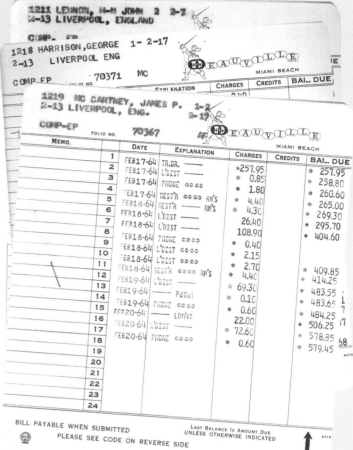

BE
BM

CABLE HOFERESQ NEWYORK

LAW OFFICES
WALTER HOFER
150 WEST 55TH STREET
NEW YORK, N.Y. 10019
JUDSON 2-5030

THOMAS R. LEVY

13 MAR 1964

March 9, 1964

Mr. Brian Epstein
24 Moorfields
Liverpool, England

Re: DEAUVILLE HOTEL

Dear Brian:

I enclose herewith for your approval, or otherwise, the bills we received from the Deauville Hotel in Miami, Florida.

With all good wishes, I remain

Sincerely yours,

WALTER HOFER

SH/njw

enc.

DATE	DESCRIPTION	CHARGES	CREDITS	BALANCE
	BALANCE FORWARDED —			
Feb. 21	M/M John Lennon	508.41		
	James P. McCartney	579.45		
	Richard Starkey	312.51		
	George Harrison	353.47		
	Brian Somerville	460.27		
	Neil Apinall	211.22		
	Robert Freeman	141.18		
		$2566.51	$2566.51	

Fact

The main hotel bill for the Beatles stay at the Deauville was taken care of at the time of the group's departure; however, individual charges made by the group, Brian Sommerville, Neil Aspinall, Robert Freeman and Brian Epstein were not paid until later. These charges, totaling $3,185.20, consisted of purchases at the hotel's shops (swim suits, terrycloth shirts and cigarettes), long distance phone calls, room service and beverage charges at the hotel's Cyrand Lounge, Patio Bar and Cafe De LaMer. Duplicate bills of the charges were sent to Brian Epstein's attorney, Walter Hofer, for payment. Hofer forwarded the bills to Brian on March 9. In mid-April, Epstein instructed Hofer to pay the Deauville the $618.69 part of the bill representing his expenses. Apparently Brian wanted additional time to confirm the alleged charges incurred by the others.

By July, the bill still had not been paid, prompting the Deauville to announce plans to attend the Beatles concert appearance in Jacksonville, Florida, on September 22, 1964, to collect the money owed in person. On July 9, the Miami newspapers reported that the bill had finally been paid in full. *The Miami Herald* ran the following quote from hotel owner Morris Lansburgh:

"There was no apology included with the check, but we feel one was not necessary. They are busy men, and we're sure it was just a mix-up. It would be a pleasure to have them stay here again."

The Deauville documents detailing the charges made by the Beatles and their entourage survive. Interestingly, the hotel mistakenly failed to include in its master bill $71.00 in charges made by Mal Evans.

THE ED SULLIVAN SHOW REMEMBERED

"*The Ed Sullivan Show* was very important. I still get people talking to me about it now, you know. It's like where were you when Kennedy was shot?" Paul McCartney

"We were aware that *Ed Sullivan* was the big one." George Harrison

"The main thing I was aware of when we did the first *Ed Sullivan Show* was that we rehearsed all afternoon." Ringo Starr

"Good ole Eddie!" John Lennon

"The Beatles first appeared on our show on February 9, 1964, and I have never seen any scenes to compare with the bedlam that was occasioned by their debut. Broadway was jammed with people for almost eight blocks. They screamed, yelled and stopped traffic. It was indescribable. There has never been anything like it in show business, and the New York police were very happy it didn't and wouldn't happen again." Ed Sullivan

"On the day of the broadcast...there was complete pandemonium. Mass hysteria. I don't think the Beatles believed what was happening. No one believed it." Vince Calandra, *Sullivan* Production Assistant

"They were four great guys who were really enjoying all the attention. They just couldn't believe their good fortune." John Moffitt, *Sullivan* Associate Director

"The Beatles were very relaxed and pleasant, having a good time riding the wave." Bill Bohnert, *Sullivan* Set Designer

"We took them to Ed's office and quizzed them about everything. They were a bunch of down-to-earth kids who thought it was all a lark, a flash in the pan that wouldn't last. John and Paul were our favorites, the friendliest and most talkative. George was quieter. Ringo was the least congenial." Ann Cremmons, *Sullivan* Production Secretary

"All of the Beatles were witty, charming and professional; not 'entitled' in any way. Brian seemed to me just your typical red-faced Englishman. Paul sang the lyrics of *She Loves You* to me as I copied them down for the show. [See photo on page 145.] He was darling and I had such a crush on him, but I played it cool." Kathie Kuehl, *Sullivan* Production Secretary

"I never believed when Ed booked the Beatles that it would be so big. It was just another act. By the time the show went on the air, it became a piece of theatrical history. It was an agent's dream to get a reaction like that." Peter Prichard, British theatrical agent

"I was amazed that these figures on the stage could generate such hysteria." Walter Cronkite

***Sullivan* Production Secretary Emily Cole positions herself to be photographed with Paul McCartney conferring with George Martin on the Miami show stage.**

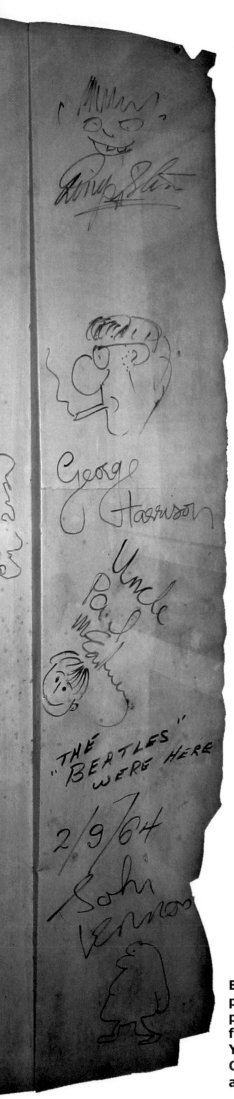

Some guests on *The Ed Sullivan Show* during the 1963-1964 season signed the back of the hard wall used on the set (see blue wall on page 154). After the wall was dismantled at season's end, the four-foot-tall section signed by the Beatles (left) was saved. For years it was in a bar in Baton Rouge, Louisiana, before being purchased by a private collector.

Beatles road managers Neil Aspinall and Mal Evans autographed hundreds of promotional pictures of the group for distribution during the first U.S. visit. The pair signed pictures from the British Beatles Fan Club (above left) on the plane flight over and Capitol promotional glossies (above right) after arriving in New York. The Beatles signed several autographs during their first U.S. visit. CONSUMER ALERT: Although hundreds of signed U.S. album covers exist, nearly all are forgeries. A rare exception is the *Meet The Beatles!* cover shown above.

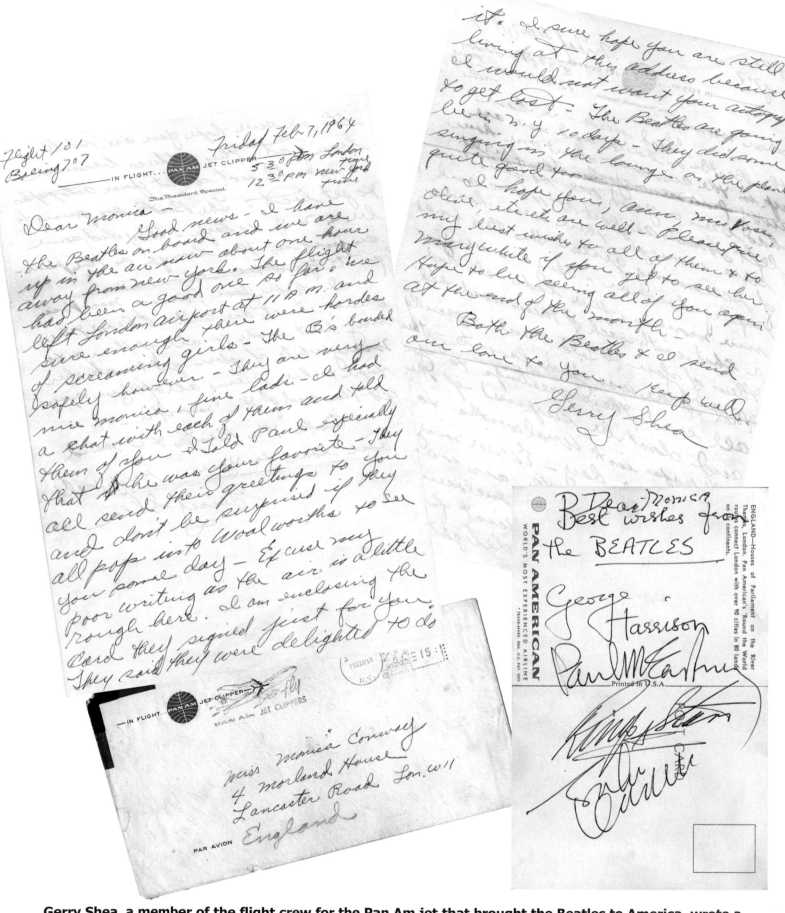

Gerry Shea, a member of the flight crew for the Pan Am jet that brought the Beatles to America, wrote a letter to Monica Conway of London as the plane was nearing New York. Shea gave Monica the good news that the Beatles were on board the plane. He told her of the hordes of screaming girls seeing them off at the airport. Shea wrote that the Beatles were very nice and that he chatted with each of them, telling the group about her. He said that he told Paul that he was her favorite and naively added that she shouldn't be surprised if they all popped into Woolworth's to see her some day. Shea told Monica that the group sang in the plane's lounge and that they were quite good. He enclosed a Pan Am post card that was autographed by the Beatles. The letter appears courtesy of *ICE* magazine's Pete Howard.

FAB FOUR FIRSTS IN AMERICA

First music industry company to express an interest in the Beatles. Would you believe Capitol Records? Well, indirectly, Capitol Records was the first. Capitol's music publishing subsidiary, Beechwood Music Corporation, set up Ardmore & Beechwood Ltd. as a British joint stock company to handle music publishing in England. Sid Colman was the company's general manager. In 1962, Colman obtained the publishing rights for the Lennon-McCartney songs *Love Me Do* and *P.S. I Love You* for Ardmore & Beechwood. Thus, a company controlled by a Capitol subsidiary became the first company to publish songs written by the Beatles. Colman had been the person who referred Brian Epstein to George Martin, head of Parlophone Records, which was owned by EMI, the company that owned Capitol. (See page 106.)

First American record company to turn down the Beatles. Would you believe Capitol Records? Even though an employee of Capitol's British publishing company was responsible for getting the Beatles signed to Parlophone, the company turned down the Beatles first two singles, *Love Me Do* and *Please Please Me*. Capitol would later turn down *She Loves You* and initially pass on *I Want To Hold Your Hand* before wising up. (See pages 11, 14, 40-41 and 72.)

First American record company to sign the Beatles. Vee-Jay Records, a Chicago company specializing in R&B and gospel recordings, entered into a five-year licensing agreement for *Please Please Me* and *Ask Me Why* on January 10, 1963. A rider to the agreement gave Vee-Jay a right of first refusal for all future Beatles recordings issued during the length of the five-year contract. (See page 14.)

First American company to obtain publishing rights for a Lennon-McCartney song. Although Ardmore and Beechwood Ltd. controlled the publishing for *Love Me Do* and *P.S. I Love You*, the American rights to the songs were not granted to Capitol's Beechwood Music Corporation until May 6, 1963. Concertone Songs obtained the American publishing rights for *Please Please Me* and *Ask Me Why* in January, 1963. (See pages 15 and 106.)

First Beatles record released in the United States. Although *Love Me Do* was the first Beatles record released in Britain, the song was not issued as a single in the United States until April, 1964. The first Beatles record released in America was Vee-Jay's *Please Please Me* single (VJ 498), which was issued on February 7, 1963, exactly one year prior to the Beatles arrival in America. This record has *Ask Me Why* on the B side and should not be confused with the later issued VJ 581, which has *From Me To You* on its flip side. (Although *My Bonnie* was released on Decca 31382 on April 23, 1962, the disc is not a Beatles record. The song is by Tony Sheridan backed by the Beatles, who are identified as "the Beat Brothers" on the label. When MGM later issued the song in January, 1964, the record was misleadingly credited to "THE BEATLES with Tony Sheridan.") (See pages 15 and 91.)

First Beatles song played on the radio in the United States. *Please Please Me* on WLS (Chicago) in February, 1963, played by Dick Biondi, WLS. (See page 17.)

First Beatles song heard on American television. *Please Please Me* (VJ 498) was reportedly played on ABC TV's *American Bandstand* hosted by Dick Clark in the spring of 1963. A staff member recalls it averaging a score of 81⅔ on the show's Rate-A-Record segment. (See page 46.)

First song written by the Lennon-McCartney team to hit a national American chart. *From Me To You* entered the *Billboard Hot 100* on June 29, 1963, at number 96. But it was the Del Shannon cover version of the song that charted. The Beatles recording of the song could do no better than 116 on the *Billboard Bubbling Under The Hot 100* listing. (See pages 30-31.)

First disc jockey to interview a Beatle for an American radio station. High school student Marcia Shafer interviewed George Harrison live on WFRX in West Frankfort, Illinois, during George's September, 1963, visit to America. (See page 48.)

First performance by a Beatle in America. George Harrison joined the Four Vests on stage during the band's September 28, 1963, concert at the VFW Hall in Eldorado, Illinois. (See pages 48-49.)

First image of the Beatles to appear on American television. Dick Clark recalls showing viewers a picture of the group during a September, 1963, broadcast of his *American Bandstand* show when he played the group's latest single, *She Loves You*. (See page 46.)

First American television appearance of the Beatles. Although most people think the Beatles first American television appearance was on *The Ed Sullivan Show*, this is not correct. While the February 9, 1964, *Sullivan Show* was the group's first live performance on American television, a clip of the band performing *She Loves You* was shown on the January 3, 1964, *Jack Paar Program*. This, however, was not the first time the Beatles were shown performing *She Loves You* on American television. The February 24, 1964, issue of *Newsweek* referred to a story on the Beatles that ran on the *CBS Evening News with Walter Cronkite* on December 10, 1963. The story, filed by Alexander Kendrick, contained concert footage of the Beatles filmed on November 16, 1963, in Bournemouth, England. For nearly 40 years Beatles experts believed this to be the group's first appearance on American TV; however, documents stored at the Library of Congress indicate that NBC ran a Beatles story filed by Edwin Newman on the November 18, 1963, *Huntley-Brinkley Report*. (See pages 60-61, 87-89 and 148-157.)

First Beatles album issued in North America. Capitol of Canada released *Beatlemania! With The Beatles* on November 25, 1963. (See pages 66-68.)

First Beatles album issued in the United States. Vee-Jay Records released *Introducing The Beatles* on January 10, 1964. The record was not, as often reported, issued in the summer of 1963. Still, it hit the stores more than a week before the official release date of Capitol's *Meet The Beatles!* (See pages 94-96.)

First disc jockey to play *I Want To Hold Your Hand* on American radio. On December 17, 1963, Carroll James of WWDC played the song on the Parlophone 45. (See page 82.)

First Beatles song to reach number one on a national American chart. The *Cash Box Top 100* for January 25, 1964, reported *I Want To Hold Your Hand* at number one. The song topped the *Billboard Hot 100* on February 1, 1964. (See pages 83 and 112-114.)

First Beatles album to top the charts in America. The *Billboard Top LP's* chart for February 15, 1964, reported *Meet The Beatles!* as the number one album in America. (See page 118.)

First Beatle off the plane in New York. George Harrison, who had been the first Beatle to set foot on American soil back in September, 1963, was the first Beatle to set foot on the Kennedy Airport tarmac on February 7, 1964. He was directly preceded by Pan Am stewardess Betty Harrison (no relation) (see page 2).

First Beatles press conference in America. The Beatles first faced the U.S. media during a press conference held at Kennedy Airport shortly after their arrival in New York on February 7, 1964. (See pages 5, 132 and 135.)

First national news program watched by the Beatles in New York. At 6:30 p.m. on February 7, 1964, the Beatles watched the *CBS Evening News with Walter Cronkite*. At the end of the broadcast, the Beatles were shown exiting the plane, standing on the tarmac and answering questions at their airport press conference. *The First U.S. Visit* video shows the group watching themselves on the show, as does the photograph on page 138. The image on the television set is that of Pan Am stewardess Betty Harrison (left) standing with the Beatles on the tarmac.

First song performed by the Beatles in front of an American audience. During the dress rehearsal for the Sunday, February 9, 1964, *Ed Sullivan Show*, the Beatles played the same songs that they would later perform during the live broadcast of the show. The first song was *All My Loving*. (See pages 153 and 155.)

First performance of the Beatles seen live on American television. The Beatles appearance on the February 9, 1964, *Ed Sullivan Show* was seen by a then-record American television audience of over 73 million people. The group performed *All My Loving*, *Till There Was You* and *She Loves You* to open the show and *I Saw Her Standing There* and *I Want To Hold Your Hand* during their second segment. (See pages 148-157.)

First Beatles concert in America. The Beatles first American concert took place on February 11, 1964, at the Washington Coliseum, a boxing arena in Washington, D.C. (See pages 176-183.)

First song performed by the Beatles during their first American concert. The Beatles opened their first American concert with George singing lead on *Roll Over Beethoven*. (See pages 180 and 182.)

First song to end the Beatles 14-week run at the top of the *Billboard Hot 100* singles chart. *I Want To Hold Your Hand* became the first Beatles single to top the *Billboard Hot 100* on February 1, 1964. It remained number one for seven weeks before being replaced by *She Loves You*, which held the number one spot for two weeks before *Can't Buy Me Love* began its four-week run. Finally, on May 9, 1964, the Beatles surrendered the top spot to Louis Armstrong's recording of *Hello, Dolly!*

First Capitol Records stock ad promoting the first Capitol Beatles album, *Meet The Beatles!* Capitol prepared the above ad for record stores to use for newspapers. Liberty Music shops ran the ad in the January 12, 1964, *New York Times* (see page 118).

HOW VEE-JAY SQUEEZED 16 OR SO RECORDS FROM 16 BEATLES SONGS

Although most people think of Capitol Records when they think of the Beatles U.S. albums and singles, the very first American discs containing Beatles songs appeared on Vee-Jay, a Chicago-based independent label that specialized in R&B and gospel recordings. As detailed earlier in this book, Vee-Jay ended up with the Beatles shortly after Capitol turned down the group's second single, *Please Please Me*. When George Martin pushed EMI to get the disc issued in the States, New York attorney Paul Marshall, who represented both EMI and Vee-Jay, set up a five-year licensing agreement between Vee-Jay and EMI's U.S. agent, Transglobal Music Co., Inc. Although the contract specifically covered only the masters for *Please Please Me* and *Ask Me Why*, an attached rider gave Vee-Jay a right of first refusal to all Beatles masters controlled by EMI for the length of the five-year deal.

VJ 498, which contains *Please Please Me* and *Ask Me Why*, was released on February 7, 1963. The record received minimal airplay and sold approximately 5,650 copies in 1963. The song did not chart nationally, but made the top forty in Vee-Jay's hometown Chicago (#35 on WLS). Initial pressings of the 45 are much sought after by collectors not only for the disc's historical importance and scarcity, but also because the group's name is misspelled with two Ts as "THE BEATTLES" (see page 6).

Vee-Jay exercised its right of first refusal under the agreement for the group's next single, *From Me To You* and *Thank You Girl*. The company issued the 45 on or about May 6, 1963, on VJ 522 (see page 28). This time the group's name was spelled correctly, and the single sold a little bit better (approximately 12,675 units by summer's end). Although the song did not chart nationally, it was a top forty hit in Los Angeles (#32 on KRLA).

Vee-Jay most likely received the mono and stereo master tapes for the Beatles 14-song *Please Please Me* LP in April or early May, 1963. Because U.S. albums normally had 12 selections, Vee-Jay dropped *Please Please Me* and *Ask Me Why* from the lineup as the two songs had already been released as a single in America (and perhaps because the 45 sold poorly). With *Please Please Me* excluded from the disc, a new title was needed. Vee-Jay chose *Introducing The Beatles* and touted the band as "England's No. 1 Vocal Group" on the cover. In June of 1963, Vee-Jay took steps towards the release of the album, including the manufacture of the metal parts to press the records and the printing of 6,000 front cover slicks.

The album was scheduled for release in the summer of 1963; however, it was cancelled when Vee-Jay ran into financial difficulties. By failing to issue the LP that summer, Vee-Jay forfeited its rights to release the album. When Vee-Jay failed to provide Transglobal with royalty statements or payments for sales of the two Beatles singles,

Transglobal unilaterally terminated the licensing agreement in August and demanded that Vee-Jay cease manufacture and distribution of all Beatles records. (It was later determined that Vee-Jay owed only $859 in royalties on sales of Beatles records.) Amid all the financial concerns and confusion at Vee-Jay, the company forgot all about the Beatles.

In December of 1963, Vee-Jay learned that Capitol had signed the Beatles to an exclusive contract and was planning on spending a significant amount of money promoting the band. The company knew they had signed a licensing agreement for the group's records, but could not find the contract. Vee-Jay had New York attorney Walter Hofer determine its rights regarding the Beatles masters. Hofer advised Vee-Jay that they had the rights to the four songs previously issued on the two singles, but probably not to the 12 songs on the unreleased album.

Vee-Jay was in desperate financial condition and realized that sales of Beatles records would improve cash flow even if the company later had to pay Capitol and/or EMI royalties and damages. A new single (VJ 581) pairing the two A sides *Please Please Me* and *From Me To You* was rush released during the first days of 1964. Vee-Jay prepared a picture sleeve for the record (see page 86). The company also decided to release its *Introducing The Beatles* LP (see page 94) on January 10, 1964, even though it knew that Capitol would take legal action to prohibit Vee-Jay from selling the album. Details regarding the different back cover variations of the album are discussed on page 97.

When Capitol learned of Vee-Jay's plans to issue a Beatles album, the Hollywood-based company hired outside counsel to prepare an injunction barring Vee-Jay from manufacturing and distributing Beatles records on the grounds that Capitol had signed an agreement with EMI in late November, 1963, for the exclusive right to distribute the Beatles recordings in the United States. Capitol filed its lawsuit in Chicago on January 13, 1964. Vee-Jay filed a similar suit in New York on January 14, arguing that the January, 1963, licensing agreement was still valid and gave the company the exclusive rights to the Beatles until January, 1968. Details regarding the litigation are covered on pages 100-109. On January 15, 1963, the Chicago court issued a temporary injunction against Vee-Jay. During the next few months, the injunction would be removed and reinstated several times, giving Vee-Jay brief opportunities to press and distribute Beatles records.

Although the injunction adversely affected the distribution of Vee-Jay's records, *Please Please Me* sold over one million copies and peaked at number three on the charts behind Capitol's *I Want To Hold Your Hand* and Swan's *She Loves You*. The *Introducing The Beatles* LP also sold over one million units and peaked at number two behind Capitol's *Meet The Beatles!* LP.

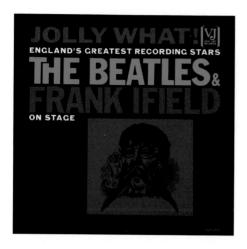

Litigation between Vee-Jay and Capitol's publishing subsidiary, Beechwood Music Corporation, resulted in Vee-Jay issuing two different versions of *Introducing The Beatles*. Version One, released on January 10, has the songs *Love Me Do* and *P.S. I Love You*. Beechwood owned the publishing rights to those songs and refused to grant Vee-Jay permission to issue the songs. To get around this hurdle, Vee-Jay removed and replaced the two Beechwood songs with *Ask Me Why* and *Please Please Me*. Because the Version One discs with *Love Me Do* and *P.S. I Love You* had a very limited run, they are much rarer than the Version Two albums with *Ask Me Why* and *Please Please Me*.

Legal considerations were also behind *Jolly What! The Beatles And Frank Ifield On Stage*. This album was a fallback record that contained songs that Vee-Jay clearly had the right to release. It combined the four Beatles songs previously issued on Vee-Jay singles (*Please Please Me, Ask Me Why, From Me To You* and *Thank You Girl*) with eight Frank Ifield songs previously issued on Vee-Jay singles. The album's cover features a drawing of an English statesman wearing a Beatles wig. Although the album's title implies live stage performances, all of the songs on the disc are the standard studio versions.

Vee-Jay had done something similar with its 1961 album *Jimmy Reed At Carnegie Hall*. The record was not, as its title implied, a live concert recording of Jimmy Reed. In 1961, no promoter would have booked a delta blues singer in the prestigious venue. The LP wasn't titled *Jimmy Reed Live At Carnegie Hall*. It was called *Jimmy Reed At Carnegie Hall*. And that's what it was. The album's cover featured a picture of Jimmy Reed **at** Carnegie Hall.

The back liner notes to the *Jolly What!* album contain a humorous misuse of the English language by referring to the compilation album as a "copulation." While the album had initial sales of over 50,000 units, over half of the discs were returned. Perhaps potential purchasers of the "copulation" album realized Vee-Jay was trying to screw them as the LP contained only four Beatles songs, all of which had previously been released.

Vee-Jay's next Beatles record was a single pairing *Twist And Shout* with *There's A Place*. At the time the 45 was released in late February, 1964, *Please Please Me* was still receiving heavy airplay. In addition, disc jockeys were busy spinning Capitol's *I Want To Hold Your Hand*, Swan's *She Loves You* and MGM's *My Bonnie*. Vee-Jay was concerned that another Vee-Jay Beatles single would confuse radio programmers, so the company created a new subsidiary label, Tollie Records (named in honor of Vee-Jay producer Calvin Tollie Carter), to issue the single. When released as Tollie 9001, *Twist And Shout* quickly moved to the top spots in *Record World* and *Cash Box*, but stalled at number two in the *Billboard Hot 100* behind *Can't Buy Me Love*. The 45 also gave Tollie a million-seller in its first release.

On March 23, Vee-Jay issued a 45 pairing *Do You Want To Know A Secret* with *Thank You Girl*. For its third Beatles single in as many months, Vee-Jay returned the Beatles to its own label, releasing the disc as VJ 587. The single gave Vee-Jay another million-seller and another number two hit in the *Billboard Hot 100*. The 45 failed to top the charts when the Beatles 14-week stranglehold of the number one spot was interrupted by Louis Armstrong's *Hello Dolly!* Many copies of VJ 587 were issued in a picture sleeve.

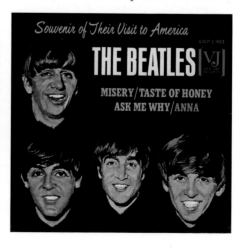

At the same time, Vee-Jay issued an Extended Play (EP) disc containing *Misery*, *A Taste Of Honey*, *Ask Me Why* and *Anna*. The record (VJEP 1-903) was packaged in a special cardboard sleeve featuring the same faces of the boys appearing on the picture sleeve for *Do You Want To Know A Secret*. With the Beatles first visit to the United States and their appearances on *The Ed Sullivan Show* fresh in everyone's mind, the EP was marketed as a "Souvenir of Their Visit to America." The record sold a respectable 78,800 units, but did not hit the national charts.

On April 1, 1964, Vee-Jay and Capitol signed a settlement agreement that gave Vee-Jay the right to continue manufacturing and distributing its Beatles discs until October 15, 1964, at which time the rights to the Beatles songs issued by Vee-Jay would revert to Capitol. It seemed like a good deal for Vee-Jay at the time because nearly everyone in the record business believed that the Beatles would be long forgotten by summer's end. And certainly the rights to the masters of songs like *Please Please Me*, *From Me To You* and *Twist And Shout* would be of little value past October 15, 1964. Most music industry insiders would have bet their careers that the Beatles popularity would not last until the next year, much less the next decade and even the next century. But, then again, the settlement was signed on April Fool's Day.

As part of the settlement agreement, Capitol's Beechwood Music subsidiary granted Vee-Jay permission to release the songs *Love Me Do* and *P.S. I Love You*. Vee-Jay quickly prepared the two songs for release as their fourth Beatles single of the year. The record was released on April 27, 1964, as Tollie 9008. Because Vee-Jay pulled the two songs from its mono master tape of *Introducing The Beatles*, the version of *Love Me Do* released on the Tollie 45 is the one with Andy White on drums and Ringo relegated to the tambourine. The single was issued in an attractive picture sleeve featuring a hand-drawn portrait of the

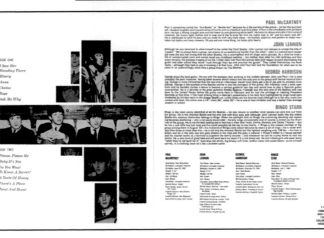

boys based upon a Dezo Hoffmann photograph. Capitol of Canada originally released the songs on Capitol 72076 in early 1963. The Canadian single, which has the version of *Love Me Do* with Ringo on drums, was imported into the United States prior to release of the Tollie single. Although *Love Me Do* was a modest hit in England (it peaked at number 17 on December 27, 1962), Americans were so hungry for new Beatles product that the Tollie 45 topped the charts on May 30, 1964, and sold over one million copies, accounting for its inclusion on the *Beatles 1* collection.

After the release of the *Love Me Do* single, Vee-Jay was faced with a horrifying dilemma. It had the most popular group of all time, but only had the rights to 16 previously released Beatles songs. And even those limited rights would expire on October 15, 1964. Vee-Jay somehow had to find a way to meet demand for new Beatles product at a time when it had no new product to offer.

In May, 1964, Vee-Jay developed plans to repackage its *Introducing The Beatles* album with a fancy gatefold cover designed to mimic the numerous teen magazines devoted to the Beatles. The elaborate cover's inner sleeve features color-tinted pictures and personal liner notes about the boys. When EMI and Capitol were told of Vee-Jay's plans to effectively issue a "new" Beatles album titled *Songs, Pictures And Stories Of The Fabulous Beatles*, Capitol demanded that Vee-Jay not market the redesigned album. Vee-Jay went to court and was victorious as the judge ruled that the company had the unqualified right to advertise and promote its Beatles masters in any cover, jacket or package which Vee-Jay deemed appropriate. Shortly after the ruling, Vee-Jay began limited distribution of *Songs, Pictures And Stories* in late July of 1964. Although the cover listed the album as VJ 1092, the record inside had the same labels as *Introducing The Beatles*. The repackaged album sold nearly 400,000 copies and peaked at number 63 on the charts.

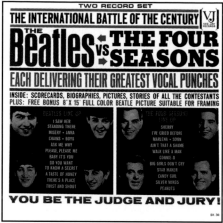

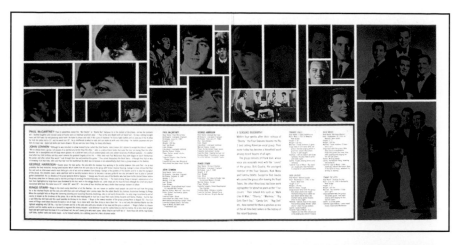

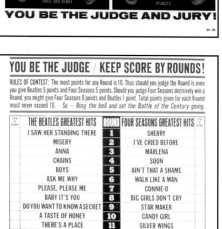

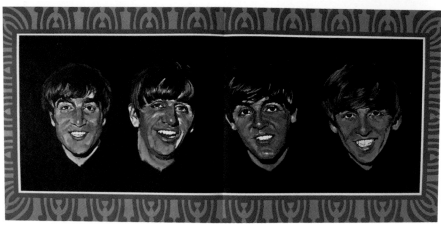

The court battle over *Songs, Pictures And Stories* taught Vee-Jay that it had the right to repackage its albums in different covers. Although EMI and George Martin had previously objected to Vee-Jay's request in late April to issue an album mixing songs of the Beatles and the Four Seasons, the company realized it could legally market an "international battle of the bands" LP by placing an *Introducing The Beatles* record and a *Golden Hits Of The Four Seasons* disc into a double gatefold cover. The resulting album, *The Beatles Vs. The Four Seasons* (DX-30), was released in late August, 1964, with deluxe packaging that included an 11½" x 23" poster. Because the double album had a relatively high list price and offered no new songs by either the Beatles or the Four Seasons, the album sold less than 20,000 copies and only reached number 142 on the *Billboard Top LP's* chart. As only 725 stereo copies were shipped to distributors, the stereo version of the album is a rarity.

After twice repackaging *Introducing The Beatles*, Vee-Jay turned its attention to the ill-fated *Jolly What!* compilation album. The problem was to find a way to sell an existing album which contained only four Beatles songs and was being returned by retailers and distributors due to poor sales. The solution was to repackage the album focusing on its strengths and downplaying its weaknesses. Put simply, *Jolly What!* had eight things going for it, namely John, Paul, George, Ringo, *Please Please Me*, *Ask Me Why*, *From Me To You* and *Thank You Girl*. It also had eight things against it, namely the eight Frank Ifield songs, which young Beatles fans viewed as a nuisance. Vee-Jay redesigned the album's cover to focus on the Beatles and their four songs.

The reissue cover features the striking portrait of the group previously used on the *Love Me Do* picture sleeve and the prominent placement of the titles to the four Beatles songs. The silly-looking English statesman, along with the "Jolly What!" language, is nowhere to be seen. Despite Vee-Jay's efforts, consumers were not fooled this time around. The so-called "portrait cover" album, which was probably released in late September, 1964, sold only a few thousand mono and a few hundred stereo copies. Thus, it the rarest of the Vee-Jay Beatles albums.

When sales of their Beatles singles began to slow down in August, 1964, Vee-Jay decided it was time to issue their four 1964 singles on their Oldies label. While it may seem strange to consider a song an oldie when it was issued only a few months before, this marketing ploy was effective. By issuing the 45s on the Oldies label, Vee-Jay was able to get new life out of the singles by obtaining placement of the discs in the oldies section of record and department stores. During August and September, Vee-Jay reported total sales of 18,086 copies of Beatles 45s on the Oldies label.

To further stimulate sales and squeeze out additional product before the October 15, 1964, cutoff date, Vee-Jay prepared a special holiday picture sleeve for its Beatles singles. The sleeve has "The Beatles" printed at the top followed by "We wish you a Merry Christmas and a Happy New Year" and features the same familiar faces of the boys that appeared on the picture sleeve to *Do You Want To Know A Secret*, the jacket of the EP and the cover to the *Songs, Pictures* LP. Vee-Jay ordered 200,000 of the Beatles Christmas sleeves, which shipped to factories in early October.

These sleeves were issued primarily with Oldies singles. In all likelihood, some fans re-bought at least one of the Oldies 45s to get the sleeve. Vee-Jay's marketing ploy was successful as total sales for the Beatles Oldies singles for October, 1964, exceeded 130,000 units.

In early November, 1964, Vee-Jay issued *Hear The Beatles Tell All*, an album containing Jim Steck's interview with John Lennon on one side and Dave Hull's interviews with John, Paul, George and Ringo on the other side. The record sold approximately 21,000 units.

Vee-Jay also issued an album containing an impressive lineup of 14 songs written by John Lennon and Paul McCartney and one song by George Harrison. The deceptively packaged and titled *The 15 Greatest Songs Of The Beatles* actually contained performances by the Merseyboys. It was issued in the summer of 1964 and is believed to have sold less than 3,000 copies.

The history of the Beatles on Vee-Jay is a fascinating story (fully detailed in the author's *The Beatles Records on Vee-Jay*) about how a small independent record company acquired and ultimately lost the rights to the most popular group of all time. It is also a lesson on what can be done with limited product and creative marketing. In less than two years, Vee-Jay issued six singles (including two on its Tollie subsidiary), four Oldies 45s, an EP, two versions of *Introducing The Beatles*, a reissue of *Introducing The Beatles* with a new gatefold cover, a compilation album with four Beatles songs and eight Frank Ifield songs, a reissue of the compilation LP and a double album combining *Introducing The Beatles* with *Golden Hits Of The Four Seasons*. Although Vee-Jay's executives produced this incredible catalog for the company's financial gain, they inadvertently created a colorful batch of singles and albums for collectors.

BEATLES AMERICAN DISCOGRAPHY 1962-1964

Release Date	Record No.	Title
04/23/1962	Decca 31382	My Bonnie/The Saints (45 by Tony Sheridan and the Beat Brothers)
02/07/1963	VJ 498	Please Please Me/Ask Me Why (45)
05/06/1963	VJ 522	From Me To You/Thank You Girl (45)
09/16/1963	Swan 4152	She Loves You/I'll Get You (45)
12/26/1963	Capitol 5112	I Want To Hold Your Hand/I Saw Her Standing There (45)
01/03/1964	VJ 581	Please Please Me/From Me To You (45)
01/10/1964	VJLP(S) 1062	Introducing The Beatles (LP) (Version One)
01/20/1964	Capitol (S)T 2047	Meet The Beatles! (LP)
01/27/1964	MGM K-13213	My Bonnie/The Saints (45) (Both sides have Tony Sheridan lead vocal)
02/03/1964	MGM (S)E 4215	The Beatles With Tony Sheridan And Guests (LP) (Contains the four Beatles and Tony Sheridan songs released on the MGM 45s plus two more Tony Sheridan songs and two by the Titans)
02/10/1964	VJLP(S) 1062	Introducing The Beatles (LP) (Version Two)
02/20/1964	VJLP(S) 1085	Jolly What! The Beatles And Frank Ifield On Stage (LP) (Contains four Beatles songs and eight Frank Ifield songs)
02/20/1964	Tollie 9001	Twist And Shout/There's A Place (45)
03/16/1964	Capitol 5150	Can't Buy Me Love/ You Can't Do That (45)
03/23/1964	VJ 587	Do You Want To Know A Secret/Thank You Girl (45)
03/23/1964	VJEP 1-903	Souvenir Of Their Visit To America (EP)
03/27/1964	MGM K-13227	Why/Cry For A Shadow (45) (A side has Tony Sheridan lead vocal; B side is an instrumental written by George Harrison and John Lennon)
04/10/1964	Capitol (S)T 2080	The Beatles' Second Album (LP)
04/27/1864	Tollie 9008	Love Me Do/P.S. I Love You (45)
05/11/1964	Capitol EAP 1-2121	Four By The Beatles (EP)
05/21/1964	Swan 4182	Sie Liebt Dich/I'll Get You (45)
06/01/1964	Atco 6302	Sweet Georgia Brown/Take Out Some Insurance On Me Baby (45) (Both sides have Tony Sheridan lead vocal)
06/13/1964	UAL 3366/UAS 6366	A Hard Day's Night (Soundtrack LP)
07/06/1964	Atco 6308	Ain't She Sweet/Nobody's Child (45) (A side has John Lennon lead vocal; B side has Tony Sheridan lead vocal)
07/13/1964	Capitol 5222	A Hard Day's Night/I Should Have Known Better (45)
07/20/1964	Capitol 5234	I'll Cry Instead/I'm Happy Just To Dance With You (45)
07/20/1964	Capitol 5235	And I Love Her/If I Fell (45)
07/20/1964	Capitol (S)T 2108	Something New (LP)
07/??/1964	VJ 1092	Songs, Pictures And Stories Of The Fabulous Beatles (LP) (Gatefold jacket album is a repackaging of *Introducing The Beatles*)
08/10/1964	Oldies OL-149	Do You Want To Know A Secret/Thank You Girl (45)
08/10/1964	Oldies OL-150	Please Please Me/From Me To You (45)
08/10/1964	Oldies OL-151	Love Me Do/P.S. I Love You (45)
08/10/1964	Oldies OL-152	Twist And Shout/There's A Place (45)
08/24/1964	Capitol 5255	Matchbox/Slow Down (45)
08/??/1964	VJ DX-30	The Beatles Vs. The Four Seasons (LP) (Two album set containing *Introducing The Beatles* disc and *Golden Hits Of The 4 Seasons* disc)
09/??/1964	VJLP(S) 1085	The Beatles & Frank Ifield On Stage (LP) (Portrait Cover)
10/05/1964	Atco (SD) 33-169	Ain't She Sweet (LP) (Contains the four Beatles and Tony Sheridan songs released on the Atco 45s plus eight songs by the Swallows)
11/??/1964	VJLP 202 PRO	Hear The Beatles Tell All (Interview LP)
11/23/1964	Capitol 5327	I Feel Fine/She's A Woman (45)
11/23/1964	Capitol (S)TBO 2222	The Beatles' Story (2 LP documentary)
12/15/1964	Capitol (S)T 2228	Beatles '65 (LP)

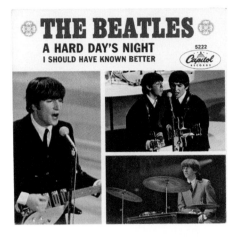
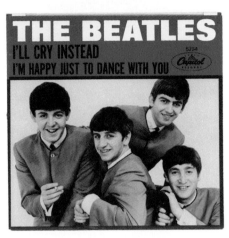

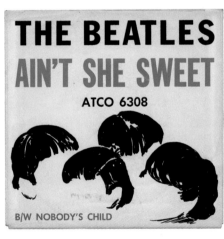

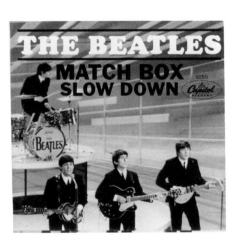

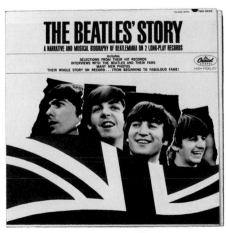

The history of the Beatles American records is fully detailed in the following books by Bruce Spizer: *The Beatles Records on Vee-Jay* (1998); *The Beatles' Story on Capitol Records, Part One: Beatlemania & The Singles* (2000); *The Beatles' Story on Capitol Records, Part Two: The Albums* (2000); *The Beatles on Apple Records* (2003); and *The Beatles Swan Song - "She Loves You" and Other Records* (2005).

OTHER ALBUMS OF INTEREST

The first three albums shown here were released by acts who shared the bill with the Beatles at the Washington Coliseum. The back of the Caravelles album states that the duo acquired its name from a new French jet airliner. (The Caravelle has two jet engines mounted on the rear fuselage and is similar in appearance and size to the DC-9.) Prior to their stardom, 19-year-old Lois Wilkinson and 17-year-old Andrea Simpson were office workers in London. Lois played guitar in their act. Andrea was a clarinetist.

The left cover on the bottom row was released by the Briarwood Singers, who opened for the Beatles at Carnegie Hall. The right cover on the bottom row is a fantasy piece that answers the question, "What if Vee-Jay Records had signed the Briarwood Singers?"

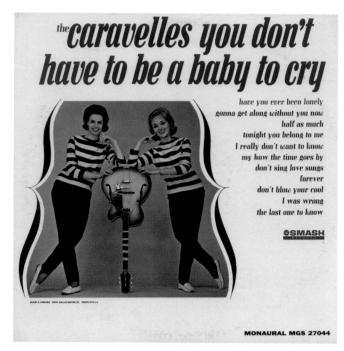

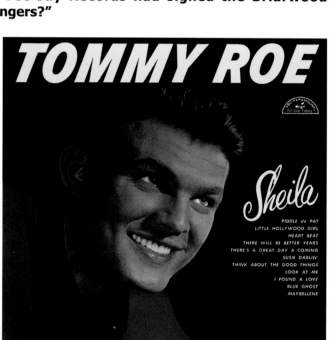

BOOKS OF INTEREST

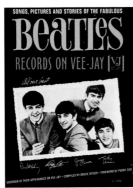

The Beatles Records on Vee-Jay,
Bruce Spizer

The Beatles' Story on Capitol
Records, Part 1, Bruce Spizer

The Beatles' Story on Capitol
Records, Part 2, Bruce Spizer

The Complete Beatles Chronicle,
Mark Lewisohn

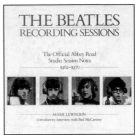

The Beatles Recording Sessions,
Mark Lewisohn

The Beatles as Musicians - The
Quarry Men through Rubber Soul,
Walter Everett

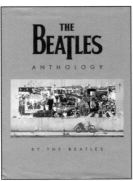

The Beatles Anthology, The Beatles

Beatles Gear, Andy Babiuk

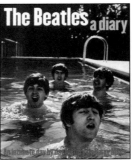

The Beatles a diary, Barry Miles

Beatles '64, A Hard Day's Night In
America, A.J. S. Rayl and
Curt Gunther

The Beatles Files, Andy Davis

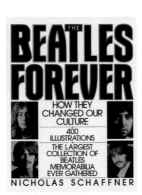

The Beatles Forever,
Nicholas Schaffner

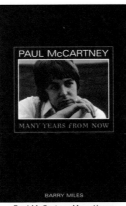

Paul McCartney Many Years
From Now, Barry Miles

Way Beyond Compare
John C. Winn

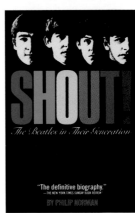

Shout! The Beatles in Their
Generation, Philip Norman

The Beatles, Hunter Davies

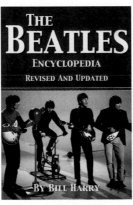

The Beatles Encyclopedia,
Bill Harry

The Beatles,
Rolling Stone Magazine

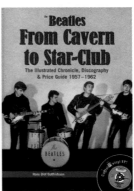

The Beatles From Cavern to Star-
Club, Hans Olof Gottfridsson

With The Beatles, Dezo Hoffmann

Official Price Guide to the Beatles Records & Memorabilia, Perry Cox

The Beatles Memorabilia Price Guide, Jeff Augsburger, Marty Eck & Rick Rann

The Beatles On Record, Mark Wallgren

All You Need Is Ears, George Martin

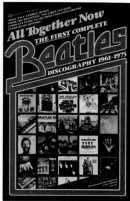

All Together Now, Harry Castleman and Walter J. Podrazik

The Beatles, An Oral History, David Pritchard & Alan Lysaght

The Beatles, Allan Kozinn

A Hard Day's Wrote, Steve Turner

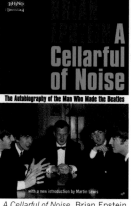

A Cellarful of Noise, Brian Epstein (with comparative narration by Martin Lewis)

In My Life: The Brian Epstein Story, Debbie Geller

Capitol Records 50th Anniversary 1942-1992, Paul Green

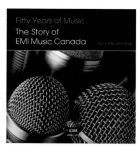

Fifty Years of Music. The Story of EMI Music Canada. Nicholas Jennings

Not Just The Beatles..., Sid Bernstein as told to Arthur Aaron

How They Became The Beatles, Gareth L. Pawlowski

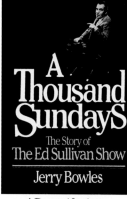

A Thousand Sundays Jerry Bowles

The Beatles Book No. 9. April 1964

The Beatles At Carnegie Hall.

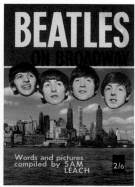

Beatles On Broadway, Sam Leach

Teen Talk (Beatles Issue)

Teen Pix Album (Beatles Issue)

Reference books from Joel Whitburn's Record Research:

Billboard Top 10 Album Charts

Top Pop Albums

Top Pop Singles

Top R&B Singles

The Billboard Hot 100 Charts

Bubbling Under Singles and Albums

is for Apple

B is for Blue Jay Way Galleries

Store Address:
9027B Florence Ave., Downey, CA 90240
Business By Appointment
Phone 562-862-2570, FAX 562-622-5835
Mailing Address: P.O. Box 896, Downey, CA 90241-9998

www.bluejaywaygalleries.com

Beatles4me.com
"Your #1 Beatles Source since 1977"

"Hundreds" of Images

used in

all of Bruce Spizer's Beatles Books

were taken from our vast inventory!

Over 20,000
Original 1960's Beatles Items
for sale!

LARGEST INVENTORY
of the
"Highest Quality"
Original Beatles Items
on the
East Coast!

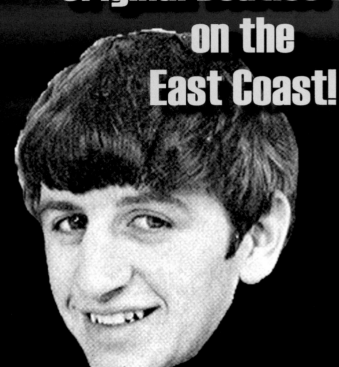

BUY - SELL - CONSIGN
"Latest" 20+ page Beatles Catalog: $2 (Overseas: $5)

HEIN'S RARE COLLECTIBLES

P.O. Box 179, Little Silver, NJ 07739-0179 USA
(732) 219-1988, FAX (732) 219-5940
e-Mail: GaryMHein@comcast.net

L.A.'s Best Collectibles

PLUS AN INCREDIBLE SELECTION OF USED COMPACT DISCS, DVD'S, RECORDS, BOOKS, MEMORABILIA, T-SHIRTS & MORE!

$ TOP PRICES PAID $
For rare vinyl, posters and memorabilia. Will travel worldwide for valuable collections.

ROCKAWAY RECORDS
2395 Glendale Blvd. • Silverlake, CA 90039
323-664-3232   sales@rockaway.com
Mon. - Sat. 10AM - 9:30PM, Sun. 12PM - 8PM

www.rockaway.com

YOUR ONE-STOP SHOP FOR BEATLES

Original Memorabilia
Collectables
Records, Tapes & CD's
Videos & DVD's
Books & Magazines
Buttons & T-Shirts
Lots of other FAB stuff!

PEPPERLAND *Music*

When in Southern California, visit our retail store or call our mail order department

Open 11:am daily

850 N. Tustin Street
Orange, California 92867

www.pepperlandmusic.com
phone: 714.639.0909 fax: 714.639.1015 email: order@pepperlandmusic.com

Your Finest Source for the Very Best in Quality Of Original 1960's Beatles Items

Website is Updated Daily !

Visit our new Office and Collector's Showroom
(By Appointment Only).
Shop through our vast Inventory of
LP Albums, EPs, Picture Sleeves, 45 Singles, Memorabilia,
Concert Tickets & Ephemera, Group & Solo Autographs
and Unique Beatles Artifacts !

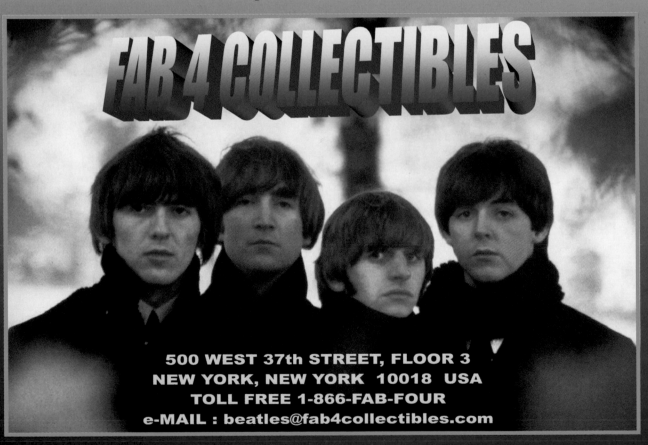

500 WEST 37th STREET, FLOOR 3
NEW YORK, NEW YORK 10018 USA
TOLL FREE 1-866-FAB-FOUR
e-MAIL : beatles@fab4collectibles.com

Order your copy of our extensive
BEATLES CATALOG
$6.00 US / $10.00 Overseas

The Beatles on [VJ] VEE-JAY RECORDS

The Beatles on *Capitol* RECORDS

The Beatles on *Apple*

The Beatles on mobile fidelity sound lab

The Beatles on

Blackbird Records

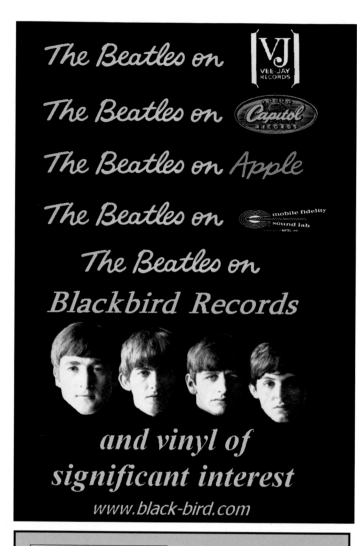

and vinyl of

significant interest

www.black-bird.com

Beatlefan

For 25 years, the voice of Beatles fandom, with the most complete news available and exclusive interviews!

For subscription rates, go to
www.beatlefan.com
Call 770-492-0444
E-mail
goodypress@mindspring.com
or send a SASE to
P.O. Box 33515-A
Decatur GA 30033

Daytrippin'

International Beatles Fan Club

Join the most FAB Beatles Fan Club

One year membership includes:
• Subscription to Daytrippin' magazine
(published 4 times a year)
• Beatlemaniac's Guide to the Internet
• Monthly on-line Beatles newsletter
• Discounts on Beatles events & merchandise
• Special promotions and giveaways
(Individual and electronic subscriptions available also!)

Join today and receive a
free Beatles bumper sticker!

U.S. residents: $26.95 US
Canada/Mexico: $32.95 US
Overseas: $39.95 US
Only U.S. funds and credit cards accepted.

Daytrippin'
P.O. Box 114
Edgewater, NJ, 07020 USA

Order on-line at
www.daytrippin.com

Daytrippin'
Special Macca
Birthday Issue
Paul turns 60!

Paul McCartney
Rocks the USA!
Detailed tour reports

Heather Mills
Revealed
Learn all about
her life
before Paul

ALSO: Garland Appeal / Nils Lofgren / UPA Student

BEATLEBAY

A Great Way To Buy and Sell Original 1960's Beatles Memorabilia
and Recordings! Each Item is Pre-Screened For Authenticity and
Your Satisfaction Is Guaranteed!

BUY - SELL –TRADE

*Check out our online Reference Library featuring the Largest
Collection of 1960's Beatles and 1960's Yellow Submarine
Memorabilia in the World !*

We are always looking to buy good original 1960's Beatles items such as
in-store record promotional posters/displays, autographed items, one of
a kind items, toy instruments, 1960's memorabilia, Yellow Submarine
items, Apple Records Promo Items, Capitol Records Promo Items.

Visit us at http://www.beatlebay.com

Email us at sales@beatlebay.com

THE BEATLES MOBILE MUSEUM IS BUYING!

I am a permanent, serious buyer of original 1960's Beatles memorabilia. I will buy one item or an accumulation. Common items such as gumcards and magazines must be in excellent condition. Rare items such as the Beatle banjo, bongos, and record player will be bought in any condition.

Primary wants

• Toy musical instruments • Concert tickets, unused or stubs • Jewelry pieces, especially on original cards
• Gumcards, display boxes, uncut sheets • Record and merchandise promotional posters and displays
• All Yellow Submarine merchandise • Movie posters and lobby cards • Radio station and fan club surveys, giveaways, promotional materials • Promotional records, 45 rpm picture sleeves, unopened 60's albums • Lunch boxes, dolls, and other 3-D items

The Beatles Mobile Museum

Jeff Augsburger, 507 Normal Ave., Normal, IL 61761
Ph. 309-452-9376 Fax 309-664-1771   Email: beatles.normal@verizon.net

---

MARK AND CAROL LAPIDOS PROUDLY PRESENT

THE FEST FOR BEATLES FANS 2004

NEW YORK METRO
APRIL 2-4, 2004
NJ CROWNE PLAZA MEADOWLANDS

CHICAGO
AUGUST 20-22, 2004
HYATT REGENCY O'HARE

OTHER DATES TO BE ANNOUNCED

As fans celebrate the 40th Anniversary of The Beatles arrival in America, we celebrate our 30th Anniversary, 97 National Conventions since 1974!!

In addition to the Annual Fans Celebrations, we also have the World's Largest Beatles Mail Order Catalogue. Over 1,000 items including Books, DVDs, CDs, Shirts, Hats, Ceramics, Jewelry, Posters, Ties, Blankets, Puzzles, Watches, Collectables. It can be viewed on line at www.thefestforbeatlesfans.com. Our Toll Free # 1-866-THE FEST.

THE FEST FOR BEATLES FANS-P.O. BOX 436, WESTWOOD, NJ 07675-0436
"A Splendid Time Is Guaranteed for All!"

The Beatles "Shea" Jackets

For the first time made stitch-for-stitch from Paul McCartney's original jacket!

R.W. Lease, Ltd., is presenting The Beatles "Shea" jacket. The famous British tan military styled stage coat has NEVER before been reproduced with such exact stitch-for-stitch detail faithful to the original.

This project has taken approximately six months to complete. R.W. Lease, Ltd., (owner of McCartney's original jacket) has painstakingly replicated every design facet of Paul's original—right down to the buttons cast from the original and imported from Europe.

This attention to detail has resulted in a finely tailored, quality garment indistinguishable in any way from The Beatles four original custom made jackets.

Available in sizes 38 to 46 in regular and long, and in both regular and European fits. Available in two colors, the original British tan and black.

By special arrangement Wells Fargo minted Badges identical to The Beatles' originals are also available.

Additional Beatle stage suit models will be made available as ready.

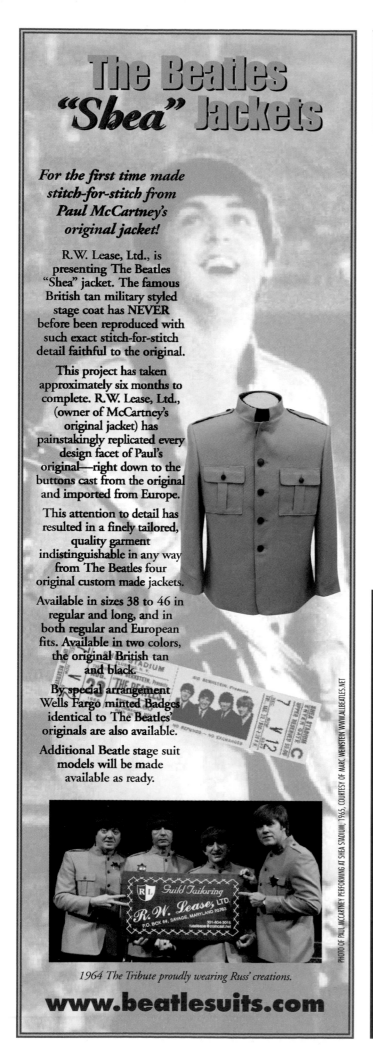

PHOTO OF PAUL MCCARTNEY PERFORMING AT SHEA STADIUM, 1965, COURTESY OF MARC WEINSTEIN WWW.ALLBEATLES.NET

1964 The Tribute proudly wearing Russ' creations.

www.beatlesuits.com

Joe Johnson's Beatle Brunch .COM

"Here's Another Clue For You All ....."
Go to our website Station Page and link to CISL ... they stream **Beatle Brunch** every Sunday!

Parisi

Beatlology
MAGAZINE

Recognized around the world as one of the best magazines for Beatles fans, Beatlology is more than just a magazine!

Beatlology Magazine – publishing since September 1998 each issue contains full colour feature articles on rare Beatles collectibles, current events and history. Visit our web site or call to order a subscription and back issues today!

Beatlology Publishing – publishing all kinds of books for Beatles fans including publisher Andrew Croft's *Collecting Beatles Sheet Music & Songbooks* and two companion guides with complete lists and values for the U.K. and the U.S., *The Beatles Canadian Discography 1962–1970 Part 1 – 45 RPM & Other Special 7" Discs*, by Piers Hemmingsen, and more titles on the way! Visit our web site to order!

Beatlology Online Auctions – Beatlology's own moderated auction site where buyers and sellers of Beatles memorabilia come together in a safe environment to buy and sell their collectibles with the support and knowledge of experienced collectors and appraisers. Check our web site for more details.

Beatlology's This Day In Beatles History – subscribe to Beatlology's **This Day In Beatles History** daily e-mail. Check our web site for more details.

Subscriptions – 6 issues per year – **U.S.** $24USD **INT'L** $36USD
Back issues and **sample issues** – $6USD ea.

U.S. orders: Beatlology, Box 400, 119 W. 72nd St., New York, NY 10023 U.S.A.
All others: Beatlology, Box 90, 260 Adelaide St. E. Toronto, ON, M5A 1N1 Canada
Tel. **416-360-8902** • Toll Free **1-888-844-0826** Mon–Fri, 9–5 EST

www.beatlology.com